NEW YORK REVIEW BOOKS
CLASSICS

T0013843

WRITTEN ON WATER

EILEEN CHANG (1920–1995) was born in Shanghai to an
aristocratic family and educated in both Chinese and English
from an early age. Her flamboyant mother spent extended
periods in Europe, leaving her and her younger brother in the
care of their opium-addicted father throughout much of their
childhood. Chang attended the American Episcopal school
for girls in Shanghai and was enrolled at the University of
Hong Kong, studying English and history, when the bloody
Battle of Hong Kong broke out in December 1941. By the
next spring she was living in war-ravaged Shanghai and
concentrating on writing. Two volumes published in 1944,
when Chang was not yet twenty-five, established her as a
literary sensation: *Romances*, a collection of short fiction, and
Written on Water, a book of essays. In 1952, Chang returned
to Hong Kong, where for three years she worked for the
United States Information Agency, translating the likes of
Ernest Hemingway, Washington Irving, and Ralph Waldo
Emerson into Chinese and translating Chinese propaganda
into English. During this period she also wrote two novels,
The Rice Sprout Song and *Naked Earth* (in both Chinese and
English versions). From 1955 on, Chang lived in the United
States, dying quietly in her apartment in West Los Angeles
in 1995. Although the books she published in her adopted
country initially failed to find a broad audience, her work has
remained the object of fervent admiration among Chinese-
speaking communities, inspiring numerous theatrical,

operatic, and cinematic adaptations. In recent years the publication of formerly unpublished manuscripts, among them novels, essays, letters, and notes, has encouraged a scholarly reevaluation of Chang as a bilingual writer. In addition to *Written on Water*, NYRB Classics publishes three books by her: *Love in a Fallen City*, *Naked Earth*, and *Little Reunions*. *Time Tunnel*, a new collection of her writing, translated by Karen Kingsbury and Jie Zhang, is forthcoming.

ANDREW F. JONES teaches modern Chinese literature and culture at the University of California, Berkeley. His books include *Circuit Listening: Chinese Popular Music in the Global 1960s* and *Developmental Fairy Tales: Evolutionary Thinking and Modern Chinese Culture*. He has also translated two volumes of fiction by Yu Hua.

NICOLE HUANG is a professor of comparative literature at the University of Hong Kong. She is the author of two monographs on Eileen Chang: *Women, War, Domesticity: Shanghai Literature and Popular Culture of the 1940s* and *Hong Kong Connections: Eileen Chang and Worldmaking*.

WRITTEN ON WATER

EILEEN CHANG

Translated from the Chinese by
ANDREW F. JONES

Edited by
ANDREW F. JONES *and* NICOLE HUANG

Afterword by
NICOLE HUANG

With illustrations by the author

NEW YORK REVIEW BOOKS

New York

THIS IS A NEW YORK REVIEW BOOK
PUBLISHED BY THE NEW YORK REVIEW OF BOOKS
207 East 32nd Street, New York, NY 10016
www.nyrb.com

Originally published in Chinese as *Liuyan*.
Originally published in Chinese by Crown Publishing Company Ltd., Taiwan

First published as a New York Review Books Classic in 2023.

Library of Congress Cataloging-in-Publication Data
Names: Zhang, Ailing, author. | Jones, Andrew F., editor and translator |
    Huang, Nicole, editor.
Title: Written on water / by Eileen Chang; translated from the Chinese by
    Andrew F. Jones; edited by Andrew F. Jones and Nicole Huang.
Other titles: Liu yan. English
Description: New York: New York Review Books, [2023] | Series: New York
    Review Books
Identifiers: LCCN 2020058337 (print) | LCCN 2020058338 (ebook) |
    ISBN 9781681375762 (paperback) | ISBN 9781681375779 (ebook)
Subjects: LCSH: Zhang, Ailing—Translations into English. | LCGFT: Essays.
Classification: LCC PL2837.E35 L58613 2021 (print) | LCC PL2837.E35 (ebook) |
    DDC 895.14/52—dc23
LC record available at https://lccn.loc.gov/2020058337
LC ebook record available at https://lccn.loc.gov/2020058338

ISBN 978-1-68137-576-2
Available as an electronic book; ISBN 978-1-68137-577-9

Printed in the United States of America on acid-free paper.
10 9 8 7 6 5 4 3 2 1

CONTENTS

Editors' Acknowledgments

THIS TRANSLATION of *Written on Water* has unfolded over the course of twenty years of friendship and collaboration. We would like once again to thank our many friends and colleagues who contributed in ways great and small to the publication of the first edition of *Written on Water* in 2005. We remain grateful for the steadfast support of Jennifer Crewe at Columbia University Press and Professor David Wang. Eileen Cheng, Louisa Chiang, Theodore Huters, Leo Ou-Fan Lee, Deborah Tze-Lan Sang, the anonymous reviewers for Columbia University Press, and many other friends and colleagues read, corrected, and helped to improve the initial drafts of the translation. One seldom gets a second chance in life, and we thank our editors at NYRB, Edwin Frank and Sara Kramer, for giving us the time and opportunity to revisit Eileen Chang's essays with fresh eyes, and with the benefit of insights gleaned from nearly two decades of new scholarship in the field. James Brook was an astute and insightful reader of the revised manuscript. We are especially grateful to Silvano Zheng, whose incisive, thoughtful, and generous commentary set into motion an extensive revision of the original translation. We hope that this new and improved edition will allow even more readers to hear Eileen Chang's inimitable voice, and enter into her literary world.

WRITTEN ON WATER

FROM THE MOUTHS OF BABES

IT USED to be that when people celebrated Chinese New Year, they would paste red strips of paper on the wall with maxims like THINGS ARE LOOKING UP and FROM THE MOUTHS OF BABES written across them. When I hark back in my title to the guileless discourse that emerges from the "mouths of babes," I don't mean to imply that I am about to spit out something that ought not to be said. It's just that I would like to indulge in talking about myself for a while. When a child in grade school comes home after school and excitedly begins to narrate everything he's seen and heard that day—how partial the teacher is to certain students and how Wang Debao was late to school and how the classmate who shares a bench with him was taken down a few points for being untidy—grown-ups, while disinclined to take him up on any of it, will let him talk on and on. I must have known the sorrow of this sort of situation when I was small for I've made it a taboo ever since to talk when no one is listening. Even now, I am happiest when someone else talks and I listen. When I'm talking and someone else is listening, I am invariably left with the uneasy suspicion that I've made myself quite tiresome. If one is really bursting with things to say and has no one to say them to, perhaps the only recourse is to go forth and accomplish earth-shattering deeds, so that when the time comes for an autobiography, one need no longer be concerned that no one will take any notice. This is a childish fantasy, of course, of which I have been disabused as I have slowly come to realize that I have scant hope of becoming a celebrated public figure worthy of a best-selling autobiography. Better, then, to write a little about myself and let off some steam, so that I don't become an insufferable chatterbox when I get old.

Still, the kind of familiar writing that's full of "me me me" from start to finish ought to be taken to task. I recently came across a couple of lines in an English book that might serve as a rather fitting jibe at authors excessively interested in themselves: "They not only spend a lifetime gazing at their own navels but also go in search of other people who might be interested in gazing along with them." Unsure as to whether what follows constitutes a navel exhibition, I have chosen to write it all the same.

MONEY

I don't know whether the custom of drawing "life lots" is common in other places besides here. When I was one year old, a group of objects were duly placed in front of me on a lacquer tray in order to predict my future career. What I picked was money—I think it was a little one-pound gold coin. That is how my aunt remembers the story, although there was also a maidservant there who still insists that I chose a pen, and I am not entirely sure which of the accounts ought to be trusted. In any case, I have been very fond of money ever since I was small. My mother was shocked to discover this propensity, and would shake her head and mutter, "Their generation . . ." My mother is a noble sort of person. When she had a lot of money, she made no mention of it, and even later, when she was in desperate need of money, she treated it with thorough indifference. I found her purity and detachment provoking and took the opposite tack. As soon as I learned the word "Mammonism," I insisted on calling myself a Mammonist.

I like money because I have never suffered on its account—certainly, I've experienced a few minor nuisances to do with money, but nothing compared to what others have suffered—and know nothing of its bad side and only the good.

When I lived at home, I did not have to worry about food and clothing, and my tuition, medical costs, and recreational expenses were all taken care of for me. But I never had any money of my own. There was the worry that children would spend any ready cash on snacks, so my father always made us give back the New Year's coins that had been put under our pillows after the holidays were over, and we never thought to protest. I never bought anything for myself in a store until I turned sixteen. I never had a chance to buy anything, and without the habit, I never developed a desire to do so.

Coming out of the cinema, I felt like a child in custody at the gendarmerie as I stood on the curb waiting for the family chauffeur to find me and take me home. (I could never find him because I was never able to memorize the number on the license plate of our family car.) This is my only memory of what it feels like to live in luxury.

The first time I ever earned any money was during middle school, when I drew a cartoon and submitted it to the *Shanghai Evening Post and Mercury*.[1] The newspaper office gave me five dollars, which I promptly used to buy a little tube of Tangee lipstick. My mother thought I should have saved the five-dollar bill as a souvenir, but I was not so sentimental. As far as I am concerned, money is merely money: it allows me to buy all the things I want.

There are some things I believe ought to belong to me simply because I am able to appreciate them better than anyone else, because they give me an incomparable delight. I dream night and day about a new outfit I have designed in my head, turning it over and over in my imagination, and when the time finally comes to buy the material, I stall, deliberating still more over the purchase to come. This is a process in which pain mingles with delight. If I had too much money, there would be no need for deliberation. Nor would deliberation be of any use if I hadn't any money at all. The painful pleasure I derive from the exercise of restraint is characteristic of the petite bourgeoisie. Whenever I see the phrase "common city people," I am promptly reminded of myself, as if I had a red silk placard hanging from my chest printed with these very words.

For the past year, I have been a self-supporting petite bourgeoise. Speaking of professional women, Su Qing once said: "I look around and see that I paid for every single thing in my apartment all by myself, down to the last nail. But where's the happiness in that?"[2] This declaration ought to be made into a maxim, but only after turning it over in one's mind a few times does the bleakness of its message begin to strike home.

I once overheard a woman puffing up her chest and declaring: "I've been on my own since I was seventeen. Now I'm thirty-one, and I have yet to take any money from a man." Might this statement that appears worthy of pride also border on resentment?

For the present, I still enjoy my self-sufficiency to the fullest, perhaps because it remains a novelty for me. I am unable to forget how I had to ask my father to pay my piano teacher's salary when I was little. I stood in front of the wicker opium couch, waiting, waiting for ever so long, and still no reply came. Later, I left my father and went to live with my mother. At first, the act of asking my mother for money had an intimate charm. This was because I had always loved my mother with a passion bordering on the romantic. She was a beautiful and sensitive woman, and I had had very little opportunity to be with her because she had gone abroad when I was four, coming home only infrequently and going away again soon after each visit. Through a child's eyes, she seemed a distant and mysterious figure. There were a couple of times she took me out when, merely by taking my hand in hers as we crossed the street, she would send an unfamiliar thrill through my body. But later, despite the straits in which she found herself, I had to press her for money every second or third day. The torments I suffered on account of her temper and my own ingratitude little by little extinguished my love for her in a stream of petty mortifications, until nothing was left of it.

To love someone enough that you are able to ask for spending money: that is a strict test, indeed.

Although the work can be grueling, I like my profession very much. "Skills civil and martial, sold for the emperors' gold." The literati of the past relied on the ruling class for their daily bread, but things are a little different nowadays. I am delighted that the guardians of my living are neither emperors nor kings but the magazine-reading masses. I don't mean to butter them up, but I must say that the masses are a most lovable sort of boss. They are not nearly as fickle as the aristocracy ("heavenly power is inscrutable" as the saying goes), they do not put on airs, they will give you their sincere support, and, in return for a good turn or two, they will remember you for five, or even ten, years. Most important, the masses are abstract. If you must have a master, it stands to reason that an abstract one is much to be preferred.

Although I don't make quite enough money to get by, I have managed to collect a little hoard of valuable things. Last year, I heard a friend of mine make a prediction to the effect that the georgette chiffon that has sold so poorly in recent years is bound to become fashionable again soon, because in today's Shanghai there's no way to come up with new variations on women's fashions, and people must look instead for inspiration in the styles they remember from five years ago. So I saved a few hundred yuan and bought a bolt of georgette. I have held on to it ever since. Now, I see that georgette has indeed come back into vogue, so I have taken the fabric to a consignment shop. Yet I almost hope that they won't be able to sell it, so that I can keep it for myself.

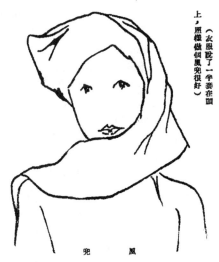

Hood.
Take a sweater halfway off and wrap it around your head. It makes a nice hood.

Full of such contradictions, I venture into the streets to buy groceries, perhaps with something of the romantic pathos of an aristocratic gentleman fallen on hard times. But recently, as an old vegetable vendor weighed my purchases and helped pack them for me, he held on to the handle of my mesh bag with his mouth to keep it open. As I lifted the now-dampened handle to carry my purchases away, I felt nothing out of the ordinary. And having discovered that something within me was different from before, I was happy: some real progress had been made, although I could not tell how or why.

CLOTHES

Zhang Henshui represents most people's ideals in this regard.[3] He likes a girl who wears a refreshingly plain, blue cotton coat, one that merely hints at the red silk cheongsam underneath. Amid modesty and innocence, a suggestion of seduction. But I have neither the qualifications nor the ambition to become a character in one of his novels.

Because my mother was inordinately fond of having new clothes made, my father once muttered under his breath, "People aren't just clothes hangers!" One of my earliest memories is of my mother standing in front of a mirror, pinning a jadeite brooch onto a green, short-waisted jacket. Standing to one side, I looked up at her, awash with envy and unable to wait until I grew up. I once said: "When I'm eight, I want to wear my hair in a wave; at ten, I want to put on high heels; and when I'm sixteen, I'll eat sticky rice wraps and sweet dumplings and everything else that's hard to digest." The more impatient I became, the more I felt that the days went by all too slowly. And thus the long days of childhood coursed sluggishly onward, like a warm sun shining on the thick, pink lining of an old cotton-padded shoe.

But there were also occasions when I resented the days for going by too fast, like the time when I grew so much and so suddenly that I never got to wear my new foreign-style suit of scallion-green brocade, not even once. Whenever I thought about that outfit later, I felt a deep sadness and saw its loss as one of the greatest regrets of my life.

For a time, when I was living under the regime of my stepmother, I had to choose things to wear from among her hand-me-downs. I will never be able to forget a certain dun-red, thinly quilted gown. It was the color of chopped beef, and I wore it for what seemed like forever, looking as if my whole body was covered with chilblains, and even when winter had passed, the scars from the sores still remained—the gown was that hateful, that shameful. Mostly on account of the fact that I was ashamed of my own appearance, my life in middle school was unhappy, and I rarely made any friends.

After I graduated from middle school, I lived with my mother. My mother put forward a very equitable proposition: if I were to marry early, there would be no need to continue my studies, and I could use the money that would have been spent on tuition to dress myself in the latest fashions. But if I kept on studying, there would be nothing left over for clothes. After I went to Hong Kong for college, I was awarded two scholarships, and because I had saved my mother a substantial sum of money, I decided that I could finally indulge myself by having a few outfits made precisely to my specifications. And ever since then, I've been indulging myself in clothes.

When it comes to harmonizing color and tone, Chinese people have only recently learned the principles of "contrast" and "matching" from the West. The common, crudely simplified conception of contrast is red against green, while matching is green with green. But what most people do not realize is that the clash between two different shades of green is extraordinarily clear: the more closely the two shades encroach upon one another, the more unsettling the vision. The contrast between red and green can be delightfully provocative, but if the contrast is too direct, if the red is too bright and the green too saturated, the effect may resemble a Christmas tree in its utter lack of subtlety. In the past, Chinese people did pay attention to strong contrasts. There is a line in an old children's song: "Red and green really fit / purple and red look like shit." In the *Golden Lotus*, the servant's wife, Song Huilian, is wearing a bright red tunic with which she matches a borrowed purple skirt. When the master, Ximen Qing, sees her, he is so disturbed that he digs through his trunks in search of a bolt of blue silk for a new skirt.[4]

Modern Chinese often say that people in times past had no idea of how to match colors. But the sorts of contrasts they used were never unequivocal. Instead, they were layered: sapphire blue and apple green, tender yellow and bright red, scallion green and peach red. We have already forgotten what they once knew.

The reticent charm and complex harmony of the past can now only be found in Japanese fabrics. That is why I love to go shopping in Hongkew; I regret only that the fabrics there are stored in bolts, like the scrolls of ancient paintings, so that one cannot examine them at will and must instead ask a store clerk slowly to unroll each sample.[5] To make a mess of a whole store and still not buy a single thing is no small embarrassment.

The tailoring of kimonos is extremely elaborate, and the patterns printed across broad swaths of fabric are often buried underneath the folds. For these sort of patterns, using the simpler lines of the Chinese cheongsam would in fact create a far clearer profile.

Japanese printed fabrics, each bolt a painting. Every time I buy some fabric and bring it home, I unroll it again and again to admire the images before finally handing it over to the dressmaker. A small Burmese temple half obscured by the leaves of a palm tree, rain falling incessantly through the ruddy haze of the tropics. A pond in early summer, the water covered with a layer of green film, above which floats duckweed and purple and white lilac petals toppled from their stems. Perhaps a fitting scene for a short lyric set to the tune "Lament for the Southland."[6] Yet another bolt, which might be titled "Flowers in the Rain": on a white background, big gloomy purple blossoms, dripping with moisture.

I even remember the fabrics I have seen but could not buy. There was a rich olive-green silk across which stole an enormous black shadow, laden with the wind and thunder of an approaching tempest. And another sort of silken fabric, pale aquamarine, shimmering with ripples reminiscent of wood grain and lake water; above which floated at regular intervals a pair of plum blossoms as big as tea bowls, iron-edged and silver-filigreed, like the multihued stained-glass windows of a medieval church, its translucent red panes set between leaded borders.

The most common colors on the market are the kinds you cannot name, the not quite blues, not quite grays, and not quite yellows that are used only for background and referred to as neutral colors, camouflage, "civilized colors," or secondary colors. Amid these secondary colors, there are splashes of enigmatic brilliance and coy allure, like the sun of another world shining on one's body. But I always feel that even these splashes are never enough, never enough, like Van Gogh, who always bemoaned that his colors were not strong enough, until he painted sunflowers suffused in the intense sunlight of southern France and was finally compelled to pile colors on top of one another in such staggering amounts that layers of oil paint began to protrude from the canvas, transforming painting into a sort of sculpture in relief.

For people who are too shy to speak, clothes are a kind of language, a "pocket drama" they can carry wherever they go. Surrounded by this dramatic ambience of our own making, do we become "people in cases"? (Chekhov's "Man in a Case" always wears a raincoat and carries an umbrella in order to insulate himself completely from the outside world. Even his watch has a watch case. In fact, everything he owns has its own special case.)[7]

The transformation of life into drama is unhealthy. Growing up in the culture of the city, many of us see pictures of the sea before we see the sea itself; we read of love in romance novels long before we experience it in life. Our experience is quite often secondhand, borrowed from artificial theatricals, and as a result the line between life and its dramatization becomes difficult to draw.

There was a night, under the moon, when I strolled down a corridor in a school dormitory with a classmate. I was twelve and she was a couple of years older. She said: "I'm very fond of you, but I don't know how you feel about me." Because there was a moon, and because

I was a born storyteller, I softly and solemnly said to her: "I . . . my mother aside . . . you are all I have." At the time, she was deeply moved by my words. And I had even managed to move myself.

There was another incident of this sort that still makes me uneasy. It was even earlier. I was five years old. At the time, my mother was not in China. My father's concubine was a prostitute, older than he, and known by the sobriquet Big Eight. She had a pale oval face shaped like a melon seed framed by a long drooping fringe. She made me a stylish skirt and jacket in lilac velvet in the very height of fashion and said: "Look how nicely I treat you! When your mother had clothes made for you, she always used odds and ends and old scraps. She certainly would have never parted with a whole bolt of velvet. Who do you like more, me or your mother?" I said: "I like you." What rankles most when I think back to that time is that I was not lying.

FOOD

When I was a child, I would often dream of eating "cloud-layer cakes," but when I finally ate the thin wafers they seemed to turn to paper in my mouth, and even worse than the astringent flavor was the melancholy sense of disillusionment.

I've always liked to drink foamed milk. When I drink milk I always find a way to gulp down the little white beads on the edge of the bowl before touching any of the rest.

In *Dream of the Red Chamber*, Grandmother Jia asks Xue Baochai what plays she enjoys watching and what things she likes best to eat.[8] Baochai knows all too well that people getting on in years like their drama loud and lively and their snacks soft and sweet and answers accordingly, just to indulge her. I am just like old people in that I enjoy foods that are sweet and tender. I will have none of those crunchy, savory things such as pickled vegetables, preserved turnips, seaweed crisps. I can't crack open melon seeds. I lack the dexterity needed to handle fine foods such as fish and prawns. I am instead a most complacent carnivore.

Shanghai's butcher shops are really quite lovely: snow-white, sparklingly clean, with dark, rose-colored paper signs hanging from tiled walls: "stew meat XX yuan," "filet mignon XX yuan." Big, white, globe-shaped lamps hang from the ceiling, shrouded with black air-raid shades yet still positively bright and cheery on account of the red lining inside the fixtures. The shop clerks in white aprons gleam with ruddy good health, their plump faces grinning as they stand with one foot propped on a stool, reading the tabloids. Their eggplants are especially big, their onions are especially sweet, and their pigs are especially ripe for slaughter. A bicycle cart stops out front, and two pigs are brought inside, laid out neatly and as yet uncarved, with only traces of blood around their snouts and a light incision around their bellies, revealing the red lining underneath. I do not know why, but such a sight makes me not the slightest bit uneasy. It is as just as appropriate as could be, and as lawful, and as right. I would be quite happy to take up a post at a butcher shop, to sit behind the cash register and collect the money as it rolls in. These places are like mental sanitoriums, full of fresh air. It wouldn't do to think too much about any one thing in particular.

PERFECT GENTLEMEN

When sitting in a tram, I sometimes happen to glance up at a gentleman standing in front of me, looking as grand as could possibly be, elegantly attired, refined, clearly a breed apart. But only seldom are such men's nostrils clean. Thus the phrase: "No man can be a hero in the eyes of those below."

LITTLE BROTHER

My little brother is very beautiful, and I am not beautiful at all. From when I was very little, not a single person in my family did not bemoan the fact that his little mouth, his great big eyes, and his long eyelashes had been wasted on a boy. The grown-ups in the family loved to tease him: "Lend me your eyelashes for a while, will you? I'll give them back tomorrow." But he would always refuse. Once, when everyone was talking about how pretty so-and-so's wife was, he asked, "Is she as good-looking as me?" Everyone used to make fun of his vanity.

He was jealous of the pictures I drew, and when no one was look-ing he would tear them up or smear two big black marks across them. I can imagine the psychological pressure he felt. I was one year older than he was, I knew how to talk better, I was stronger and healthier, and he could neither eat the things I was allowed to eat nor do the things I was allowed to do.

When we played together, I was always the one who set the agenda. We were two stalwart and valiant warriors of "Jin Family Village." I was called Moon and he was called Apricot. I wielded a fine sword, and he had two copper cudgels. And along with us came a whole legion of make-believe warriors. It was always around dusk when the curtain rose. Old Mrs. Jin was in the kitchen chopping vegetables for our last meal before going off to battle. We would cross the mountains by the light of the moon, ambushing the barbarians under cover of night. On the way, we would dispatch two tigers and steal their spawn. The tiger eggs would be like big embroidered balls, and when you broke open the shells, the insides were as white as soft-boiled eggs, except the yolks were round. My little brother quite often would refuse to obey my commands, and we would quarrel. He could "nei-ther make orders nor take them." Yet he was so lovable and such a pretty boy that I would sometimes let him make up a story of his own—"There was a traveler being chased by a tiger, so he ran and ran and ran, running like the wind, with the tiger roaring at his back ..."—but before he could even finish, I would collapse into laughter and kiss his little cheeks, as if he were merely a plaything.

After we got a stepmother, most of my time was spent away at boarding school; I could go home only infrequently and had very little idea of what sort of life my little brother was living. Once, when I came home for vacation, I was astounded to see him grown tall and thin, wearing blue cotton overalls that were none too tidy, and reading a stack of comics rented from a bookstall. At the time, I was reading Mu Shiying's *Nanbei ji* (Poles apart) and Ba Jin's *Miewang* (Annihilation) and was of the opinion that his reading habits were greatly in need of revision.[9] But he merely flitted in front of me before slipping off somewhere else. Everyone at home proceeded to give me a detailed account of his many ignominious deeds, his failure to attend classes, his disobedience, and his lack of ambition. I was even angrier than they were and railed against him in like manner until even they urged moderation.

Later, at the dinner table, over a very trivial matter, my father slapped my little brother across the face. I gave a violent start, hid my face behind a rice bowl, and felt my tears come pouring down. My stepmother began to laugh. "Well? What are *you* crying about? It's

Youth.
Youth: filled with laughter, clamor, sincerity, and anguish. When you still have it, you're not aware of it. Once you become aware of it, it's already quickly ebbing away.

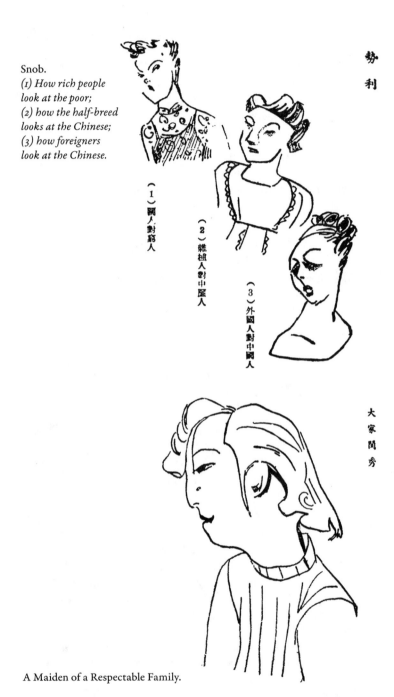

Snob.
(1) How rich people look at the poor;
(2) how the half-breed looks at the Chinese;
(3) how foreigners look at the Chinese.

勢
利

（1）闊人對窮人

（2）雜種人對中國人

（3）外國人對中國人

大
家
閨
秀

A Maiden of a Respectable Family.

A Passion for Philanthropy.
An American lady of the type of Mrs. Roosevelt.

太 太 國 美 的 型 人 夫 羅 斯 羅

not like he was scolding you. Will you look at that! He's the one who got hit, but you're the one that's crying." I dropped the bowl, ran to the adjoining bathroom, and bolted the door behind me, sobbing silently all the while, standing in front of the mirror and staring at my own distorted face, watching the tears roll down, just like a close-up in a movie. Then I clenched my teeth together and swore to myself: "I want revenge. One day, I shall have my revenge."

The bathroom window overlooked the balcony. With a popping noise, a little leather ball slapped against the window glass and bounced back onto the balcony. My brother was playing kickball out there. He had already forgotten everything that had just happened. He was used to this sort of thing. I did not cry anymore. All I felt was a chilling wave of sadness.

WRITING OF ONE'S OWN

ALTHOUGH I write fiction and essays, I usually pay very little heed to theory. Recently, though, I suddenly feel as if I have a little something to say, so I have written it down here.[1]

I have always thought that literary theory comes after literary works. That is how it has been in the past, that is how it is in the present, and in the future I'm afraid it will remain the same. If we desire to enhance writers' awareness of their own craft, it would naturally be of some help to extrapolate theory from literary works themselves in order to use this knowledge as a gauge for further creation. But as we go about this process of gauging our creations, we must also remember that, in the process of literary development, work and theory are like two horses sharing the same yoke, jockeying back and forth as they drive each other forward. Theory is not a driver seated on high, brandishing a whip.

These days, it seems that literary works are impoverished, and so literary theory is impoverished as well. I have discovered that literary writers tend to favor the uplifting and dynamic aspects of life over the placid and static, not realizing that the latter are the foundation of the former. That is, they concentrate for the most part on struggle and neglect the harmonious aspects of life. In reality, people only engage in struggle in order to attain harmony.

An emphasis on the uplifting and dynamic smacks more or less of the superman. Supermen are born of specific epochs. But the placid and static aspects of life have eternal significance: even if this sort of stability is often precarious and subject at regular intervals to destruction, it remains eternal. It exists in every epoch. It is the divine aspect of humanity, and one might also say, of femininity.

Very few works in the history of literature plainly sing in praise of the placid, while many emphasize the dynamic and uplifting aspects of human life. The best of these works, however, depict the dynamics of human life unfolding against a backdrop of inherent placidity. Without the grounding of stability, uplift, like froth, has no substance. Many works are forceful enough to provide excitement but unable to offer any real revelation, and this failure results from not having grasped this grounding.

Struggle is stirring because it is at once grand and sorrowful. Those who struggle have lost their harmony and are in search of a new harmony. Struggle for the sake of struggle lacks resonance and, when transformed into writing, will never produce great literary works.

I find that, in many works, strength predominates over beauty. Strength is jubilant and beauty is mournful, and neither can exist without the other. "Life and death are so far apart / I make my vow to you / and take your hand / to grow old together."[2] This is a mournful poem, but how very affirmative is its posture toward human life. I do not like heroics. I like tragedy and, even better, desolation. Heroism has strength but no beauty and thus seems to lack humanity. Tragedy, however, resembles the matching of bright red with deep green: an intense and unequivocal contrast. And yet it is more exciting than truly revelatory. The reason desolation resonates far more profoundly is that it resembles the conjunction of scallion green with peach red, creating an equivocal contrast.

I like writing by way of equivocal contrast because it is relatively true to life. In "Love in a Fallen City," Liusu escapes from her corrupt traditional family, but the baptism of the Battle of Hong Kong does not transform her into a revolutionary. The Battle of Hong Kong does affect Fan Liuyuan in the sense that it steers him toward a more settled existence and finally marriage, but marriage does not make him a saint or compel him to abandon completely his old habits and ingrained tendencies. Thus, although Liusu and Liuyuan's marriage is healthy in some ways, it remains prosaic, earthbound, and, given their situation, it could be nothing more.

There are very few people, after all, who are either extremely perverse or extremely enlightened. Times as weighty as these do not allow for easy enlightenment. In the past few years, people have gone on living their lives, and even their madness seems measured. So my fiction, with the exception of Cao Qiqiao in "The Golden Cangue," is populated with equivocal characters. They are not heroes, but they are of the majority who actually bear the weight of the times. As equivocal as they may be, they are also in earnest about their lives. They lack tragedy; all they have is desolation. Tragedy is a kind of closure, while desolation is a form of revelation.

I know that people are urgent in their demand for closure and, if they cannot have it, will be only be satisfied by further excitement. They seem to be impatient with revelation in its own right. But I cannot write in any other way. I think that writing in this manner is more true to life. I know that my works lack strength, but since I am a writer of fiction, the only the authority I have is to give expression to the inherent strength of my characters and not to fabricate strength on their behalf. Moreover, I believe that although they are merely weak and ordinary people and cannot aspire to heroic feats of strength, it is precisely these ordinary people who can serve more accurately than heroes as a measure of the times.

In this era, the old things are being swept away and the new things are still being born. But until this historical era reaches its culmination, all certainty will remain an exception. People sense that everything about their everyday lives is a little out of order, out of order to a terrifying degree. All of us must live within a certain historical era, but this era sinks away from us like a shadow, and we feel we have been abandoned. In order to confirm our own existence, we need to take hold of something real, of something most fundamental, and to that end we seek the help of an ancient memory, the memory of a humanity that has lived through every era, a memory clearer and closer to our hearts than anything we might see gazing far into the future. And this gives rise to a strange apprehension about the reality surrounding us. We begin to suspect that this is an absurd and anti-quated world, dark and bright at the same time. Between memory and reality there are awkward discrepancies, producing a solemn but subtle agitation, an intense but as yet indefinable struggle.

There is an unfinished sculpture by Michelangelo, called *Dawn*, in which the human figure is only very roughly hewn and even the facial features are indistinct. But its expansive spirit symbolizes the imminent advent of a new era. If such works were to be produced today, one would be entranced, but none exist, nor indeed can they exist, because we are still unable to struggle free of the nightmare of the era.

And it is this era that constitutes my artistic material, one for which I believe the technique of equivocal contrast is appropriate. I use this method to portray the kinds of memories left behind by humanity as it has lived through each and every historical epoch. And by these means, I provide to the reality that surrounds me a revelation. This is my intention, although I do not know if I have accomplished it. I am incapable of writing the kind of work that people usually refer to as a "monument to an era" and I do not plan to try, because it seems that the concentration of objective material needed for such a project has yet to become available. And, in fact, all I really write about are some of the trivial things that happen between men and women. There is no war and no revolution in my works. I think that people are more straightforward and unguarded in love than they are in war or revolution. War and revolution, by their very nature, make more urgent demands of rationality than sensibility. Works that portray war and revolution often fail precisely because their technical prowess outstrips their artistry. In contrast with the unguarded freedom of love, war is inexorably imposed on us from the outside, whereas revolution often forces the individual to drive forward by dint of will alone. A real revolution or a revolu-tionary war, I believe, should be as emotionally unguarded and as able to penetrate into every aspect of one's life as romantic love. And it should bring one back into a state of harmony.

I like forthright simplicity, but I must portray the rich duplicity and artifice of modern people in order to set them off against the ground of life's simplicity. This is why my writing is too easily seen by some readers as overly lush or even decadent. But I do not think it possible to use the elemental approach of a book like the Old Testament. This is the altar on which Tolstoy was sacrificed in his waning years. Nor do I approve of the aesthetes who advocate Beauty above all else. I think that their problem lies not in their beauty but in their failure to provide the figure of Beauty with a ground. The water in a mountain stream is merely light and frolicsome, but seawater, though it may seem to ripple in much the same way, also contains within it the prospect of vast oceanic swells. Beautiful things are not necessarily grand, but grand things are always beautiful. And yet I do not place truthfulness and hypocrisy in direct and unequivocal contrast; instead, I utilize equivocal contrast as a means of writing the truth beneath the hypocrisy of modern people and the simplicity underneath the frivolity, and this is why I have all too easily been seen as overly indulgent and criticized for lingering over these beguiling surfaces. Even so, I continue to write in my own style and can only feel ashamed that I have yet to perfect my art. I am, after all, just a neophyte when it comes to literature.

When readers of the old school read my works, they find them rather diverting but also more unsettling than they should be. New-style people find them reasonably absorbing but not quite as serious as they might be. But that is the best I can do, and I am confident that my art is not compromised. I only demand of myself that I strive for an even greater degree of truthfulness.

Further, because I rely on a particular conception of equivocal contrast in my writing, I do not like to adopt the classicist manner in which good and evil, spirit and flesh, are always posed against each other in stark conflict, and thus the theme of my works may sometimes seem vague and unsatisfactory. I think the theory that a literary work needs a main theme could do with some revision. In writing fiction, one ought to have a story. It is better to let that story speak for itself than fabricating a plot in order to fit a certain theme. Readers often pay very little heed to the original themes of the great works that have come down to us through the ages, because times have changed, and those concerns no longer have the power to engage us. Yet readers of these works may at any time extract new revelations from the stories themselves, and it is only thus that the eternal life of any given work is assured. Take *War and Peace*, for instance. Originally, Tolstoy intended his story to revolve around the religious and collectivist philosophies of life that were popular at the time, but, as it turned out, the unfolding of the story itself eventually vanquished his pre-determined theme. This is a work that was rewritten seven times, and with each revision the predetermined theme was forfeited still further. In the end, what remained of the theme was little more than an aside, becoming in fact the most awkward section of the novel, and there was no new main theme to replace it. This is why Tolstoy felt himself somewhat at a loss after having finished the novel. In comparison with *Resurrection*, the main theme of *War and Peace* does seem rather indistinct, but it remains much the greater work. Even now, every inch of the text comes alive as we read. The difference between modern literary works and those that came before also seems to rest on this distinction. No more does the emphasis lie principally on a main theme; instead, the story is allowed to give what it can and readers to take what they are able.

This is how I have and will continue to write *Chained Links*. In that work, the absence of a main theme is conspicuous, but I hope that people will like it for the story alone. My original idea was very simple: I would describe these sorts of things as they are. Modern people for the most part are exhausted, and the modern marriage system is irrational as well. Thus silence reigns between husbands and wives. There are those who look for relief by engaging in sophisticated flirtation, so as to avoid having to take responsibility for their actions, and those who revert to animal desires by patronizing prostitutes (but these are only beastly men and not beasts and are thus all the more horrifying). Then there is cohabitation, which is not as serious a bond as marriage, involves more responsibility than sophisticated flirtation, and is not so lacking in humanity as whoring. People who go to extremes are, in the final analysis, the minority, and so living together out of wedlock has become a very common phenomenon in recent years.

The social status of the men who support these kinds of arrangements is roughly middle class or below; they work hard and live thriftily. They can't afford to let themselves go but aren't so reserved that they are willing to let themselves sink into boredom, either. They need vibrant, down-to-earth relationships with women, relationships that are just as vibrant and down-to-earth as the other aspects of their lives. They need women to look after their homes and are consequently less perverse in their dealings with them. In *Chained Links*, Yaheya is the proprietor of a midsized silk shop who still must work the counter himself. If Nixi could get along with him in peace, peace would continue to reign in their relationship for years to come and nothing would prevent the two from growing old and gray together. The failure of their life together out of wedlock arises from Nixi's own character flaws. Her second lover, Dou Yaofang, is the relatively prosperous owner of an herbal medicine shop, but he lacks the swanky air of a big-time capitalist. The petty official with whom Nixi lives has no more than a touch of the bureaucrat about him. Neither man is especially perverse when it comes to Nixi. What transpires between her and them is very human. And thus it should come as no surprise that these relationships are full of genuine affection.

As for women who live with men out of wedlock, their social position necessarily starts out somewhat lower than that of men, but most of them possess a fiery will to live. Still, the seductive power they have over their lovers is no more and no less than the charm of a healthy woman. If they were really as perverse as they are often imagined to be, they would not satisfy the needs of these men. Such women can work for attention, can be jealous, show off, and fight; they can be quite savage but never hysterical. They have only one problem: that their status remains forever in doubt. And because of this gnawing insecurity, they become selfish and mercenary as time goes on.

This sort of cohabitation is more prevalent in China than it is in the West, but no one has yet attempted to write about it. The Mandarin Ducks and Butterflies writers find these types of people lacking in the sentimentality traditionally evoked by "talented scholar and beautiful maiden" romances.[3] The new-style writers, on the other hand, dislike that these relationships seem to resemble neither love nor prostitution and are thus neither healthy enough nor sufficiently perverse to lend themselves to the articulation of an unmistakably clear main theme.

What moves me about Nixi's story is the purity of her passion for material life, a life that she must struggle with all her might to retain. She wants the love of men but also desires security, cannot have both simultaneously, and ends up in possession of neither. She feels she can depend on nothing and invests everything in her children, hoping thereby to reap the bounty of their labor: a most inhuman sort of reward.

It is not that Nixi lacks feeling. She wants to love this world but never finds an opening. Nor is it the case that she is unloved, but the love she receives is merely the leftover stew and cold table scraps from someone else's meal, as in Du Fu's poem: "Leftover stew and cold scraps / everywhere bitterness concealed."[4] But she is above all a vital, healthy woman and never resorts to beggarliness. She resembles instead someone who chews greedily on cakes made from leftover soybean dregs, fried in too much oil: even though she has a very strong constitution, and the meal might have a modicum of nutritional value, she'll end up with an upset stomach. That a human being is made to eat the dregs usually intended for beasts is the real tragedy.

As for the fact that I have adopted phrases and diction from traditional fiction in writing *Chained Links*—where Cantonese and foreigners of fifty years ago speak like characters from *The Golden Lotus* or when the Chinese people in Pearl Buck's fiction sound just like characters from old English literature when they open their mouths to speak—all these borrowings were for the sake of expedience and less than ideal as such. My original intention was this: the romantic ambience of Hong Kong as envisioned by Shanghai people would set up one sort of distance and the temporal divide between the present and the Hong Kong of fifty years ago would create another.

So I adopted an already antiquated sort of diction in order to represent better these two kinds of distance. There are times when it may seem contrived and overdone. I think I will be able to make some corrections in the future.

NOTES ON APARTMENT LIFE

ON ENCOUNTERING the line "I long to ride the wind home / but fear those coral towers and jade domes / for high places are unbearably cold," the majority of apartment dwellers who live on the top floor might well feel a shudder of recognition run down their spines.[1] The higher the apartment, the colder. Ever since the price of coal went up, radiators have become purely decorative. The "H" on the hot water tap may be an indispensable feature of a bathroom's design, but as things stand now, if you mistakenly turn on the hot water instead of the cold, a series of wails and hollow thumps emerges from the "Nine Springs" of the netherworld somewhere down below. That is the sound of the apartment building's terribly complicated and capricious hot water system losing its temper. Even if you don't engage in deliberate provocation, this god of thunder might well make an appearance at any time. It comes at you out of nowhere with an evil, elongated buzz followed by two blasting sounds, exactly like an airplane circling over the roof of the building before dropping two bombs. Having lost my courage in the terror of wartime Hong Kong, this sound used to throw me into a panic when I first got back to Shanghai. Early on, the pipes still went about their work conscientiously, laboriously transporting hot water up to the sixth floor, where it arrived with a gurgle or two. That was easily forgiven. But nowadays there is loud thunder but very little rain, and we are lucky if we get two drops of rusty brown mud ... but there isn't much else I can say; the unemployed are so full of bile

In the rainy season, the foundation of the tall building sinks into the topsoil from its weight, such that the deepest puddles are clustered right around the front entrance. The street will be completely dry, but we still have to spend money hiring rickshaws to cross the vast and misty moat that rings the building. When there is too much rain, the apartment itself will flood. We take turns coming to the rescue, using old towels, burlap bags, and sheets to block up the cracks in the window. When these things get wet through, we wring them out and put them back, squeezing the dirty water into wash basins and then pouring it into the toilet. After two days and two nights of work, a whole layer of skin has been rubbed off our palms, but water still pools at the base of the walls, and the patterned wallpaper is dappled with water stains and spots of mildew.

If the wind is not blowing in our direction, however, rain at the top of a tall building is actually quite lovely. One day, it rained around dusk. I had forgotten to close the windows on my way out, and when I came home and opened the front door, the apartment was full of the sound of wind and the smell of rain, so I looked out the window. It was a deep blue, raindrop-spattered night, with a few pale lamps swaying in the distance. Most of the houses had yet to turn on their lights.

I am often astounded by how extraordinarily clearly one can hear street noises from the sixth floor, as if it was all happening right beneath one's ears, resembling the way memories of trivial incidents from childhood become increasingly clear and close the older and more distant they become.

I like to listen to city sounds. People more poetic than me listen from their pillows to the sound of rustling pines or the roar of ocean waves, while I can't fall asleep until I hear the sound of trams. On the hills in Hong Kong, it was only in the winter when the north wind blew all night long through the evergreens that I was reminded of the charming cadence of a tram. Those who have lived their whole lives amid the bustle of the city do not realize what exactly they cannot do without until they have left. The thoughts of city people unfold across a striped curtain. The pale white stripes are trams in motion, moving neatly in parallel, their streams of sound flowing right into subconscious strata.

Our apartment is near the tram depot, but I've never been able to tell exactly what time they come home. The phrase "trams coming home" doesn't seem quite right—everyone knows that trams are soulless machines and that the words "coming home" all but overflow with sentimental associations. But have you ever seen the strange spectacle of trams going into their garage? One after another, like small children waiting in line, noisy, squealing, hoarse bells happily sounding out: "cling, clang, cling, clang." Amid the noise, a sense of a docility born of exhaustion, like children before bedtime waiting for their mothers to help them wash up. The lights in the trams shine bright white. Vendors hawk bread to tram ticket collectors coming off the late shift. Every once in a while, when all the trams have gone inside, a single one is left parked outside, mysteriously, as if it had been abandoned in the middle of the street. Seen from above, its exposed white belly gleams in the moonlight in the depths of the night.

The vendors around here rarely sell any particularly fancy snacks. Nor have we ever lowered a basket out the window to the street to buy things from them. (Which reminds one of Violet Koo in the movie *Nong ben chiqing* [I'm a fool for you]. She makes a rope out of silk stockings, attaches a paper box to the end, and lowers it out the window to buy noodle soup. No real silk stockings could ever survive such an ordeal! In the current climate of rationing and "resource conservation," this is a shocking extravagance that sets one's pulse racing). Maybe we should try lowering a basket to the street. Every time we hear the vendor who sells stinky tofu coming down the street, we have to grab a bowl, race down six flights of steps, give chase down the street, and, having finally located our man several long blocks away and made our purchase, take the elevator back home. All this seems faintly ridiculous.

Our elevator man is a real character, well read and erudite, of rare cultivation, a man who keeps meticulous tabs on the comings and goings of each family in the building. He doesn't approve of his son becoming a ticket collector on a streetcar because it's not a sufficiently classy profession. On even the hottest of days, no matter how urgently someone is ringing the electric buzzer, he still insists on donning a neatly ironed silk vest over his sleeveless undershirt before emerging from his room. He refuses to operate the elevator for visitors who dress sloppily. His thinking may incline too much toward the out-moded ideals of the traditional gentry, but at least he thinks. True, he leaves his little room only to step into the little room of an eleva-tor. One fears that his whole existence will be consumed shuttling back and forth between these two cells. As the elevator rises, layer after layer of darkness moves past the brass grillwork, patterned after the Chinese character for man (人). Brown darkness, rusty brown darkness, darkest darkness, and, set against these variations, the grizzled head of the elevator operator.

When he has a moment off, he goes to the back courtyard and cooks stir-fried dishes and griddle cakes on a little coal-burning stove. He taught us how to cook wild red rice: after the rice comes to a boil, kill the flame, and let it sit for ten minutes before continuing. What results is rice that is soft, cooked through, but not the least mushy or lacking in texture.

I once asked him to buy soy milk for us and gave him a used milk bottle for that purpose. After having made these purchases by proxy for two weeks, he rather matter-of-factly reported: "The bottle's gone." Whether it was broken or merely stolen, we didn't know. A little later on, he brought us a slightly smaller bottle full of soy milk: "Oh? The bottle's back?" He replied: "It's back." We could never ascertain whether this new bottle was meant to compensate us for the lost one or was merely on loan. These sorts of incidents have something of a socialistic tinge to them.

He invariably glances through the *Xinwen bao* (Daily news) before delivering it to our apartment every morning. He must read the tabloids rather more carefully, for we rarely get to see them before eleven or twelve noon. He doesn't read the English, Japanese, German, or Russian papers, which is why, bright and early each morning, they are rolled up and stuck in the crook above everyone's doorknobs.

No one steals the papers, but the metal facing over the doorbells was once pried off and taken away. There are actually two guards responsible for securing the front entrance. They are not twins, but they seem to share the same sawdusty yellow faces sticking out above button-down collars and sawdusty yellow knees sticking out between their shorts and the tops of their high socks. They doze on wicker chairs in front of the mailboxes during their shift. Whenever you want to check the mail, they block the way so that you must solicitously push your face close to theirs, as if to enquire whether their acne has shown any improvement lately.

Perhaps only women can fully appreciate the advantages of apartment life: the problem of hired help becomes much less pressing. The cost of living is high, and even if you can afford a maid, you have to prepare for her to be annoyed by your shortcomings. Domestic life is a relatively simple matter in an apartment. You can arrange for a company to come by once every two weeks and do a thorough cleaning, thus eliminating the need for hired help. Not having to have a maid is one of the best things in life. Leaving any notions of the ideal of equality aside, it's terribly annoying, if not utterly ruinous in terms of one's appetite, to have someone who has not yet eaten standing over you and watching as you eat at mealtimes, always at the ready to give you more rice. There are so many little chores that are inherently pleasurable to perform. If you can't see eggplants growing in a garden, it's almost as lovely to see them at the vegetable market: an intricate and glossy shade of purple next to the pale green of new peas, the ruby ripeness of peppers, and the golden yellow of gluten shining like soap bubbles in the sun. Every time one washes spinach and drops it into the wok, there are always one or two broken leaves stuck to the bottom of the bamboo basket, and no matter how hard you shake, they refuse to budge. In the light, the fresh emerald leaves displayed against the rectangular weave of the basket call to mind snow pea flowers on a trellis. And why must we call other things to mind at all? Isn't the beauty of the basket itself sufficient? None of this is intended as a display of my fealty to the National Socialist Party and its efforts to coax women back into the kitchen.[2] There is so little point in coaxing, and if one must coax, it would only be right to urge men into the kitchen for a visit as well. Obviously, when people who have hired a cook start to hang around the kitchen, they will be looked on with some distaste. We must be careful not to infringe upon the prerogatives of our betters.

Sometimes, one also feels rather acutely the bitterness of life without help. There were weevils in the rice crock, so I sprinkled white pepper inside: apparently weevils do not appreciate the pungent aroma, and you can remove the peppercorns before soaking the rice. I mistook the head of a fat weevil for a peppercorn and squeezed it between my fingers. Once I realized my mistake, I could not help letting out an appropriately dismayed squeal, dropping the pot, and running away. In fact, when I saw a snake in Hong Kong once, it was much the same. All I saw of that snake was his upper half, stretching to a height of nearly two feet, just after it had slithered from out of a hole. I was holding a stack of books as I walked rapidly down a hill when I came face to face with it. It gazed quietly at me and I gazed quietly back, and it was only after a long pause that I screamed, turned, and fled.

Speaking of insects, there are hardly any flies up on the sixth floor, but every so often a few mosquitoes do make an appearance. If they were endowed with the slightest bit of imagination, surely they would faint dead away upon flying to the window and looking down to the ground far below? Unfortunately, these mosquitoes are all too similar to the English in their indifference and self-satisfaction. Even in the jungles of Africa, an Englishman still wears tails to dinner.

An apartment is an ideal retreat from the world outside. Often, people who are weary of metropolitan life yearn for the quiet harmony of the countryside, longing for the day when they might retire to their old country home, keep bees, plant a few crops, and enjoy a well-earned rest. Little do they know that in the countryside the mere purchase of a half pound of smoked meat elicits storms of idle gossip, whereas in an apartment on the top floor, you can change clothes right in front of the window without anyone knowing the difference!

Even so, the secrets of everyday life must be made public at least once a year. In the summer, each and every family throws its doors wide and brings rattan chairs out into the hallway to take the breeze. Someone over there is talking on the telephone. The servant boy across the hall is ironing some clothes as he translates the telephone conversation into German for the benefit of his little master. There is a Russian man downstairs noisily giving Japanese lessons. The woman on the second floor seems to be locked in mortal combat with Beethoven, gritting her teeth as she repeatedly pummels the piano, against which a bicycle is precariously propped. Someone somewhere is making beef stew, and someone else simmering a Chinese herbal brew that counters indigestion.

Mankind is naturally inclined to mind other people's business. Why shouldn't we take the occasional stealthy glance at one another's private lives, if the person being looked at suffers no real damage and the one who looks is afforded a moment of pleasure? In matters involving the provision and procurement of pleasure, there's no need to be overly fussy. What, in the end, is there to fuss about? Misery endures, but life is short.

The kids in the building sometimes skate in the roof garden, and when they are in high spirits, the scraping sound of their motion back and forth can go from morning to evening, sounding like nothing so much as dishes rasping against each other or a sleeper steadily grinding his teeth, setting your own teeth on edge, like the sour little pips of a green pomegranate that drop to the ground with a flick of a finger. The foreign gentleman next door rushes furiously up the stairs to give them a piece of his mind. His wife warns: "They won't understand what you're saying, anyway. It's a waste of time." He balls his fists and rolls up his sleeves: "No matter. I'll make them understand." A few minutes later, he descends the stairs with the wind knocked out of his sails. The kids upstairs aren't so young anymore, and they're female, and they are pretty.

Speaking of public-spiritedness and morality, we cannot really claim to be any better than anyone else. We sweep the dust on our balcony down to the balcony below us without the slightest hesitation. "Oh, they've put their carpet out to dry on the railing. It would be such a shame to dirty it. Let's wait until they take it back in before we sweep." One kind thought such as this, and a glimmering halo materializes around one's head. This, then, is our not so very thorough sense of ethics.

BUGLE MUSIC FROM THE NIGHT BARRACKS

TEN O'CLOCK at night, and I am reading a book by lamplight when the bugle in the army barracks near my home starts to play a familiar melody. A few simple musical phrases, slowly rising and then descending, with a purity of heart altogether rare in this vast crucible of a city.

I say, "They're playing the bugle again, Auntie. Didn't you hear it?" My aunt says, "I wasn't paying attention." I am afraid of hearing that bugle every night, because I am the only one who ever listens to it.

I say, "Oh, they're playing again." But for some unknown reason, this time the sound is very soft, as slight as a strand of silk, breaking off several times before once again picking up the thread. This time, I don't even ask my aunt whether she has heard it. I begin to doubt whether there really is a bugle at all or if this is merely a memory of something I've heard. Above and beyond my sense of desolation, I feel frightened.

But then I hear someone outside whistling loud and clear, picking up and following the bugle's melody as he goes along. I spring to my feet, full of joy and empathy, and rush over to the window. Yet I have no desire to know who it is, whether it's coming from an apartment upstairs or down below or from a passerby on the street.

Foreigners (1).
(1) The English;
(2) the Germans;
(3) the French.

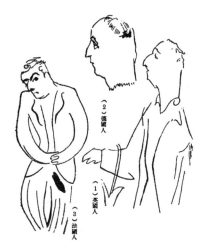

（２）德國人

（１）英國人

（３）法國人

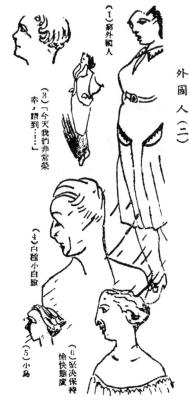

（１）窮外國人

外國人（二）

（２）英國太太碰到天災人禍，事無大小，總叫你：親愛的，鎮靜一點。

（３）「今天我們非常榮幸，讀到……」

（４）白種小白臉

（５）小鳥

（６）堅決保持愉快態度

Foreigners (2).
(1) A poor foreigner;
(2) "An English lady, no matter what calamity she encounters, be it serious or inconsequential, will always tell you, 'Remain calm, my dear'";
(3) "Today, we are very fortunate to have the honor of...";
(4) a pale, feminine Caucasian man;
(5) a little bird;
(6) "Steadfastly hold to a positive attitude."

Foreigners (3).
(1) A Western lady;
(2) a crazed artist;
(3) a ballet dancer;
(4) a Japanese dandy;
(5) a girl named Yukiko.

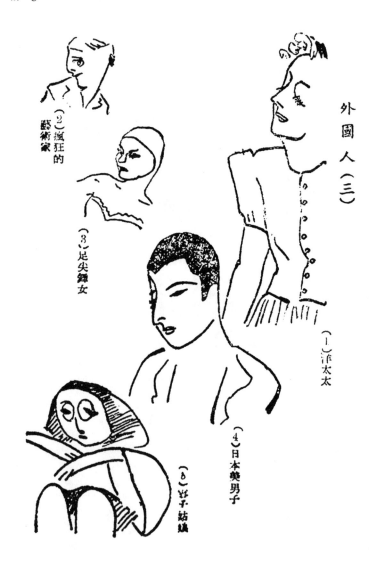

外國人（三）

（一）洋太太

（二）瘋狂的
藝術家

（三）足尖舞女

（四）日本美男子

（五）雪子姑娘

"WHAT IS ESSENTIAL IS THAT NAMES BE RIGHT"

I MYSELF have an unbearably vulgar name, am well aware of the fact, and have no plans to change it. Even so, I remain extremely interested in people's names.[1]

To give someone a name is a simple and small-scale act of creation. When the patriarch of days gone by would sit in winter with his feet propped up on a foot-warming brazier, smoking a water pipe, and pick out a name for a newly arrived grandson, his word was all. If the boy was called Guang-mei (Brighten the Threshold), he would end up doing his best to redound honor on the gates of the family house. If he was called Zuyin (Ancestral Privilege) or Chengzu (Indebted to the Ancestors), he would be compelled to frequently remember his forebears. If he was called Hesheng (Lotus Born), his life would take on something of the coloring of a pond in June. Characters in novels aside, there aren't many people whose names adequately describe what they are like in reality (and often the opposite is the case and the name represents something they need or lack—nine of ten poor people have names like Jingui [Gold Precious], Ah Fu [Richie], Dayou [Have a Lot]). But no matter how or in what manner, names inevitably become entangled with appearance and character in the process of creating a complete impression of a person. And this is why naming is a kind of creation.

I like to give people names, even though I have yet to have an opportunity to do so. It seems that only parents and schoolmasters in the countryside have this right. Besides these, we must also include venerable gentlemen and grand dames who buy servant girls and dancehall madams who procure young women. Such a shame that these people are so sloppy in their execution of these duties, since they rely entirely on precedent: little kids are invariably called Maotou (Kid), Er Maotou (Kid Number Two), San Maotou (Kid the Third); servant girls become Ruyi (As You Wish); and taxi dancers are given foreign-sounding names like Manna.

Catholic priests and Protestant pastors also give babies names when they're baptized (this must be one of the most compelling of their duties), but they never seem to stray very far from the common round of George, Mary, and Elizabeth. I once compiled two or three hundred commonly used English names for girls, and I'm afraid that my list pretty much exhausts the possibilities, even if there are a few that I left out. Customs are handed down, and names are inevitably selected from folkloric traditions and religious history, to the point where one runs everywhere into people with the same names—what a bore! There's an old joke: someone flips through the entire Bible in search of a relatively distinctive name. He triumphantly informs his pastor that he's decided on a name no one else has ever used before: Satan.

As for Chinese people, we have all of Wang Yunwu's great big dictionary of Chinese in which to search for just a couple of characters to represent ourselves.[2] With such an abundance of choices, it seems unforgivable that there are some people who are willing to let themselves be called things like Xiuzhen (Precious) and Zijing (Quiet).

Appropriate names need be neither novel, nor erudite, nor dignified. What is important is that they create a clear image that resonates with a person's identity. When I read the newspaper, I like looking through the classified ads, sports pages, and lists of recipients of scholarships and small business loans, because I will usually find some good names there. Chai Feng-ying (Firewood Phoenix Flower) and Mao Yi-jian (Frugal Thatch), for instance. Can't you see the flesh-and-blood figures just waiting to emerge from behind the names? One need hardly mention Mao Yi-jian's miserable penury. Chai Feng-ying not only sounds like the epitome of the proverbial "precious daughter of a humble home"; her name sounds like it has a story just wriggling to get out, a folksy tale of a beautiful girl rising above her station. I would love to write a story in the near future in which Chai Feng-ying is the heroine.

Some people say that a name is merely a cipher, without any intrinsic significance. But those who make this argument in print are themselves writing under the imprint of their own carefully crafted pen names. Of course, this is a natural impulse. Who among us does not desire to distinguish himself from the crowd? Even if we lived in an idealized future world in which every citizen was assigned a number like a prisoner and there were no names beyond the numbers themselves, each number would still inescapably take on its own distinct connotation. Three and seven are smartly handsome numbers, while two clearly comes off as rather staid. In Zhang Henshui's *Qinhuai shijia* (The house of Qinhuai) the mischievous girl is called Xiaochun (Little Spring), while Erchun (Second Spring) is her modest and retiring sister. In *Ye shen chen* (Deep is the night), there is the virtuous Ding Erhe (Second Harmony Ding) and the cautiously conventional Second Miss Tian.[3]

Although a movement to promote the use of signs instead of names could never be pushed through to successful conclusion, it is not an entirely unreasonable notion given the excessive complexity of Chinese names. As soon as your feet hit the ground, you are given a pet name. In the past, pet names were chosen with great care, unlike the perfunctory sorts of endearments common today, such as Nannan (Girlie) and Baobao (Baby). For the vast majority of girls, the pet name is the only name they will ever get. Since they are never going to go to school anyway, there is little use giving them an impressive "school name," and once they marry they will immediately lose whatever sense of identity they might once have had, becoming merely Miss Zhang née Li or the like. Everything about a woman should carry with it a touch of mystery, and for this reason, a woman's pet name is never given out lightly. In the boudoir poetry of women writers, we can see that a newlywed groom who openly calls out the bride's childhood name is seen as being rather remiss and his lapse deserving of a pouting reproach.

Little boys write out their school names in painstakingly neat characters on their first character primers. If a boy should grow up to be an official, this name then becomes an official title, the invocation of which will be restricted to superiors in the bureaucracy, parents, and teachers. He also has a more informal "style name" for use by friends and relatives belonging to the same generation as himself. There is also a third name that is kept in reserve but never used. These literary sobriquets are relatively free of restriction. Such a name can be changed in honor of the purchase of a particularly fine antique. It can be changed after moving house. It can be changed when he becomes wildly infatuated with an actress and wants to make the liaison public. If names are meant to suggest states of mind, why shouldn't they shift at any time or any place in accordance with someone's ever-changing moods?

In *Ernü yingxiong zhuan* (The story of lovers and heroes), Young Master An has an "East Chamber Wife" and a "West Chamber Wife."[4] He commissions a carved plaque to be placed above the door to the eastern chamber that reads "Banxiang shi" (Fragrant petal boudoir) and one for the western chamber that reads "Banxiang shi" (Fragrant companion boudoir). He goes on to call himself the Banban zhuren (Petal companion lord). When Old Man An sees these signs, he is most perturbed, viewing them as dubious markers of descent into the degenerate frivolity of romance. This passage often fires readers with indignation against the tyranny of the old-style family, so ubiquitous and invasive that even when a son chooses a perfectly harmless sobriquet, the patriarch still feels compelled to interfere. Surely all the name signifies is the son's desire to enjoy his own wives? And was it not his own father who arranged his union with these women? Despite these objections, however, I still have quite a bit of sympathy for Old Man An, if only because creating superfluous sobriquets is, after all, a rather inane occupation.

What if we were to analyze the question on a more fundamental level? Why ever would someone feel compelled to have several names in the first place? Because, it seems, each individual is multifaceted. What a father sees in a person and what the foreigner at the office sees of the very same person are completely different matters, made so through differentials of power and relative position. Some people like to plaster their walls with mirrors from the ceiling to the floor so that they will always be able to take stock of their own image from several different angles, never tiring of the view. Taking extra names is a similar sort of self-inflation.

But if self-inflation does no harm to others, what's wrong with using it as a means of amusing oneself? A sort of spiritual superfluity it may well be, but we Chinese have always had a penchant for profligate indulgence in beauty.

The desire for those in the world outside to take an interest in one's name is an altogether different matter. Perhaps we really believe that when a reader sees our latest incarnation, they say "Oh, Gongyang Huan. When his first piece was published, he was still going by the name Zang Sun Didong, and when he submitted a manuscript to such and such magazine, he went by Ming Di, but he's also been called Bai Bo, referred to on occasion as Mu Lian, and apparently the writer who goes by Ying Yuan is really him, too, as is Duan Dai, at least according to some people. In such and such a newspaper, his byline is Dongfang Maozhi, but when he's acting as the editor for a women's magazine, he temporarily takes on an appropriately feminized Lin Yanchan, also known as Nü Gui."[5] Even a prominent public figure who counted on people to commit so many names to memory might be accused of unduly extravagant expectations. How much the more so a writer?

If people do what they are expected to do, they receive the expected amount of recognition. And after ten years or so, when they have finished the job they have set out to do or simply can't do it anymore, they are forgotten. Society has a short memory, and that is as it should be, and no one really has a right to complain . . . even though there are many things out there that people ought, but do not, remember!

When I was still in school, there were at least two other people who had the same name as I did, and no one seemed to think it was funny or lacking in good taste. When the Chinese teachers called out the roll, they never mispronounced my name; when the English teachers read out a name like Wu Wanyun they invariably ran into difficulties, as if their tongues were tied in a butterfly knot. But when they read my name, it always came to them loud and clear. No small mercy!

Recently I've begun to think that I ought to be dissatisfied with my name. Why shouldn't I adopt two lovely and profound characters to make a new one? Even if they would have no impact on whether I'm really lovely and profound myself, they might at least prevent a bad first impression on my readers. I seem to remember that someone once said: "The art of succeeding in publishing depends first and foremost on selecting a positively effulgent name." Could it be true (as Confucius said) that "if the name is incorrect, words will not follow. If words do not follow, deeds will go unaccomplished"?

China is a nation of words. When an emperor met with misfortune, he would immediately change the name of the reign period in hopes of turning the country's luck in the year to come. What used to be the Twelfth Year of the Martial Advent would suddenly become the Inaugural Year of the Era of Great Celebration, thus putting an immediate end to the sufferings of the past. An excessive faith in the power of words is our most distinctive characteristic.

Everything in China sounds just a little bit too good, rolls just a little too easily off the tongue. Certainly, not everything that sounds or looks bad from the outside is necessarily useful, but the most useful people are often the most ordinary. I am willing to keep my unbearably vulgar name as a warning to myself that I must find a way to rid myself of the fussiness with words of the typical well-read intellectual and begin to look for life through its essentials: wood, rice, oil, salt, soap, water, and sun.

This story has wound its way back to the beginning. My desire to become an ordinary person and to focus on having an ordinary name is admittedly another form of "word worship." Perhaps these are merely excuses. The reason I feel such a fond attachment to my name is tied up with my memory of how I came to be named. When I was ten, my mother proclaimed that I should be sent to school, and my father raised a huge storm of protest and refused to give his consent. Finally, my mother personally carried me to school over his loud protests, like a kidnapper. As she filled out the school registration card, she hesitated, uncertain what name to write down. My childhood name had been Ying, but to be called Ying Chang would sound a bit too reedy and dull. She propped her head against her hand and thought for a moment before saying: "Let's transcribe your English name into Chinese for the time being." She always planned to change it someday but never did; now, I wouldn't want to change it anyway.

FROM THE ASHES

THERE'S already a considerable distance between myself and Hong Kong: one thousand miles, two years, new events, and new people. I would not have known how or from where to begin speaking of what I saw and heard in Hong Kong during the war, because the experience cut too close to the bone, affecting me in an altogether drastic fashion. My mind is now somewhat more settled, at least to the extent that I am able to keep those events in some kind of order when they come up in conversation. And yet my impressions of the Battle of Hong Kong seem nevertheless to be almost entirely restricted to a few irrelevant trivialities.

I have neither the desire to write history nor the qualifications to comment on the approach historians ought to bring to their work, but privately I have always found myself wishing that they would concern themselves more with irrelevant things. This thing we call reality is unsystematic, like seven or eight talking machines playing all at once in a chaos of sound, each singing its own song. From within that incomprehensible cacophony, however, there sometimes happens to emerge a moment of sad and luminous clarity, when the musicality of a melody can be heard, just before it is engulfed once more by layer after layer of darkness, snuffing out this unexpected moment of lucidity. Painters, writers, and composers string together these random and accidentally discovered moments of harmony in order to create artistic coherence. When history insists on the same sort of coherence, it becomes fiction. The reason that H. G. Wells's *Outline of History* cannot stand as a proper history is that it is a little too rationalized, chronicling as it does the struggle between the individual and the group from start to finish.

Rigid and unswerving worldviews, be they political or philosophical, cannot help provoking the antipathy of others. What's usually called joie de vivre is to be found entirely in trivial things.

In Hong Kong, when we first received word of the advent of war, one of the girls in the dormitory[1] flew into a panic, "What am I to do? I have nothing to wear!" She was a wealthy overseas Chinese for whom different sorts of social occasions required different sorts of apparel. She had made adequate preparations for all kinds of contingencies, from dancing on a yacht to a formal dinner, but she had never considered the possibility of war. She managed eventually to borrow a baggy dress of black quilted cotton, which she figured would not be the least bit attractive to the fighter planes circling overhead. When the time came to flee, all the students in the dormitory went their separate ways. After the battle, when I ran into her again, she had cut her hair short in the boyish Filipino style that was all the rage in Hong Kong at the time, so that she could look more like a man if need be.

The psychological response of different people to the war did, in fact, seem to have something to do with their clothes. Take Sureika, for instance. Sureika was the reigning beauty of a remote little town on the Malay Peninsula, a skinny girl with dark brown skin, heavy-lidded and languorous eyes, and slightly protruding front teeth. Like most girls who have been educated in a convent, she was almost shamefully naive. She chose to study medicine. Medical students have to dissect corpses, but do the corpses wear clothes? Sureika was concerned about this question and made inquiries. This became a standing joke around campus.

When a bomb fell next door to our dormitory, the warden had no choice but to order us to evacuate down the hill. Even at the height of the crisis, Sureika did not neglect to pack up her most luxurious clothes and, in defiance of the earnest counsel of many wise people, found a way to transport them down the hill in a large and unwieldy leather trunk in the midst of an artillery barrage. Sureika later participated in defense work, becoming a substitute nurse for a Red Cross medical unit. She would squat down on her haunches to gather firewood and light bonfires, clad all the while in a copper-red brocade gown, embroidered in green with the character for "longevity." And though it was something of a shame to wear such a nice dress under those circumstances, the brilliance of her attire allowed her an unprecedented degree of self-confidence, without which she would have been unable to mix so well with her male coworkers, and this made it worthwhile. As she shared their hardships and braved danger alongside them, sharing jokes, chatting, and growing accustomed to the work, she gradually became a skilled old hand. For her, the war was a rare sort of education.

For most of us students, however, our attitude toward the war could be summed up by a simile: we were like someone sitting on a hard plank bench, trying to take a nap. Although in terrible discomfort, and ceaselessly complaining of it, we managed to fall asleep all the same.

What we did not have to pay attention to we managed to ignore. As we passed through life-and-death situations, navigating the most colorful experiences imaginable, we remained ourselves, untouched, maintaining our everyday modes of life. Occasionally, someone might do something that seemed somewhat out of the ordinary, but after careful analysis, one could see that it was in fact entirely in character. Evelyn, for instance, was from the interior of China and had witnessed plenty of combat in her time. By her own account, she was hardy, tough, and entirely accustomed to frightening experiences. When the military garrison next to our dormitory was bombed in an air raid, though, Evelyn was the first to lose control, bursting into hysterical sobs and loudly relating her stock of terrifying war stories for the benefit of the other female students until their faces turned ghostly pale with fright.

Evelyn's pessimism was a healthy sort of pessimism. When the grain reserves in the dormitory were almost gone, Evelyn began to eat more than usual and urged us all to do the same, since there would very soon be nothing left to eat at all. We had actually thought of making a serious bid to cut down our food intake and even ration our supplies, but she did her best to obstruct these efforts, eating more than her fill and sitting to one side and sobbing, all of which eventually resulted in a bad case of constipation.

We congregated in the basement of the dormitory, and in the pitch dark stood between stacks of trunks, listening to the sound of machine gun fire crackling like raindrops on water lotus leaves. Because the little scullery maid was afraid of ricocheting bullets and refused to go near the window to wash the vegetables in the light, our soup was full of little wriggling insects.

Yanying was the only one of my classmates who had any guts.[2] She risked her life to go into town to see a movie—a Technicolor cartoon—and, when she got back to the dormitory, went upstairs all alone to take a bath. When a ricocheting bullet shattered the bathroom window, she remained calm, leisurely humming a tune as she continued to splash in the tub. The warden was furious when he heard her singing. Her indifference seemed to make a mockery of everyone else's terror.

When the University of Hong Kong shut down, out-of-town students were forced to leave the dormitories—driven, in effect, into homelessness. There was no way to solve the problem of room and board save to join the defense effort. I went with a large group of fellow students to register at the Air-Raid Precaution headquarters. As soon as we were done, emerging with newly issued badges in hand, we managed to run right into an air raid. We jumped off the tram we had been riding and made a beeline for the sidewalk, flattening ourselves against a doorway, wondering whether we had fulfilled our duties as Air-Raid Precaution volunteers in the process. (Before I had managed to find out what the duties of an Air-Raid Precaution volunteer might be, the battle was already over and done.) The doorway of the building was crammed with people, bulky in their winter clothes, and smelled of naptha. Looking above their heads, I saw a brilliantly clear pale blue sky. The emptied tram sat in the middle of the street. The space outside the tram was full of pale sunlight; the tram, too, was filled with sunlight. In that moment, the lone tram possessed a sort of primitive desolation all its own.

I felt terribly uncomfortable—would I die amid a crowd of strangers? Yet what would be the good of being blown to bits and scraps alongside my own flesh and blood? Someone barked a command: "Hit the deck! Hit the deck!" How could one possibly find a place to hit the deck surrounded by such a lot of people? And yet we somehow managed to collapse against each other's backs and tumble to the ground. An airplane dived through the air and with a bang was right over our heads. I covered my face with an Air-Raid Defense helmet, and only after a long moment of darkness did I begin to realize that we had not died after all. The bomb had landed on the other side of the street. A young store clerk who had been wounded in the thigh was being helped across the street, his pants leg rolled up to reveal a trickle of blood. He was very happy, because he had become the focus of the crowd's attention. At first, the people outside the doorway tried to force the door open, but it wouldn't budge. With the clerk's arrival, they fell to again with the courage of newly discovered moral conviction and began to shout: "Open the door! Don't you know there's a wounded man out here! Open up!" One could hardly blame whoever was inside for not opening the door, because our little group was a rabble and might be capable of anything. The indignation of the crowd grew to such a pitch that they began to curse the people inside for "heartless beasts." Finally, the door opened, and the crowd surged inside with a great shout, received by a couple of old ladies and their maids, who stood woodenly in the entrance hall and held their peace. It's hard to say whether all the chests and storage baskets lining the corridor remained in place when everything was over. The plane continued to drop bombs on other parts of the city, receding gradually into the distance. And when the air-raid alert was finally lifted, the entire crowd made a mad dash for the tram car, for fear of forfeiting the price of a ticket if they couldn't get on in time.

We received word that Professor France of the history department had been shot dead—by his own men.[3] Like the rest of the English, he had been requisitioned by a military garrison. That day, he had come back to the barracks after nightfall. Perhaps he was lost in thought, for when he failed to respond to the sentry's call, the sentry opened fire.

France was an open-minded and magnanimous fellow, thoroughly sinicized, who wrote a passable hand in Chinese (although he did have problems with stroke order), loved to drink, and had once gone on a trip with a group of Chinese professors to Canton, where they visited with the little nuns at a Buddhist nunnery of less-than-sterling repute. He had built himself a place with three bungalows well off the beaten track. One of the buildings was entirely given over to raising hogs. There was neither electricity nor running water at his house, because he did not approve of material civilization. He did, however, have a beat-up old automobile, which the house boy used for grocery shopping.

He had a childishly ruddy face, porcelain blue eyes, and a prominent round chin, his hair had already begun to thin, and he wore a tattered length of Nanking silk, printed with Buddhist swastikas, as a necktie. He smoked like a chimney during class. As he delivered his lectures, a cigarette would always dangle precariously from his lips, shuttling up and down like a seesaw but never falling to the ground. When he tossed his cigarette butts out the window, they would whiz past the girls' billowy perms: a not inconsiderable fire hazard.

He had his own unique take on historical research. He read official documents to us with such rhetorical flourish that they became very funny. We derived a sense of being close to history from him, as well as a cogent worldview, and we could have learned so very much more, but he died—an entirely purposeless death. His life could not be said to have been sacrificed for the good of his country. And even if he had died for king and country, so what? He had very little sympathy for England's colonial policies and didn't take them all that seriously either, perhaps because he felt that it was only one of the world's many follies. Whenever it was time for the volunteer corps to drill, he would always say, "I won't be able to see you next Monday, children. I've got to practice my martial arts." Little did we know that "practicing

大學即景（一）

旁講：先生在黑板上寫字。

Campus Scenes (1).
During the lecture, when the professor is writing on the blackboard.

martial arts" would one day take his life. A good teacher, a good man. The waste of humanity...

Many others have already pointed to the chaos and destruction of every sort of public amenity during the siege of Hong Kong. The cooling ducts of the government cold stores broke down, but the authorities allowed the mountains of beef stored inside to rot rather than distributing it. Volunteers in the defense effort were given rice and soybeans but no oil and no fuel for cooking. The officers of the Air-Raid Precaution corps spent their time looking for firewood and rice with which to provision those under their command and had no time to spare for taking care of bombs. For two days running, I ate nothing and went to work with the floating gait usually associated with immortals unencumbered by base desires. Of course, someone as derelict in duty as I probably deserved to suffer. I finished reading *An Exposé of the Bureaucrats* during an artillery barrage.[4] I had read it when I was little, before I was able to appreciate its virtues, and had always wanted to read it again. As I read, I worried whether I would be allowed to finish the book. The print was minuscule, and the light poor, but if a bomb were to fall, what would I need my eyes for, anyway? "When there's no skin," the saying goes, "where do you put the hair?"

Throughout the eighteen days of the siege, was there anyone who did not experience that unbearable, half-past-four-in-the-morning feeling? Waking to another trembling dawn, surrounded by fog, cowering from the cold, with nothing to depend on. No way home. And if or when you got home at all, you might not find it there anymore. Homes can be destroyed, money transformed into worthless paper in the bat of an eyelid, other people can die. And one's own life? Precarious at best. As the Tang poem puts it: "Bleakly I leave those near and dear / moving into distant misty veils."[5] But even lines like these cannot describe the untenable and unmoored quality of that emptiness and despair. It was intolerable to most people. Some were so anxious to grasp on to something solid that they decided to get married.

A couple came to our office to borrow a car from the Air-Raid Precaution branch director so that they could go to collect their marriage license. The man was a doctor and probably not a very kind person in ordinary circumstances, but now he gazed constantly toward his bride, his eyes brimming over with a devotion so dogged that it was almost tragic. The bride was a nurse, petite and rather pretty, with rosy cheeks glowing with happiness. Unable to obtain a proper wedding dress, she wore instead a sleeveless pale green silk robe, hemmed with dark green lace. They came in several times and were made to wait several hours on each occasion. They would sit quietly across from one another, gazing into each other's eyes, and so unable to suppress their smiles that we all smiled along with them. We really ought to have given them a better return for the gratuitous happiness they brought us.

Eventually, the battle came to an end. It was a bit difficult to adjust to its absence after the cease-fire. Peace came as a kind of disturbance, acting on us like too much wine. To see airplanes in the blue sky above and know that one could enjoy watching them fly without risking a bomb falling on one's head—this was enough to make them seem lovable. Forlorn, sparse winter trees spreading their hazy canopies like pale yellow clouds, clear water flowing from a faucet, electric lights, busy street life: all these things belonged to us again. Time itself had been restored to us: the light of day, the dark of night, the four seasons. For the time being, our lease on life was allowed to continue. Wasn't that enough to make people beside themselves with joy? It was precisely because of this peculiar psychological state that the postwar years in Europe became the Roaring Twenties.

I remember how we scoured the streets in search of ice cream and lip balm after Hong Kong fell. We went into every store we saw to ask whether they had ice cream. Only one place conceded that it might perhaps have some the next day. We trooped several miles back to the store to honor the engagement and were given a plate of expensive ice cream, chock-full of little ice crystals that made a crunchy noise with each mouthful. The streets were full of makeshift stalls selling rouge, Western medicines, canned beef and mutton, stolen suits, cashmere sweaters, lace curtains, cut glass, whole bolts of woolens. We went to the city every day to go shopping. We called it shopping but really did no more than look. It was at that time that I first learned how to transform shopping into a pastime; no wonder the majority of women never tire of it.

Hong Kong discovered anew the joy of eating. Strange how the most natural, the most fundamental of functions, when suddenly accorded excessive attention and subjected to the glare of intense emotion, can come to seem sordid and even perverse. In Hong Kong after the battle, there were people every five or ten paces along the sidewalks, dressed in the immaculate fashion of those employed by foreign firms, squatting by little stoves cooking yellow biscuits that were as hard as iron. Hong Kong is not quite as can-do as Shanghai, and new entrepreneurial opportunities are exploited only very slowly. For what seemed like ages, these yellow cakes continued to monopolize the street-food market. Only very gradually did experimental varieties such as sweet rolls, samosas, and rather dubious-looking coconut cakes begin to make an appearance. Schoolteachers, shopkeepers, legal clerks—everyone had suddenly become a snack vendor.

We stood at the stalls eating turnip cakes fried in bubbling hot oil, while barely a foot away lay the discolored corpse of a pauper. Would winter in Shanghai be just the same? At least Shanghai would not seem to tolerate such a harsh scene. Hong Kong lacks Shanghai's sense of its own cultivation.

Because of the shortage of petrol, garages were turned into restaurants, and you could hardly find a silk shop or a medicine shop that wasn't selling pastries on the side. Hong Kong had never before been so gluttonous. The students in the dormitory talked of nothing the whole day except food.

In this euphoric atmosphere, only Jonathan stood alone, brimming over with disdain and fury. Jonathan was another overseas Chinese classmate who had joined the ranks of the Volunteer Corps and fought in combat. He wore an open-necked shirt under his greatcoat, his face was wan, and a lock of hair dangled between his brows in a manner reminiscent of Byron—such a shame that his pallor was merely the result of a bad cold. Jonathan knew all about what had happened during the fighting in Kowloon. What made him angriest was that they had sent two undergraduates to the trenches to carry an English soldier back from the front: "Two of our lives weren't worth one of theirs. They promised special treatment when they recruited us, said we would be supervised by our own professors, but they broke every single one of their promises." As he had thrown aside his scholar's brush to join the ranks, he must have thought the war would resemble an excursion to Kowloon chaperoned by the Young Men's Christian Association.

After the cease-fire, we worked as nurses in a makeshift hospital at the university. Aside from a few regular patients moved from the larger hospitals, most were coolies hit by stray bullets and looters who had been injured as they were being arrested. There was a tuberculosis patient who had a bit more money than most and hired another patient to serve as his valet, sending him out into the streets in his baggy, wide-sleeved hospital gown to run errands. The hospital chief felt that this represented a lapse of decorum, flew into a rage, and threw them both out. Another patient was found to have secreted a roll of gauze, several surgical knives, and three pairs of hospital trousers under his pillow.

Moments of drama were rare. The patients' days passed so slowly that they were driven to distraction. The higher-ups sent word that they were to sift rice, picking out the little pebbles and chaff, and because they really had nothing else to do, they seemed to take to this monotonous task. In time, they even began to grow fond of their own wounds. In the hospital, each patient's wounds came to represent the sum of his individuality. Each morning when ointments were applied and dressings changed, I watched as they gazed with adoring eyes at the new flesh forming around the wounds, with something resembling the love of a creator for his handiwork.

They lived in the dining hall of the men's dormitory. In the past, this room had always been bursting with noise: a gramophone playing the Brazilian ballads of Carmen Miranda, students breaking plates and cursing the cook at every turn. Now some thirty silent, seething, and smelly men occupied the room, unable to move their legs, unable to stir their minds, unaccustomed to thought. There weren't enough pillows so their beds were pushed up against the columns, and they lay with their heads propped against them, their necks at right angles to the rest of their bodies. They sat with their eyes wide open, waiting to be served two portions of brown rice per day, one dry, one gruel. With continued exposure to the elements, most of the air-raid protection paper pasted over the glass doors had begun to flake away, and when the sun shone through the glass, the white shreds looked like paper voodoo dolls. At night, these grotesque little white goblins were silhouetted against the deep blue of the glass panes.

We didn't mind the night shift, because even though it was ten hours long, very little had to be done. When the patients needed to urinate or move their bowels, all we had to do was to call for one of the orderlies: "Bedpan for number 23" (using the Cantonese Anglicism "pan"), or "Piss-pot for number 30." We sat behind a screen reading, and we even had late-night snacks of specially delivered milk and bread. The only drawback was that eight or nine times out of ten, patients would die during the night.

There was one man whose tailbone was rotting with gangrene, exuding an evil stench. When his suffering was at its worst, his facial expression actually seemed almost ecstatic: eyelids drooping, mouth pulled into the smile of someone who has an itch he can't quite scratch. He called out all night long, "Miss! Oh, miss!" The syllables were drawn out, quavering, even melodic. I paid no attention. I was an irresponsible, heartless nurse. I hated him, because he was suffering terrible things. Eventually, every patient in the room was roused from sleep, and, unable to ignore him, they began to call out in unison, "Miss." I could only walk over, stand sullenly by his bed.

"What do you want?"

He thought for a while, then moaned, "Water." All he really wanted was for someone to wait on him; the task didn't matter. I told him there was no boiled water in the kitchen and walked away. He sighed, fell silent for a moment, and then began to call out again, until he couldn't manage anything but a kind of low moan:

"Miss ... Oh, miss ... Hey, miss ..."

At three in the morning, as my colleagues slept, I went to boil milk, heedlessly carrying the fat white milk bottle through the hospital ward and down to the kitchen. Most of the patients were awake, and they stared wide-eyed at the bottle, which to them was even more beautiful than a lily blossom.

Hong Kong had never had such a bitterly cold winter. As I washed the old, coverless copper pot with a bar of soap, my hands felt like they were being cut by a knife. The pot was sticky with grime and grease. The orderlies used it to make soup, and the patients to wash their faces. I poured the milk, and the copper pot sat atop the blue gas flame, like an image of Buddha sitting astride a blue lotus flower, pure and luminous. But that interminable drawl of "Miss...Oh, miss" pursued me all the way to the kitchen. One white candle illuminated the small room as I kept watch over the milk as it came to a boil, as flustered and angry as a hunted beast.

The day the man died we were all happy enough to dance. Just as the sun began to rise, we entrusted his funeral arrangements to a professional nurse and retreated to the kitchen. One of my companions used coconut oil to bake some bread that tasted a bit like Chinese fermented rice cakes. A cock was crowing over another icy white morning. Selfish people such as ourselves went nonchalantly on with living.

Besides work, we studied Japanese. The teacher they sent was a young Russian whose yellow hair was cropped close to his skull. Each time we went to class, he would begin the lesson by asking a female student her age in Japanese. If she hesitated, he would hazard a guess: "Eighteen? Nineteen? No more than twenty, I should think. Which floor do you live on? May I come and visit you sometime?" As the student contemplated how to discourage his advances, he would chuckle: "No English allowed. You have to answer in Japanese. All you know how to say is 'Please come in and sit down. Have something to eat.' You don't know the Japanese for, 'Get out of here!'" When he had finished his joke, he himself would be the first to blush. At first, students jostled for a place in the lecture hall, but gradually fewer and fewer students showed up for his class. When the numbers had dwindled to embarrassing lows, he quit in a fit of pique and was replaced by another teacher.

This Russian teacher saw my drawings but had eyes only for a portrait of Yanying wearing a corset. He was willing to part with five Hong Kong dollars for it, but when he saw how reluctant we were to sell, he quickly relented, "Five dollars—not including the frame."

The special atmosphere during the war inspired me to draw a lot of pictures. Yanying colored them in. Going into transports over one's own sketches might be unseemly, but the fact is that these pictures were actually quite good. They didn't seem anything like my own work, and I can never dream of drawing the likes of them again. My

大學即景之（二）

Campus Scenes (2).

only reservation is that people found them somewhat baffling. I could have spent a lifetime writing annotated biographies for those pell-mell character sketches and never regretted a moment. For example: the irascible subletter's wife, crossed-eyed, her pupils protruding like two water faucets; the young matron whose head and neck are the barrel of an electric hair dryer at a salon; a prostitute with an infectious disease squatting like a lion or a dog, garters and the tops of her red silk stockings showing beneath her dress.

I especially liked the colors Yanying used for one picture in particular, all different blues and greens, reminiscent of the line in the poem: "Blue seas lit by the moon, a pearl sheds tears / Indigo fields warmed by the sun, jade gives rise to mist."[6]

I sketched with the knowledge that I would very soon lose the ability to do so. And from this I derived a lesson, an old lesson. If there is something you want to do, do it right away; even then, you might already be too late. Man is the most changeable of creatures.

There was a young Annamese classmate who had a minor reputation as a painter among his fellow students. He complained that in the wake of the battle, his line was not nearly as forceful as it had once been, since he was now compelled to cook for himself, which left his arms fatigued. It pained us terribly to watch each day as he fried aubergines (for fried aubergine was the only dish he knew how to cook).

When the war broke out, most Hong Kong University students were overjoyed, because December 8 also happened to be the first day of exams, and to be excused from exams for no reason was an almost unprecedented godsend. That winter, we suffered through a fair amount of hardship and through these trials gained a better sense of our priorities. But priorities are difficult to define. Once you dispose of all the specious ornaments of culture, what seems to remain is merely "food and drink, man and woman." Human civilization does its best to transcend the realm of the bestial, but could it be that several thousand years of work have been nothing but wasted effort? So it seems. Students from overseas, stranded in one spot with nothing at all to do, spent their days grocery shopping, cooking, and flirting—and not the gentle sort of flirting that normally takes place among students, leavened with a touch of sentimentality. In the dormitories after the war, a male student might lie on a girl's bed playing cards deep into the night and then come back the very next morning before she had even awoken and sit himself right back down on the edge of the bed. From next door, one would hear her coy cries of "No! Didn't I say no? No, I will not" and so on until she was dressed. This sort of phenomenon produced different reactions in different people and may even have compelled some of us to retreat in horror to Confucius's side. In the end, one cannot dispense with restrictions. Primitive people may well have had a certain innocence, but, in the final analysis, they weren't completely human, either.

The hospital director was extremely worried by the prospect of illegitimate war babies. One day, he happened to catch sight of a female student sneaking out of the dormitory with a rectangular bundle in her arms and thought his nightmare had already become reality. Only later did he learn that she was carrying rice she had gotten at work to sell on the black market but had disguised the sack as a baby to forestall the possibility of being mugged by the hoodlums who filled the streets.

In point of fact, what we had were over eighty young people who had narrowly escaped with their lives and for that reason were all the more full of vitality. There was food, there was shelter, and there were none of the usual entertainments outside to distract us. There were no professors (in truth, most professors are eminently dispensable), but there were lots of books: the pre-Han philosophers, *Shijing* (The classic of poetry), the Bible, Shakespeare. This was, in short, the ideal environment for higher education. And yet our classmates treated it as a tedious transitional period; behind them lay the ordeal of battle and ahead the moment when they could finally sit at their mothers' knee and sob out their sorrows. In the meantime, the best they could do was listlessly scribble the legend "home sweet home" across a dusty windowpane. Getting married, even if out of boredom, was at least a somewhat less passive approach to the situation.

That people who have neither professions nor pastimes find solace in marriage was attested to by the endless parade of marriage announcements in the Hong Kong newspapers. Some of the students among us got married as well. Students typically have very little understanding of the realities of human nature. When they have had for the first time an opportunity to peel away someone else's surface, revealing the timid, pitiful, or laughable being underneath who shrinks from the slightest touch, they almost always fall in love with this first discovery. There is no question, of course, that they had everything to gain and nothing to lose by love and marriage, but willingly to limit their own horizons when still so young seems rather tragic.

The vehicle of the times drives inexorably forward. We ride along, passing through thoroughfares that are perhaps already quite familiar.

Against a sky lit by flames, they are capable nevertheless of shaking us to the core. What a shame that we occupy ourselves instead searching for our reflections in the shop windows that flit so quickly by—we see only our faces, pallid and trivial. In our selfishness and emptiness, in our smug and shameless ignorance, every one of us is like all the others. And each of us is alone.

SHANGHAINESE, AFTER ALL

WHEN I returned to Shanghai a year ago, my first impression of the Shanghainese from whom I had been separated for so long was that they were fair and plump. In Hong Kong, eight or nine of every ten Cantonese are dark and skinny. The East Indians are even darker, and the Malays even skinnier. Having grown accustomed to seeing them, each and every Shanghainese seemed as fat and white as a gourd, like the children in powdered milk advertisements.

The second thing that struck me about the Shanghainese was their knowingness. The popular literature of the Hong Kong masses is best represented by the celebrated bus stop placard: "If the bus should stop, it would be here." Shanghai is of an entirely different order. When I first got back to Shanghai, I often found myself exclaiming: "They're Shanghainese, after all." I went to buy soap and heard a little shop apprentice explaining to his partner: "Hey, the character you want is the *xun* [merit] in the name Zhang Xun, or 'work of merit,' not the *xun* [fragrance] in the word 'xunfeng' [scented breeze]." The *News* printed an advertisement for the grand opening of a department store that was written in a genuinely compelling mixture of parallel and free-style prose in the manner of the Qing dynasty Yanghu School.[1] On the dangers of selecting the wrong gift, the advertisement had this to say: "When friendship hangs in the balance, how great the stakes?" Seemingly a parody, yet quite true nonetheless, and not at all overstated.

The knowingness of the Shanghainese is not limited to their facility with language and proficiency in the ways of the world. One can also find specimens of spontaneously spirited and unaffected writing almost anywhere in the city. Last year, one of the tabloids printed a doggerel verse by an author whose name I have already forgotten, although I will never forget the poem itself. Two actresses had invited the author to share a meal, and the occasion prompted him to write: "At table with two of the greats / Miss Zhang and Miss Yun share lovely traits / After eating my fill I continue to sing their praise / Such an opportunity doesn't come every day." Such a lovably roundabout sort of self-deprecation! There is helplessness, magnanimity, and indulgence here—an indulgence born of exhaustion, when one looks down on others but also looks down on oneself and yet still retains a sense of intimacy with both oneself and others. I saw another couplet on a streetcar that expressed the same sentiment with even greater clarity. The words had been scratched with a finger across the black coating on the window of the tram: "Grandpa and Grandma each have their reasons, men and women their equal rights." The saying has always been "Grandpa has his reasons, and Grandma says she's right," so why bother to ascertain who's really wrong? Both of them are in the right. And what with the years of trouble caused by the proposition that "men and women have equal rights," why not just *let* them be equal? Once again, this is a case of an indulgence that stems from sheer exhaustion. The grin stretched across a face covered in sweat and grime is emblematic of Chinese-style humor.

Shanghainese are traditional Chinese people tempered by the high pressure of modern life. The misshapen products of this fusion of old and new culture may not be entirely healthy, but they do embody a strange and distinctive sort of wisdom.

Everyone says Shanghainese people are mean, but their meanness is measured. Shanghainese know how to flatter and deceive, how to curry favor with those in power, how to fish in troubled waters. But because they also understand the arts of life, their practice of these arts never goes beyond the bounds of propriety. And as far as meanness goes, the only thing I know for certain is that every fiction needs a villain. Good people like to hear stories about mean people, but bad people most certainly do not enjoy stories about those who are good. This is why none of my stories has for its main character a saint.

There is only one girl who might be said to approach the ideal, being kind, compassionate, and righteous, but if she weren't so pretty, I am afraid she might end up being more than a little annoying. Even with her beauty, many readers might well feel like telling her to go back to the fairy tale where she came from. She might have a place in a story like "Snow White" or "Cinderella." But Shanghainese people are not that naive.

I have written a book of Hong Kong romances for Shanghainese readers, including the seven stories "Aloeswood Ashes: The First Incense Brazier," "Aloeswood Ashes: The Second Incense Brazier," "Jasmine Tea," "Heart Sutra," "Glazed Roof Tiles," "Sealed Off," and "Love in a Fallen City."[2] The entire time I was writing these stories, I was thinking of Shanghainese people, because I wanted to try to observe Hong Kong through Shanghainese eyes. Only people from Shanghai will be able to truly understand the parts where I wasn't able to make my meaning clear.

I like Shanghainese people, and I hope the Shanghainese will like my book.

SEEING WITH THE STREETS

THERE was a foreign girl who spent two years in China. Having never paid her respects to the Forbidden City, the Great Wall, the Monte Carlo of the Orient, or the Venice of the East and lacking any interest whatsoever in China's new culture and new cinema, she did, however, develop an appreciation for Chinese children: "So beautiful, especially in winter, bundled up in their padded jackets, padded pants, padded gowns, and padded overalls until they are so short and so round, wobbling this way and that. Oriental eyes look nice in the first place, and on the little yellow faces of the children, those wondrous slanted eyes look even more wonderful. I wish I could take one home to Europe with me!"

Intellectually earnest fellow nationals felt that she was treating the future masters of our country as mere playthings, that her language was clearly insulting to China, and that it would be necessary to lodge a protest with the embassy. More mischievous souls were able to joke about it, saying that bringing a child with Chinese blood back home wouldn't be so terribly difficult, if she were so inclined.

Having heard her words, however different our reactions to them might have been, we could not help looking anew at Chinese children, for we had never thought there was anything particularly remarkable about them before! When people in the family are an annoyance to others, we are usually so accustomed to them that we don't notice anything amiss; when family members are lovable or ought to be held in high regard, we often fail to realize this until after we have been told it by people outside the family. To be sure, we cannot expect to receive such compliments all the time, for we have far too many fail-

64

ings that urgently need fixing and ought really to concentrate our energies on absorbing some hard-sounding but honest truths, as a means of self-admonition. And yet, if we spend our days sweating with self-hate and contemptuously telling ourselves we don't deserve to live, what exactly *is* the point of living? We may as well select a few of our happier traits and take a look.

It is better to walk ten thousand miles than to read ten thousand books. When we go from home to work, to school, to the market, we walk at least a mile a day. After ten or twenty years, we will have covered several thousand miles. And if each time we walk down that street as if it were the first time we had ever seen it, if we see afresh and with new eyes, without succumbing to the blindness of familiarity, we will have done something like walking ten thousand miles, without even sailing the four seas.

There are a lot of things worth looking at on the streets. At dusk, a rickshaw rests by the side of the road, with a woman sitting at a slant on the seat, a mesh bag in her hands, full of persimmons. The rickshaw man squats on the ground, lighting the wick of an oil lamp. The sky darkens, and the lamp at the woman's feet gradually grows bright.

The braziers used to roast yams have the same shape and dusky color as the roasted yams themselves.

Little restaurants will often cook pumpkins just outside the front door, and while you couldn't really say that it's a nice smell, the hot pumpkin steam and their "eye-brightening" red imparts a sense of "warmth for the old and comfort for the humble" to those who pass by.[1]

On cold mornings, there are usually people squatting on the sidewalk lighting little braziers, sending forth billows of white smoke as they fan the flames to life. I like to walk through that smoke. There are similarly sweet, warm, and overpowering clouds of smoke outside the garages that dispatch cars retrofitted to run on naptha instead of petrol. Most people do not like burnt smells—burnt coals or spent matches, milk or cloth—but to dismiss them as "the stink of coal" or "the stench of burnt cloth" seems rather summary.

Most of the people who ride on the back of someone else's bicycle are attractive young women or, barring that, small children. But the other day, I saw a postman in his green uniform riding a bicycle with a little old lady on the back, who must have been his mother. A deeply affecting sight. And yet the era in which a Li Kui would carry his old mother on his back has passed us by.[2] The mother, unaccustomed to such lavish favors, looked somewhat ill at ease. Her feet dangled in the air as she sat carefully, her face reflecting her diffidence—like a poor relation sitting in a tall rosewood chair asking for a handout—as she rode into the wind with a smile that must have chilled her tongue.

Someone attaches a little red lamp to the wheels of his bicycle, so that all you see as he rides past is a whirling red circle, its flowing movement lovely in the extreme.

Over shop windows in the deep of night, the bars of the protective window gates form a filigree, underneath which lie layers and layers of air-raid defense paper, yellow, white, transparent, stuck in squares and diagonals atop the glass, as enigmatic as the latticed window frames and curtain rods of ancient times.

A shop has long since closed, the lights are off, and the wooden mannequin's leather coat has been stripped away. She stands with her shoulders exposed, facing away from the street. But her modesty is wasted, for even if she were facing outward, she would hardly move passersby to beautiful dreams. She was manufactured a little too cheaply and too clumsily, and there is nothing to recommend even the face or the hands or the feet that would have been exposed even with the benefit of the coat. I once saw plaster torsos of Laurel and Hardy in a boutique in Hong Kong that not only looked nothing like them but were in dreadful taste as well, especially their chubby, pale faces. The mannequins in Shanghai boutiques are not much nicer. Underneath even the most expensive wool knit hats, they are forever wearing the same inhuman grins. They are an insult to humanity, an irony even more extreme than the proverbial "monkey groomed to wear an official's cap."

If I knew how to sculpt, I would be more than willing to develop in that direction. Shop window design is an exceedingly interesting line of work, because there is a motionless drama enacted in every display. (During the middle ages in Europe, every holiday would be celebrated with dramas sponsored by the Church as a form of worship. The earliest religious dramas were extremely minimal, without even a smattering of dialogue, in which the actors playing biblical roles would don luxuriantly colorful robes, strike magnificent poses, and stand motionlessly in place. Every few minutes, they would shift position, forming a different pattern on the stage, or what was called a tableau. When Chinese people hold religious festivals, it seems to me that the performers do move around the stage as they sing, but there might well be tableau-type performances as well.)

The purpose of shop windows is to stimulate one's desire to buy things. They say that an excessively inflated desire to consume is the common affliction of modern city dwellers. In desiring to buy items they do not need, they naturally want more money than they can earn and proceed to do whatever it takes to get it. Shop windows are thus the irrational by-product of an irrational society. But such theories aside, we might speculate that the sights offered to the public by this kind of street art, however grand and aristocratic they seem, serve to relieve their audiences of the need to actually spend money. Dispensing delight and visual pleasure free of charge ought, after all, to be considered a form of public service.

On a bitterly cold winter night four or five years ago, I went to look at the shop windows on the Avenue Joffre with my cousin. Under neon lights, hats slanted across the slanted faces of the wooden beauties, atop which slanted feathers. I don't wear Western suits and had no need to wear a hat to match and no desire to buy one, but I could still gaze at the display with appreciation, neck huddled inside my coat, hands firmly ensconced in my pockets, pointing at the window with the tip of my nose and my chin, frosting the cold plate glass with white blossoms of breath. These days, the face of the city has grown leaner, and the storefronts along Avenue Joffre have lost much of their luster. And even if they were as brilliant as before, would we still be as thrilled by what they had to offer?

There is a display window for a salon that I do like. It is curtained in green fabric, and underneath the foot of the curtain there is always a tabby cat who either paces back and forth or lies curled by the window, fast asleep.

The Western-style coffee shop next door is filled with the clamor of machinery each night, lights blazing, turning out pastries and sweets. The smell of eggs and vanilla extract lingers until dawn before dissipating into the air. In a big city where "bills keep falling from the sky even when you're inside," it seems almost unreasonable that the owners allow us to enjoy the aroma without having to pay a cent. But the aroma of the cakes made by our sweet-smelling neighbor far outstrips their flavor, a fact that becomes apparent as soon as you've eaten one. Perhaps everything under heaven is the same: a cake that's done isn't as good as a cake in the process of being made. The glory of a cake is in the aroma it gives off as it bakes. Those who enjoy life lessons may well find one here.

On my way to market, I happened to run into a military blockade and was detained in an area just yards from home. So near, and yet it might as well have been the ends of the earth, as far as I was concerned. In a sunny spot, a servant woman tried to force her way past the lines, struggling as she shouted: "It's getting late! I have to get back and make dinner!" Everyone in the crowd broke into laughter. A Cantonese rice peddler sitting on the curb told her son "They'll let you go if you need to see a doctor but not to cook dinner." Her voice was so deadpan, so solemn, so very satisfied with all and sundry that it sounded like a beginner's foreign-language textbook. But for some unknown reason, her voice was somehow unsettling, as if there were a deeper meaning to what she had said. And yet there really wasn't.

Standing in front of the rope strung from a bamboo enclosure stood a man, no more than a yard away, dressed in black with a black nylon cap, very short of stature, who reminded me of the illustrations of the detectives in the novel *Xiepu chao* (Tides of the Huangpu).[3] From the other side of the cordon came three men in tight-fitting uniforms, striding with their chests thrust forward, their leather shoes sounding out crisply against the pavement. People who are able to move freely during a blockade seem almost obligated to move with their chests thrust forward and their shoes sounding out crisply against the ground. Two of the men had already crossed the line when the third darted forward and grabbed hold of the arm of the man in black, easily, familiarly, and, without a word of explanation, led him back toward the other side. The other two also made their way through the crowd, took hold of his other arm, and then, with long determined strides, vanished with him into the distance. This was the first time I had ever seen a criminal arrested. And even the authorities seemed to realize that the scene had lacked a certain suspense: in order to make up for the shortfall, they dispatched a group of MPs to the scene after it was all over to quell any unrest. From some distance away, the MPs drew their pistols and surveyed the scene before them, fully prepared to mop up any remaining resistance. I was prepared as well: to throw myself to the ground at the first sound of gunfire so as to avoid being hit by a stray bullet. But all they did was gaze from afar and, detecting no telltale signs of malfeasance or mischief, loudly voiced their disappointment in Shandong dialect and went on their way.

When the tension had subsided, the crowd struck up a debate about just what had happened. A delivery man, supporting his bicycle, bent his head down to laughingly address the woman peddling rice: "How could he possibly have gotten away? As soon as something happens, they post pictures everywhere. How could he have gotten away?" Then he turned to the rickshaw driver with a guffaw: "They nearly missed him. Those two had already walked past him, but the third guy caught sight of him." He continued: "Standing right here the whole time. But no one even noticed him!"

The rickshaw driver sat grinning on his running board, arms folded: "But why should it be that, of all the people standing here, the only one they chose to arrest was him?"

Idle roadside chitchat, taking pleasure in the misfortune of others—pathetic yet lovable all the same.

The knit blouse of a woman in the street, because she has had her hands in her pockets for a very long time, is stretched into a most inelegant bulge; when viewed from behind, it appears to be too long at the front, too short at the back.

The saying is that the "everyone on the road knows what's really in Sima Zhao's heart." In the United States, "the man in the street" is a phrase used constantly to signify the common man. Whether news reporters need to praise or cast blame, the "man in the street" is invariably summoned to bear witness: "as even the man in the street knows..." But usually the man in the street knows nothing of the sort, even in his wildest dreams.

When you watch people in the street, they usually return your gaze, so that you can't look them over at length or leisure. But if you want to force the issue, it's easy to make someone submit to a close, hard look without reciprocating. There are not many people who are stylish from head to toe, chic from top to bottom. Most ordinary people are well aware of their deficiencies and will invariably avert their eyes and look down at their feet in dejection when swiftly scrutinized from head to toe. There is another method as well. Staring fixedly at people's feet is enough to put them in a flustered state. Are their socks inside out? Is it obvious to everyone that their shoes are made of fake leather? Are they bowlegged? Pigeon-toed? When I was little, I used to listen to an old maid from Hefei tell stories about how she had hunted wolves in the countryside. She said wolves had "copper heads, iron backs, and hemp stalk legs." That was why they were able to fend off attackers with their heads or their backs but not with their legs. The psychological weaknesses of human beings also seem to be located below the trunk.

There is an army barracks in the neighborhood where the soldiers practice playing the bugle every morning and every evening, without much sign of progress. I have heard other people say that the sound is pure torture, that the exercises grate on the ears, but somehow the noise doesn't trouble me at all. Great music stands alone as a bequest to the world, belonging like all perfect things to a superhuman realm. It is only in the realm of perfect technique that the ever-tangled and tired human element is allowed a moment of rest. When one's technique has yet to be perfected, struggle, anxiety, disorder, and adventure predominate, and the human element remains strong. I like the sound of humanity because it's always about to reveal itself.

The sound of a *huqin* played by a beginner is like that, too.[4] Even when I'm listening to a master perform, I like to hear him tune his instrument. I like those tentative, fragmentary squeals and squawks. Listening to people learning to play the violin, however, is another matter: that sharp, sawtooth wave of sound is too much like the cries of a dying chicken.

One night as I walked along a desolate street, I heard a song about roasting gingko nuts: "Sweet so sweet and sticky, too." The singer was a boy about ten years old, and he had yet to really learn the song by heart so as to be able to sing it with conviction. I cannot forget that dark, gloomy, long avenue, with the boy kneeling on the ground beside his wok, his chest illuminated by the light of the fire.

A CHRONICLE OF CHANGING CLOTHES

IF ALL the clothing handed down for generations had never been sold to dealers in secondhand goods, their annual sunning in June would be a brilliant and lively affair.[1] You would move down the path between bamboo poles, flanked by walls of silk and satin—an excavated corridor within an ancient palace buried deep under the ground. You could press your forehead against brocades shot through with gold thread. When the sun was still out, this thread was warmed by the light, but now it is cold.

People in the past went laboriously about their lives, but all their deeds end up coated in a thick layer of dust. When their descendants air these old clothes, that dust is shaken out and set dancing in the yellow sunlight. If memory has a smell, it is the scent of camphor, sweet and cozy like remembered happiness, sweet and forlorn like forgotten sorrow.

We cannot really imagine the world of the past, so dilatory, so quiet, and so orderly that over the course of three hundred years of Manchu rule, women lacked anything that might be referred to as fashion. Generation after generation of women wore the same sorts of clothes without feeling in the least perturbed. At the beginning of the dynasty, because men were forced to show submission to the conquerors but women were not, women's clothing still retained the clear imprint of Ming dynasty styles. From the middle of the seventeenth century all the way to the end of the nineteenth, capacious jackets with huge sleeves were perennially popular, giving their wearers an air of statuesque repose. The jacket collar was very low, nearly nonexistent. One wore a "great jacket" on the outside. On informal occasions, the great jacket would be removed to reveal the "middle jacket." Beneath the middle jacket was a form-fitting "little jacket," which would be worn to bed and was usually of some enticing shade like peach pink or "liquid red." Atop this ensemble of three jackets, finally, would be the "Cloud Shoulder Vest Coat" of black silk, with broad edging patterned with stylized "coiled clouds."

The sloping shoulders, narrow waist, and flat chest of the ideal beauty, who was to be both petite and slender, would disappear under the weight of these layers on layers of clothing. She herself would cease to exist, save as a frame on which clothing could be hung. The Chinese do not approve of women who are overly obtrusive to the eye. Even the most spectacular virtues recorded by history—for example, a woman hacking off her own arm after having been touched by a strange man—however admired by commoners, always produced a vague sense of regretful unease among the educated class, who believed women should not draw attention to themselves, no matter the circumstances. The most spotless of reputations can be tarnished by exposure to the steamy breath of the multitudes. If even women who sought to gain distinction for themselves by such honorable means had their detractors, what of those who, in eccentrically deviating from sartorial norms, did even greater violence to accepted modes and customs?

The strictest formalization prevailed in the matter of the skirt worn outside the trousers when a woman left the house. Usually it was black, but on festive occasions a wife might wear red, and a concubine pink. Widows were restricted to black, but if the husband had been gone more than a few years and the in-laws were still in the house, lake blue or lilac were permissible. The tiny pleats in the skirt were the most exacting test of a woman's grace and comportment. Ladies of good family walked with such mincing steps on their tiny feet that, although the pleats could not be prevented from moving a little, this motion was restricted to an almost imperceptible quiver of the fabric. A pretty maiden of humble origins, unused to such attire, would almost inevitably create the unfortunate impression of being wind-blown and wave-buffeted. Even more trying were the red skirts worn by brides, which were festooned with innumerable sashes, each half an inch wide and tied at the end with a little bell. The bride was to emit no more than a faint chime as she moved, like the sound of bells on a distant pagoda carried on the wind. It was not until the 1920s, when gathered skirts with a freer and more billowy effect came into style, that these sorts of skirts were done away with entirely.

The slightest deviation in the wearing of furs was also seen as the mark of a parvenu. Each sort of fur had its own season, and the distinctions were extremely precise. In the event of an unseasonably cold October, it was permissible to wear three fur-lined jackets, but in choosing just what sort of fur to wear, one had to consider not the weather itself but the season. In early winter, one wore short-haired furs, starting with Persian lamb, purple lamb shearling, and pearly lamb shearling. Then came the "intermediate furs," such as silver squirrel, gray squirrel, "grayback," "foxleg," "sweet-shoulder," "Japanese sword," and finally, in the coldest winter months, the long-haired furs: white fox, blue fox, Western fox, darkling fox, purple sable. Purple sable could only be worn by those with official titles. Middle- to lower-class people were much more prosperous in those days than they are now, for most were able to own a sheepskin coat or a "gold and silver" robe patched together from the cheaper white and yellow fur from the belly and back of a fox.

Young ladies lent a spot of brightness to the gloom of winter months with their "Zhaojun" hoods.[2] In historical illustrations, the hood Zhaojun is wearing as she is sent off on horseback to marry the king of the Huns is of the simple, generous Eskimo type made so popular by Hollywood starlets in recent years. But the nineteenth-century version of the Zhaojun hood was absurdly colorful and gay: a black satin cap of the sort worn by men but rimmed with fur and decorated with a large red pompom on top and a pair of pink satin ribbons streaming from the back, at the ends of which were sewn two little gold seals that chimed when they came into contact with each other.

An excessive attention to detail characterized the costume of that era. In modern Western fashion, various unnecessary details cannot be said to have been eliminated, but they always have a purpose: to bring out the blue of one's eyes, to create the illusion of a larger bosom for those who are deficient in that regard, to make someone look a little taller or a little more petite, to focus attention on the waist, or to conceal the curve of the hips. The details of ancient Chinese clothes, however, were completely pointless. You might say that they were purely ornamental, but then why were even the soles of cotton shoes inscribed with intricate patterns? There was seldom an opportunity for the shoe to be revealed to view, much less the sole. Even the slightly raised edges of the heels were covered with elaborate designs.

Quilted coats came with either "three pipings and three trimmings," "five pipings and five trimmings," or "seven pipings and seven trimmings," and besides all the pipings and trimmings, the front and the hems were studded with sparkling sequins depicting plum and chrysanthemum flowers. The sleeves were finished with embroidered silk borders called "railings," which came in seven-inch strips and were cut out to form the characters for "fortune" and "longevity."

This amassing of countless little points of interest, this continual digression, reckless and unreasonable, this dissipation of energy on irrelevant matter, marked the perennial attitude toward life of the leisure class in China. Only the most leisured people in the most leisurely country in the world could appreciate the wonder of these details. It certainly took tremendous amounts of time and artistry to create fine distinctions between a hundred lineal designs that were similar but not the same and just as much effort to appreciate the differences among them.

Chinese fashion designers of old seemed not to have understood that a woman is not a Prospect Garden.[3] The heaping together of too many details will inevitably diffuse interest and result in a loss of focus. The history of Chinese fashion consists almost exclusively of the steady elimination of those details.

Things were not as simple as that, of course. There was also the wax and wane of waistlines. The first important change came around the thirty-second or thirty-third year of the reign of Emperor Guangxu.[4] The railways, no longer such a novelty, began to take an important place in Chinese life, and the fashions and fancies of the great commercial ports were swiftly introduced into the interior. The size of robes gradually dwindled, and wide trimmings and railings went out of date, replaced by extremely narrow strips of fabric. Flat piping was called "chive edges"; round piping was called "lamp wicking" or "incense stick trim." In times of political turmoil and social unrest—the Renaissance in Europe, for instance—there will always be a preference for tight-fitting clothes, light and supple, allowing for quickness of movement. In fifteenth-century Italy, clothes were so tight that they had split seams at the elbows, knees, and other joints. During the days when the revolution in China was brewing, Chinese clothes were nearly bursting at the seams. During the short reign of the "Little Emperor," Puyi, the jacket clung like a sheath to the body. And such were the wonders of the Chinese corset that even then the image of the body beneath the clothing had resembled not a real woman's body but rather that of a pre-Raphaelite poetic muse. A slim, straight robe would fall straight to the knees, from whence two tiny trouser legs dropped a timorous hint of even tinier lotus shoes attached apologetically to the ground. There was something infinitely pathetic about those pencil-slim trouser legs. In Chinese poetry, "pitiful" is just another way of saying "lovely." The instinct to protect the opposite sex, always a part of the masculine makeup, was perhaps given additional impetus by a difficult and transitional era in which the new could barely keep up with the destruction of the old. Women, formerly self-possessed in their wide robes and large sleeves, found that it would no longer do to look complacently fortunate. Instead, it was to their advantage to act the damsel in distress.

It was, moreover, an age of extremes. The evils of both our system of government and our system of family life were suddenly exposed. Young intellectuals condemned all that was traditional, even all that was Chinese. Conservatives, shocked out of their complacency, redoubled their efforts to suppress them. Wild controversies raged day in and day out, at home, in the newspapers, and in the entertainment field. Even the perfumed and powdered actors of the so-called civilization plays of whom wealthy concubines were enamored discoursed

清 末 時 裝

Late Qing Fashion.

ad lib on contemporary politics to their onstage lovers, to the accompaniment of gushing tears.[5]

It was a commotion unprecedented in the long history of a land of moderation and harmony. This atmosphere of hysterical excess gave rise to the Sycee collar, a tall, stiff affair that reached nearly as far as the nose and, like the Burmese neck rings made of gold that are piled one atop the other until they are almost a foot tall, forced women to stretch and distend their necks. This frightening and formidable collar was altogether disproportionate to the willowy limbs and delicate torso underneath. The top-heavy, unbalanced effect thus created was one of the signs of that time.

With the founding of the Republic, there was a period in which the superficial signs of enlightenment began to appear everywhere. It was a time when Rousseau's idealistic notions about human rights were taken very seriously. Students enthusiastically rallied around the right to universal suffrage, demonstrated against filial piety, and advocated the promotion of free love. Experiments were even made in the practice of a purely spiritual, Platonic love, seemingly without much success.

Fashion also exhibited an unprecedented innocence, lightness, and delight in itself. "Trumpet sleeves" fluttered fairylike, affording a view of the pale jade of a woman's wrists. Abbreviated jackets fit snugly around tiny waists. Ladies of the upper classes went out in gathered skirts but at home were clad in loose-fitting short pants ending at the knee. And because their silk stockings ended at the knee as well, there were inevitably moments of danger when a bit of flesh happened to be revealed in between. Women of a rather risqué temperament would even allow the tassels of the long, pale-colored silk sash used to belt the pants to dangle provocatively from underneath their short jackets.

Much of the inspiration for fashions in the early years of the Republic derived from the West. The collar was first reduced in height and then practically eliminated altogether. Necklines became round, square, heart-shaped, diamond-shaped; white silk scarves became suitable for all seasons; as were white silk stockings with black embroidered designs that crawled up the legs like insects. Social flowers and prostitutes wore spectacles just for the way they looked, since spectacles were a sign of modernity. Such was the extent of the indiscriminate importation of things foreign.

Warlords came and went, each trailing his own dusty wake of officials, government agencies, and legal codes. Fashion tripped behind, trying to catch up, undergoing a thousand transformations. The hem of the jacket, once square, suddenly went round, then just as suddenly V-shaped, before changing once again into a hexagon. In the past, women's clothes, like jewelry, could always be sold for ready cash, but in the Republican era, pawn shops no longer accepted them, because once they went out of fashion, they were worthless.

Quick alterations in style do not necessarily indicate mental fluidity or a readiness to adopt new ideas. On the contrary. They may reveal instead a generalized apathy, for frustration in other fields may lead to the forced flow of intellectual and artistic energy into the domain of fashion. In a time of political chaos, people were powerless to improve the external conditions governing their lives. But they could influence the environment immediately surrounding them, that is, their clothes. Each of us lives inside our own clothes.

In 1921 women first began to wear long gowns. This garment, called a *qipao*, or "banner gown," after the eight military banners under which the Manchus had invaded China in the seventeenth century, had always existed alongside Chinese fashions but went unremarked until the twentieth century. Manchu women, disliking the gown's lack of feminine grace, had once shown an inclination to switch to the more alluring Chinese-style jacket and trousers but were severely reprimanded by an imperial edict that banned this practice. With the establishment of unity among the various nationalities by the new Republic, women all over the country suddenly began to wear the *qipao*—not because they wanted to show their loyalty to the Manchu Qing dynasty or their support for its restoration but because they wanted to look like men. From time immemorial, women in China have been identified by the phrase: "hair in three tufts, clothes in two pieces," while men's clothes since the Manchu dynasty have had no break at the waist. The difference between one piece or two pieces seems slight, even inconsequential, but women in the 1920s were quite sensitive to differentiation of this sort. They had been immersed in Western cultural influence and intoxicated by its calls for equality between men and women, but the yawning gap between these ideals and the reality that surrounded them was a constant humiliation. Soured and angry, they sought to discard everything that smacked of femininity, even to the point of eliminating womanhood altogether. This was why the first *qipao* were stiff, cold, and puritanical. The political misfortunes that befell the nation one after another, within and without its borders, could not help leaving the people disillusioned.

There came a day when youthful idealism could no longer maintain itself in the face of unremitting disaster. Fashions began to retract, taking on a curt, tightened look. Trumpet sleeves narrowed into cylinders. By 1930 they had risen to the elbow, while at the same time the high collar began to make a comeback. Unlike the old Sycee collar, which had at least the virtue of cutting across the cheekbones diagonally in order to give even the most recalcitrant of faces a pleasing melon-seed shape, the new collar was like a tube pressing under the neck, providing even young women whose skin had yet to sag with a double chin. Such a collar is simply unforgivable. But it did serve quite adequately as a symbol of the deliberate, reasoned sensuality so prevalent in the atmosphere ten years ago: an upright collar separating a goddesslike head from the voluptuous and sensual body far below. This was parody; this was the mad laughter that comes on the heels of despair.

The double-breasted and belted military-style greatcoat so popular in the West at the time was perfectly suited to the sad, shrill mood in China. Chinese women, moderate to the last, softened this gallant look by wearing the masculine overcoat over a floor-length gown of sleek velveteen, with scandalously long slits up the thighs, revealing long pants of the same fabric, edged with shiny silver lace. Perhaps the person inside the outfit also represented a similarly strange combination: aggressively idealistic on the outside but a thoroughgoing materialist when it came to the point.

In recent years, the most important alteration in fashion has been the elimination of sleeves (a gradual and apparently quite dangerous procedure, undertaken with the utmost of caution over the course of twenty years). At the same time, collars became much shorter, hemlines rose, and all ornamental features such as pipings and trimmings were done away with entirely, replaced first by cloth-covered "butterfly buttons" and then by hidden metal clasps. In short, the end result was subtraction: the stripping away of all ornaments, whether necessary or unnecessary. What remained was a tight sleeveless sheath, showing the neck, the arms, and the part of the leg below the knee.

What is important now is the person: the *qipao* became nothing more than a foil faithfully setting off the contours of the figure. The garments of the era before the revolution were altogether different. The individual was of secondary concern; what mattered was the creation of a poetic sense of line, an abstract form. Thus it was that the female form was conventionalized: it was only when women took off their clothes that one could become aware of any differences among them.

Fashion in China is not an organized, planned business venture. There are no great fashion houses like Lelong's and Schiaparelli's in Paris that monopolize the market and exert influence throughout the world of white people. Our tailors lack initiative of their own and can only follow the vast, unaccountable waves of communal fancy that make themselves manifest from time to time. And it is for this reason that Chinese fashions can be more reliably read as representing the will of the people.

It is impossible to verify who really starts these fashions, because the Chinese have very little respect for copyrights and the originators do not appear to mind so very much anyway, imitation being the sincerest form of flattery. Shanghai attributes the recent arrival of medium-length sleeves—sometimes called three-quarter sleeves—to Hong Kong, and Hong Kong people, just as eager to shift responsibility on to someone else, insist that they came from Shanghai.

The billowy return of sleeves heralds a revival of formalism. These latest developments are moving in the direction of tradition. Traditional detail can never be reclaimed, but to the extent possible, traditional lines most certainly may. Utilized in a suitably dynamic manner, they can be adapted to the demands of modern environments. Those who would stretch the front of the *qipao* to apronlike proportions, for example, effectively suggest the hidden allure of spending time in the kitchen, the implications of which are worth pondering.

The modern history of men's clothing has been less eventful. There was only a very brief period—between 1915 and 1919 or 1920—when men's clothes paid a modicum of attention to foppish adornment, edging robes with little "as-you-wish" patterns and allowing for the use of fabrics usually reserved for women's clothes. The people of that era, however, felt this to be a strange and rather unsettling phenomenon. Today, Western-style men's suits are cautious and colorless, adhering as closely and as conservatively as possible to the established image of a foreign gentleman. This is notwithstanding the fact that even Chinese-style garments have been trapped for many years within a limited palette of gray, coffee brown, and dark blue and restricted as well by extremely monotonous fabrics and patterns. Men enjoy far more freedom than women, but purely on account of this single and all too conspicuous unfreedom, I would not want to be a man.

Clothes seem to be quite inconsequential. The ancient hero Liu Bei had this to say on the matter of clothes: "Brothers are like one's hands and feet; wives and children are like clothes that can be put on and taken off."[6] But it will be very difficult indeed for women to reach the point where husbands are likened to clothes. One Western author (was it Bernard Shaw?) once complained: "Most women put more careful thought and consideration into the choice of their hats than their choice of husbands." Even the most heartless of women will wax passionate when she starts to speak of "last year's quilted silk gown."

Until the eighteenth century, men in both China and abroad were still able to wear bright colors such as red and green. The proscription of color in men's clothing seems to be a signal characteristic of modern civilization. Putting aside the question of whether this proscription has negative psychological effects, one can declare at the very least that this is an unnecessary privation. Life in civilized society has many different kinds of necessary privations, and it seems to me that we should relent a little when it comes to these smaller items, as compensation. One might make another argument as well: if men were more interested in clothing, perhaps they would become a bit more complacent, a bit less inclined to use various schemes and stratagems to attract the attention and admiration of society and sacrifice the well-being of the nation and the people in the process of securing their own prestige. Of course, to argue that the task of bringing peace to the world could depend on men dressing up in gaudy splendor would obviously be somewhat ludicrous. Even an official wearing a brocade sash underneath his bright red python-patterned ceremonial robes can still play havoc with court protocols. It should be noted by way of reference, however, that in the rational

utopia of the great prognosticator H. G. Wells, male and female citizens alike wear sheer, brightly colored clothes and cloaks made of a gauzy material.

By force of habit, a man dressed even slightly out of the mold inevitably strikes one as strange. Wearing an overcoat over a Chinese-style robe is one example; it would be better instead to add another quilted jacket or a fur robe on top, despite the added bulk. Once when I was on the streetcar I saw a young man, perhaps a student or perhaps a clerk, who had tailored himself a rather tight mohair robe with green checks over a rice-colored background. He was wearing women's stockings, striped red and green, and an exquisitely carved fake ivory pipe hung from his mouth, although there was no tobacco inside the bowl. He sucked on the pipe for a moment, removed it from his mouth, took it apart piece by piece, put it back together, and then placed it back in his mouth to continue sucking, his face radiant with satisfaction. At first, I found him ridiculous, but then I thought to myself: why not, if this was what gave him pleasure. An autumnal chill as dusk approaches and vendors at a vegetable market prepare to pack up and go home. Fish scraps and pale green husks of sweet corn litter the ground. A child on a bicycle dashes down the street just to show off. He lets out a shout, lets go of the handlebars, and effortlessly shoots past, swaying atop the seat. And in that split second, everyone in the street watches him pass, transfixed by an indefinable admiration. Might it be that in this life that moment of letting go is the very loveliest?

Liveliness.
*(1) A society lady,
dripping with liveliness
from head to toe;
(2) Hong Kong coed,
slender and jaunty;
(3) a Shanghai coed, pale,
plump, and energetic.*

Hong Kong.
(1) Darling wife of an
aristocratic gentleman;
(2) social butterfly;
(3) Negro blood;
(4) Indian businessman.

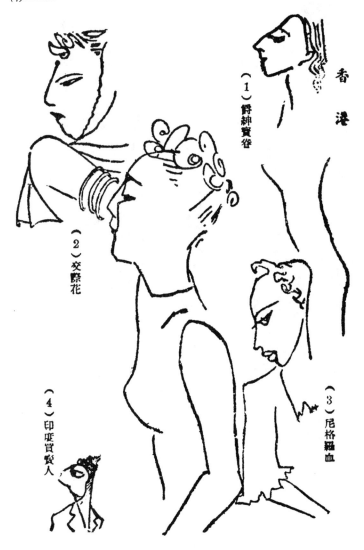

（1）爵紳寶眷

香港

（2）交際花

（3）尼格羅血

（4）印度買賣人

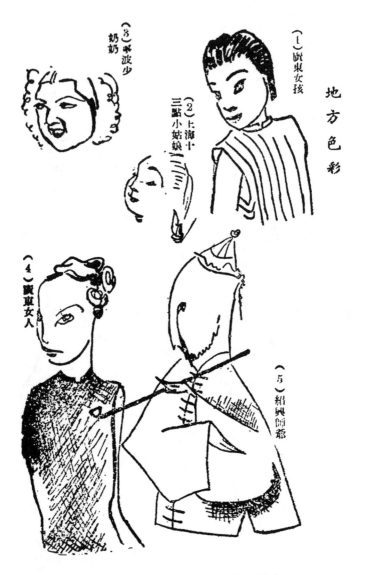

地方色彩

（1）嶺東女孩

（2）上海十三點小姑娘

（3）寧波少奶奶

（4）廣東女人

（5）紹興師爺

Local Colors.
(1) Cantonese girl;
(2) flighty Shanghainese girl;
(3) Ningbo housewife;
(4) Cantonese woman;
(5) Shaoxing secretary.

LOVE

This is true.

THERE was once a daughter of a tolerably well-off family in the country who was very lovely and sought out by many matchmakers, although nothing had come of their efforts. That year, she was only fifteen or sixteen years old. One spring evening, she stood by the back door, hands resting on a peach tree. She remembered that she was wearing a moon-white tunic. She had seen the young man who lived across the way, but they had never spoken. He walked toward her, came to a halt close by, and said softly: "So you're here, too?" She did not say anything, and he did not say more. They stood for a moment and then went their separate ways.

That was all.

Later, the girl was abducted by a swindler in the family and sold as a concubine in some far-off town, then sold several times more, passing through any number of trials and ordeals. When she was old, she still remembered that incident and often spoke of that evening in spring, the peach tree by the back door, that young man.

When you meet the one among the millions, when amid millions of years, across the borderless wastes of time, you happen to catch him or her, neither a step too early nor a step too late, what else is there to do except to ask softly: "So you're here, too?"

SPEAKING OF WOMEN

WESTERNERS call mean and treacherous women "catty." I recently came across a little English pamphlet called *Cats* dedicated to insulting women, even if you could not really say the contents were completely unreasonable. Various aphorisms about women of this sort tend to be scattered here and there and thus difficult to find. The virtue of this pamphlet is that it compiles them all in one place. I have selected and translated a portion of these sayings. Readers will no doubt react to them, whether with anger, amusement, or gratification. Men who think themselves fair-minded will probably render "even-handed judgments," comment that some of them "are a little extreme," or opine that "they're true enough, but only of a minority of women, and ought to serve as a negative example for the rest," and so on. In short, I have yet to encounter anyone who doesn't have an opinion on this topic, myself included. Shall we have a look at the original text first and then discuss it afterward?

Mr. Anonymous, the author of *Cats*, solemnly states in his preface that "nothing that is said in what follows applies to you personally, dear readers, and if you happen to be male, well, it doesn't apply to your wife, your sister, your daughter, your grandmothers, or your mother-in-law, either."

He stresses repeatedly that his motivation in writing the pamphlet was not to avenge his own disappointments in love but acknowledges later that it may serve as a way to vent anger, for "a man who has been quarreling with his wife can read the book before bedtime and derive from it a measure of comfort."

He says: "The material form of the woman is a marvel of rationality. That her spiritual constitution is rather less so is only to be expected. We cannot ask for too much."

"When a man falls truly in love, the depth and passion of his feeling are far superior to those of a woman. On the other hand, when a woman hates someone, she is able to hold a grudge for much longer than a man."

"The only difference between women and dogs is that dogs cannot be spoiled, do not wear jewelry, and—thank heaven!—cannot talk."

"In the final accounting, every man ends up spending his money on a woman."

"A man can flirt with the lowest of bar girls and not lose his standing as a gentleman. But a woman of high station cannot so much as blow a kiss at a postman without fatal consequences to her good name. From this, we can only deduce that men cannot compare with woman in at least one respect: they need not worry when bending below the waist, because they can always straighten back up."

"Generally speaking, a woman needs less stimulation in her everyday life than a man. This is why a man who strays from the straight and narrow during his day of leisure in order to rejuvenate himself, soothe his cares, assuage his annoyances, or realize unaccomplished ambitions ought to be forgiven."

"For the vast majority of women, the meaning of 'love' lies in 'being loved.'"

"Men like to love women, but sometimes they also like women to love them."

"If you promise to help a woman do something, she will do anything for you in return. But if you have already helped her, she will do nothing to return the favor. This is why one ought to agree to oblige any number of different women. You may perhaps receive something in return for your efforts that way. Women have only one kind of gratitude, which is gratitude in advance."

"A woman may be wearing an outfit that looks lovely to all the men who see her, but in the eyes of a member of her own sex, the fabric is only 'one shilling three pence a yard' and could hardly be called beautiful."

"Time is money, which is why the more time women spend in front of their mirrors, the more money they must spend in a boutique."

"If you don't flirt with a woman, she'll say you're not a real man. If you do, she'll say you aren't a gentleman."

"Men boast of victories; women boast of retreats. But the 'enemy' has usually attacked on account of her own provocation."

"Women dislike kind men but see themselves as remarkably efficient reformatories—as soon as they marry, their husbands will no doubt be transformed into saints."

"Only men have the right to propose marriage, and as long as this tradition persists, marriage will never be a level playing field, because women will always be able to exploit the fact that they once acquiesced to your demands and thus retain the upper hand in any given domestic squabble. This is, in fact, why women will always cede the right to propose marriage to men."

"Many women will never be happy until they can do something that isn't right. Marriage, apparently, isn't wrong enough."

"Women often forget this simple point: their entire education has consisted of teaching them to resist temptation—and yet they spend their entire lives doing their very best to attract it."

"Modern marriage is a form of insurance that was invented by women."

"If women were paid royalties for the stories they invent off the top of their heads, they would all be rich by now."

"If you ask a woman an unexpected question, her first answer will probably be true, and her second will be fiction."

"A woman will often argue a point with great ferocity, until she is assured of victory over her husband. But in speaking with a third party, she will cite her husband's position as an article of incontrovertible truth. Pity the husband..."

"Two women can never make friends as quickly as two men, because there are more secrets between them."

"Women are really very fortunate: no surgeon will ever be able to dissect their consciences."

"When a woman judges the quality of a man's character, her sole standard is the way the man has treated her and her alone. This is why a woman is capable of saying: 'I don't believe this man is a murderer. He never murdered me!'"

"Men make mistakes. Women endlessly contemplate the mistakes they are planning to make."

"Women don't consider the future. At the same time, they do their best to forget the past. Heaven only knows what they have left to think about!"

"When a woman sets her mind on living thriftily, she is able to forgo the necessities of life to a truly frightening degree!"

"If a woman tells you a secret, do not under any circumstances tell another woman—because it's almost certain that another woman has already told her!"

"No matter what favor you plan to do for a woman, she will believe that you really ought to lend a hand. No matter what you actually do for a woman, she will never thank you for doing it. No matter what trivial thing you forget to do for a women, she will curse you forever for not having done it. The family is not a charitable institution."

"Most women never think before they speak. Men think but don't speak!"

"If she decides not to read a novel for a second time because she already knows the story, she'll never make a good wife. If all she cares about is novelty and has no interest in style or substance, once she's surveyed her husband's character and come to understand his weaknesses and peculiarities, she'll begin to find him oppressively dreary and fall out of love with him forever."

"Your woman will build castles in the air. And if they do not actually exist, you will catch the blame!"

"It's even harder to make a woman to say 'I was wrong' than to compel a man to say a tongue twister in public."

"If you doubt your wife, she will cheat on you. If you don't suspect your wife of cheating, she will suspect you."

These are wisecracks, as is every statement that claims that all women are this way or that. The price of such so-called wisdom is a cheapening of the truth, for how could it be possible to sum up all women in a single phrase? And yet, women *are* relatively easy to sum up. Although people the world over vary in terms of their customs, habits, occupations, and environments, the majority of women are still looking after their homes and tending to their children. There is only this single, traditional mode of living, and although variations exist, they exist only within limits. This is why generalizations to the effect that women are this way or that are somewhat more reliable than those that state that men are this way or that.

I remember that at our amateur debate society at school, as soon as the question of men and women came up, everyone promptly forgot what the original topic was supposed to have been and focused intently on this single point, speaking out of turn, interrupting one another, and filling the room with raucous laughter and angry expostulations. One young woman, in tones reminiscent of the reformist New Party of the late nineteenth century, went on at some length about the desperately unfair treatment women suffer at the hands of men, about how men bully women: women, these soft and fragile creatures, endowed with an overflowing abundance of emotions, emotions that are only exploited by men in order to restrict them, to force them to submit to being mere playthings; women, whose unfavorable position in the struggle for existence is solely due to a lack of equality; and so on.[1] These are the perennial arguments women rely on in these polemical battles between the sexes. At the time, I couldn't resist challenging her. It wasn't that I wanted to play the devil's advocate but simply that I was sick of that sort of stuff. In the 1930s *Ling-lung* (Petite magazine), so beloved of co-eds, ran articles on the beauty secrets of the stars right alongside advice on how freshly beautified young ladies could resist the unwanted attentions of young men, since all men "harbor evil intentions," falling in love is a dangerous undertaking, and marriage—"the tombstone of love"—even more dangerous still.

We are all familiar with women mouthing these kinds of platitudes, and we have heard more than our fair share of complaints from men as well, who claim that women have committed unpardonable sins, crimes too numerous to mention. If not for the fact that they remain necessary for the survival of the nation, they ought to be done away with entirely.

Each camp sings its own tune, and it may be that, at least superficially, they both have truth on their side. Women are in fact petty, coy, dissembling, narrow-minded, and skilled in the arts of flattery and flirtation. (Even though proper ladies have nothing but contempt for women of easy virtue, given the opportunity to play the strumpet for a while, every one of them would jump at the chance.) Intelligent women will doubtless accept the justice of these charges, while deftly turning the tables by laying the blame for these deficiencies squarely on men. Ever since prehistoric times, women have been subjected to the naked fist of patriarchal domination because of their lack of physical strength. Several thousand years of languishing under masculine control gave rise to the "wifely way" as a means of adapting to the environment in which they found themselves. The deep-seated inferiority of women was created by the hand of man, so what on earth are men complaining about?

If the weakness of women was engendered by their environment, how is it that in modern times women who have received the very same college education as their male counterparts remain just as oversensitive and needlessly querulous as their grandmothers? Of course, habits formed over the course of thousands of years cannot be eradicated in a day. All in due time . . .

And yet asking men to shoulder all the blame doesn't seem to be a completely satisfactory solution. Not only that, it smacks of irresponsibility. Irresponsibility, of course, is yet another adjective men have long accustomed themselves to using to describe women. The author of *Cats* says: "An eminent professor once provided me with a dozen reasons why I should never take a woman too seriously. I found this somewhat troubling, because women always take themselves extremely seriously and hate to be seen as docile and irresponsible little creatures. If this professor believed that they were not to be taken seriously but they themselves refused to be docile and irresponsible little creatures, then what was I to do? They want people to take them seriously, certainly, but when they have made a serious mistake, they hope that you will shrug it off by saying, 'She's just an irresponsible little creature.'"

The reason women were made to submit, becoming slaves of a patriarchal system, was their lack of physical strength. And yet men themselves are no stronger than jackals, wolves, tigers, or leopards. How is it that the male of the species, pitted against the birds and the beasts, managed to survive in the evolutionary struggle? The argument is clearly flawed, and shifting the blame on men simply will not account for such questions.

The celebrated novelist Aldous Huxley, in his novel *Point Counter Point*, writes, "The sort of person you are determines the way you will be treated." *Point Counter Point* is about a young woman named Marguerite who is truly a glutton for punishment. She is a woman who seems to have been born to elicit other people's pity. Her husband is a kind and docile man at heart, but even he ends up having an affair with a social butterfly. Marguerite is finally driven to sorrow, despair, and lamentation.

Certainly, society's motion forward is an unimaginably vast process, bigger than the efforts of any one individual, so big that even the self-styled vanguard is caught up by its motion without understanding the whys or wherefores. And yet, at a certain level, there must in fact be an active role for the individual to play in the process. Take a look at the state of the world today, for instance. Mankind has progressed step by step, only to arrive at an intensely competitive, highly mechanized and commercial civilization, a civilization in which warfare becomes an unavoidable necessity. Even those—especially those—who run toward the fray shouting, "Don't fight! We can't fight!" will inevitably and unwittingly be roped in along with everyone else. There's no way out, and yet one could hardly argue that humanity bears no responsibility for its own impasse.

Some people say that, in their tenure as masters of the world, men have made a muddle of things. It would be better, runs this line of argument, if they would simply come clean and cede their position to women. Yet it seems that this particular prescription may have been written a little too hastily. It makes little difference if you have a strong empress like Wu Zetian or a powerful emperor like Taizong of the Tang dynasty, so long as the system remains a monarchy. Whether the emperor is a man or a woman is of no account; what matters is that with a good emperor all under heaven is at peace. The problem with monarchy is that a good emperor is hard to find. In a democratic system, on the other hand, the problem is that most women are even less able to govern themselves capably than men. Our international disputes already bear a conspicuous resemblance to the catfights of amahs. One shudders to imagine what would happen if the genuine article were allowed into the arena.

The absurd notion that if women were allowed to rule the land, they would bring peace to all under heaven—an idea that resonates nicely with the old adage about bringing the Buddhist sage into the play because there aren't any actors left onstage—does in fact have some basis in science. There are those who predict that if the current world war damages our civilization to such a degree that it is unable to recover, the new culture that will arise in its place will belong to the blacks. The white and yellow races have already made their contributions to society; only the blacks have remained innocent and unspoiled, with their energies fully intact, which is why, I'm afraid, the leading role will be theirs for the taking in the great era that is yet to come. This is not merely an alarmist sentiment. Advanced civilization, with its highly developed means of training and repression, doubtless takes its toll on our primitive vitality. Women have often been dismissed as savages or primitives. Mankind has tamed and subordinated the birds and beasts but has somehow been unable to tame women. For several thousands of years, women have always remained outside the compass of civilization. How are we to be certain that they haven't been conserving their primitive vitality in patient preparation for their next big step forward?

One great advantage for a society in which women were at the helm would be that women are much more sensible when choosing their mates. This is not, of course, an erudite branch of scholarship, but it does have direct bearing on the future prospects of humankind.

Men select their wives solely based on looks. Features and figure are undeniably important in eugenics. When women select a mate, they no doubt pay attention to looks, but not nearly so exclusively as men. They also take other qualities into account such as wisdom, health, demeanor, ability to provide for a family, and so on. Physical appearance is a secondary concern. There are those who say that the crux of the problem with modern society is that men don't know how to select their wives properly, which is why, in turn, their children are not brought up properly and their shortcomings are passed down to the next generation. It may be something of an overstatement, but I am willing to argue that if all marital unions were selected by women, we could create a nation of supermen.

The term "superman" derives from the work of Nietzsche and is frequently invoked. Even before Nietzsche, however, there are suggestions of a similar ideal in classical allegory. Strangely enough, the superman always appears in our mind's eye as a man. Why should this be? In all likelihood, because the civilization of the superman has made progress beyond our own, and our own civilization is the civilization of men. There's another level here: the superman is the culmination of an ideal, while we can actually locate superior women in reality. No matter what stage of cultural development we reach, a woman always remains a woman. Men strive toward one sort of advance or another, while women remain the same: basic, fundamental, emblematic of the cycle of the seasons, of the earth, of birth, growth, sickness, and death, of eating and reproducing. Women bind the soaring, errant souls of mankind to the solid trunk of reality.

We can find perfect women in the here and now. Perfect men are few and far between, since we have very little idea of what constitutes perfection in a man. Those in search of wealth and power have their own notions, as do those who wish to withdraw from the world in the manner of the Daoist philosophers Lao-zi and Zhuang-zi or those who are adherents of the National Socialist Party. And it seems that each of these types has its flaws. That is the problem with our overdrawn expectations of what it means to be a perfect man.

Women's lives take place in a more restricted territory, which is

SPEAKING OF WOMEN · 97

why a perfect woman can be more perfect than a perfect man. At the same time, a bad woman can be even more thoroughly despicable than a bad man. This is the truth of the matter. There are businessmen who pay absolutely no attention to professional ethics but whose family lives are beyond reproach. On the other side of the coin, there are men with an utter lack of conscience in their dealings with women who are models of probity when it comes to their occupations. An evil woman, however, is evil through and through.

The superman is male, but divinity has something female about it, because a superman and a god are not the same thing. The superman is an aggressive creature whose very being implies a reason for being, a goal. The divine, on the other hand, signifies all-encompassing compassion, limitless sorrow, perfect understanding, serenity. Along with the vast majority of people commonly referred to as intellectuals, I would like to believe in religion but find myself completely unable to do so. Were there to come a day when I became a believer, I would place my faith in an entity like the Mother Earth in Eugene O'Neill's play *The Great God Brown*.[2]

The Great God Brown is the most deeply affecting play I know. I have read it over and over again, and even after my third or fourth reading, it can still bring me to tears and leave me with an aching and sorrowful heart. O'Neill uses impressionist techniques to portray Mother Earth as a prostitute: "She is a strong, calm, sensual, blonde girl of twenty or so, her complexion fresh and healthy, her figure full-breasted and wide-hipped, her movements slow and solidly languorous like an animal's, her large eyes dreamy with the reflected stirring of profound instincts. She chews gum like a sacred cow forgetting time with an eternal end."

The way she speaks is coarse and warm and frank: "I'm so damn sorry for the lot of you, every damn mother's son-of-a-gun of you, that I'd like to run out naked into the street and love the whole mob to death like I was bringing you all a new brand of dope that'd make you forget everything that ever was for good! *(then, with a twisted smile)* But they wouldn't see me, any more than they see each other. And they keep right on moving along and dying without my help anyway." Someone dies and is buried in the earth. Mother Earth comforts the dying man: "After you're asleep I'll tuck you in."

To be in the world, one must always wear a mask of deceit, but she removes the mask for a dying man: "You can't take this to bed with you. You've got to go asleep alone."

And here I quote a section of dialogue:

BROWN: *(snuggling against her—gratefully)* The earth is warm.
MOTHER EARTH: *(soothingly, looking before her like an idol)* Ssshh! Go to sleep, Billy.
BROWN: Yes, Mother. . . . And when I wake up . . .
MOTHER EARTH: The sun will be rising again.
BROWN: To judge the living and the dead! *(frightenedly)* I don't want justice. I want love.
MOTHER EARTH: There is only love.
BROWN: Thank you. Mother . . .

After someone dies, she says to herself: "What's the good of bearing children? What's the use of giving birth to death?" She also says: "Always spring comes again bearing life! Always again! Always, always forever again!—Spring again!—life again!—summer and fall and peace again!—*(with agonized sorrow)*—but always, always, love and conception and birth and pain again—spring bearing the eternal chalice of life again!—*(then with agonized exultance)*—bearing the glorious, blazing crown of life again! *(She stands like an idol of Earth, her eyes staring out over the world)*."

This, finally, is a real goddess. By comparison, the Goddess of the Luo River who "flutters like a startled swan / spins like a roaming dragon" is just another beauty from a costume drama, the Guanyin so revered by the common crowd is just an antiquated beauty with bare feet, those magnificent Greek statues of towering nudes are merely female athletes, and the Madonna with her golden tresses is nothing more than a pretty wet nurse at whose teats the masses have been suckling for more than a millennium.[3]

To continue in this vein would be to run the risk of falling into a whirlpool of theological debates, which tend to be just as fierce as arguments about men and women, only much duller. Perhaps I ought to come to some conclusions before it is too late.

Even though women have a thousand sorts of shortcomings, they still possess the makings of Mother Earth. Lovable women are genuinely lovable. To a certain degree, lovable qualities and a graceful bearing can be manufactured by artificial means, and this is in fact the goal of every system of education in every land that desires a yield of good and virtuous girls. Even when this original intention is distorted beyond recognition, as invariably happens, producing wives and daughters more akin to those described in *Cats*, we must remain sympathetic to the original ideal.

A woman may win favor in any number of different ways. Those who are interested solely in a woman's body forgo many of the most precious pleasures in life.

Winning favor by means of a beautiful body is the oldest profession in the world and indeed the most common job description for women, because every woman who marries for economic reasons is included in this category. And there's really no need for recrimination. Those who have beautiful bodies please with their bodies, and those with beautiful thoughts please with their thoughts; it makes very little difference in the end.

Birds of a Feather.
(1) Nastiness;
(2) shallowness;
(3) stupidity;
(4) pretension.

物傷其類

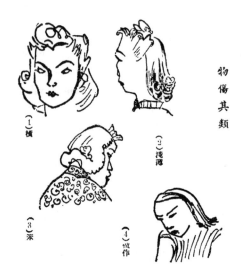

（一）橫

（二）淺薄

（三）笨

（四）做作

Master/Husband and Servant/Wife.

（一）犬主

（二）奴家

BY THE LIGHT OF THE SILVER LANTERN

THERE is a Shaoxing-style opera called *By the Light of the Red Lantern*.[1] I can't understand the lyrics, and I was never able to form any sort of idea of what the play is about, but I'm so mad for its charming and unpretentious title that I am going to adapt it here for my own use. "By the Light of the Silver Lantern" ought to suggest that I am going to borrow a mercury-vapor lamp to illuminate the everyday customs and feelings that surround us. Although the beams projected by the silver lantern often stray rather far from reality, they may well prompt us to reflect upon ourselves.

The two films I am going to discuss, *The Struggle for Spring* and *The Song of Meiniang*, are perhaps already out of date. In fact, they have already come and gone at the third-run theaters, but in the interior and in low-class entertainment centers in this city, they're still shown again and again. The people who make up these audiences may be unfamiliar to us, but the films they enjoy deserve comment.

This essay cannot be considered a film review, because what I am looking at here is not the movies, but Chinese people in the movies.

Both these films touch on the question of womanly virtue. The scope of womanly virtue can be quite broad, but most people understand it to mean the question of how to be a good wife and, in particular, how to remain cheerfully monogamous with a polygamous husband. In *The Song of Meiniang*, the husband is an amorous man who frequents a house of ill repute that employs respectable married women. The favorite nightmare of such men is that they will encounter their own wives or daughters there, suddenly recognizing them as they approach with mincing steps. A shattering encounter of this sort is clearly rife with dramatic possibilities. And that is why our writers have drawn on such scenes for almost thirty years in their so-called social novels. This, however, is the first onscreen appearance of such a scenario. Meiniang is tricked into working at the brothel, and when her husband stumbles upon her there, he slaps her across the face. Before she is able to say a word in her defense, he disowns her.

When a husband goes out on the town to philander, does a wife have the right to follow his example? Modern girls quite openly denounce one-sided notions of marital fidelity. Neither is this question unfamiliar to Chinese wives of a more traditional sort. Provoked by some trivial matter to jealousy, they may threaten to take revenge by these very means, but whatever serious threats they may issue are taken half in jest by their husbands.

In a bantering and unreflective mood, men might even acknowledge a certain primitive justice in their wives' declarations of independence. It is very difficult to persuade a Chinese man to discuss this topic with a straight face, because he considers nothing more hilarious than adultery. But if we could force him to consider the proposition, he would surely veto it. From a purely logical standpoint, two blacks do not make a white and two wrongs do not make a right. But Chinese men have no use for logic such as this in arriving at their conclusions, because they realize that for a wife to carry out such a threat would not only be impractical but also disadvantageous to her. She might have the right in theory, but some rights are better left unused.

This wisdom notwithstanding, questions of this nature are apparently just the thing for enlivening after dinner repartee in mixed company. In *The Song of Meiniang*, a married women volubly defends her presence in an ill-famed establishment in a manner reminiscent of a formal speech at a banquet. Even so, our innocent heroine has never even dreamed of such a right, let alone the notion of rights as such. Drawn into these dubious environs under false pretenses by a man who has convinced her that he is the founder of a new charity school and that he would like her to be the principal, she is immediately discovered by her husband, and the fatal misunderstanding ensues. She never has a chance to consider whether she has a right to commit an offense, cast as she is into the abyss before even reaching the rim of the question.

In *The Struggle for Spring*, the husband does not succumb to temptation until he has been filled to the gills with alcohol, and he regrets it afterward, which seems to make his act forgivable. But only the audience is aware of these mitigating circumstances. His wife never knows and never concerns herself with such questions, for it seems that she lacks even the slightest bit of curiosity. All that interests her is holding on to that fraction of him that still falls to her: in the event of his untimely death, the part of him that survives in his child, even if it is a child by another woman.

Although *The Struggle for Spring* was adapted from an American film called *The Great Lie*, it remains close to the Chinese heart. This virtuous wife—who undergoes all manner of suffering and unpleasantness to protect the fetus growing inside the belly of her husband's mistress and even stops her from having an abortion—is fundamentally Oriental in spirit, because of our deeply grounded traditional emphasis on the importance of preserving the family line.

In today's China, amid the intermingling of new and old currents of thought, Western individualism is at a considerable advantage, so the continued existence of such models of feminine propriety, if they indeed exist, are in need of explanation. Even against the backdrop of the strict moralism of ancient times, this tangled psychological complex, with its excessive emphasis on self-sacrifice merits close scrutiny. Unfortunately, *The Struggle for Spring* is too superficial by half, seeing no call for explanation of the inner lives of either the wife or the mistress and taking all these questions basically for granted. The airy narrative style of director Li Pingqian is as winning as ever. Particularly gratifying to male audiences is the scene in which the wife and mistress sleep nestled in each other's arms, in perfect harmony and tender accord.

With a story as interesting as this one, *The Struggle for Spring* could easily have served as a sidelight to several momentous social issues. But this opportunity is passed over in silence. *The Song of*

Meiniang is the same. Blissfully unaware of its progressive potential, it meanders insubstantially through familiar territory: the tragedy of the abandoned wife. Meiniang is rushed from clichéd situation to clichéd situation, like a celebrity starlet hopping from one banquet to another. She stumbles in a rainstorm, kisses her child through a windowpane, gasps for breath in a thatched hovel, dies at long last in the arms of her repentant husband, and sings a love song to him on a lake in a final flashback of their life together. The film has every tried-and-true element of a successful romantic drama, but the remarkably poor lighting seriously detracts from the effect.

In part because of the awful deficiency of the lighting, even the scenes of revelry look remarkably cold and bleak. The performance of Ma Ji, playing the madam of the brothel, suffers from the monotony of her sharp, cloying, and artificial laughter. Yan Jun, known for his villains, is fluent and effective in a straight role. Wang Xichun is not yet able to cast off completely the restrictions imposed on her by her training in Peking opera, while Zang Yinqiu steals several scenes with a brilliantly satirical portrait of an elementary school principal—the scenes that one can make out in spite of the poor lighting.

Nancy Chen tends toward the schoolgirlishly effusive in her portrayal of the heroic wife in *The Struggle for Spring*.[2] Bai Guang is limited by her lines and comes off as an unusually earnest vamp as she thrusts her glass at us over and over again, always with the same admonition: "Drink up! Drink up!"[3] She attempts to break up the monotony with flashes from her lovely eyes, but even though she is such an expert "optometrist," these efforts seem somewhat forced.

LET'S GO! LET'S GO UPSTAIRS

I WROTE a play in which a destitute man throws himself and his entire family on the mercy of their relatives. When a quarrel erupts, he leaps indignantly up with the exclamation: "I can't take any more of this. Let's go! Let's get out of here!" Mournfully, his wife interjects: "But where are we to go?" He gathers his wife and children around him and says: "Let's go! Let's go upstairs." At dinnertime, when it is announced that food is on the table, they come back down again.

Chinese people have learned how to leave home from Nora in *A Doll's House*.[1] There can be no doubt that this stylishly bleak gesture has left an extremely deep impression on a generation of Chinese youth. In the personal ads in the newspapers, bulletins for missing persons like the following appear in shocking quantity: "Since you left at nine o'clock at night on the 12th without saying goodbye, Grandma is confined to bed, Mother has had a relapse, and the faces of the whole family are awash in tears. Hurry back as soon as you see this." Leaving is one thing, but the question remains: what kind of escape counts as "braving the storm and weathering the elements," and which kind is just "going upstairs"? The conventional wisdom seems to hold that a woman who is a "flower vase" (pretty to look at but empty inside) has "gone upstairs," housewives have "gone upstairs," dreaming is "going upstairs," remaking the American film *Rebecca* is "going upstairs," copying from other books is "going upstairs," collecting antique coins is "going upstairs" (collecting modern currency counts as going downstairs), but there is in fact no single formula for making such determinations. The advantage of reality is that exceptions are so plentiful, and each individual case needs to be analyzed on its own terms. Actually, just moving from the back of the building to the front for a breath of fresh air and opening the window for a change of scenery can be quite nice. In any case, there's plenty of food for thought in all this, which is why I like that scene in my play.

There is, however, nothing else to recommend it, except that it's quite cheerful. There's grief, vexation, and acrimony, but it's cheerful vexation and cheerful acrimony. And another thing: at the very least, it's a play for Chinese people—loud and lively and fun for ordinary folk. If it were playing at a theater now, I would find a way to persuade you to go and see it. But I don't know when I'll ever get it produced. I suppose it may be too early to start advertising now. Because when the time comes—if there is a time—people might have already forgotten all about it, and the ads would be lost on them.

I wrote the play before the Lunar New Year and brought it over to Mr. Ke Ling so that he could have a look at it.[2] The structure of the thing was far too diffuse, and the last act unusable. I am grateful for Ke Ling's guidance. After several rounds of revision, the play was really much improved. But when it was finally done, I was left at a loss. They say there is a serious drought of scripts at the moment. Maybe there really aren't any scripts around, at least not the ones Cao Yu hasn't found time to write yet.[3] No one seems to have any use for scripts by people who've yet to make a name for themselves. I don't necessarily think that there's a monopoly, merely that the walls are fortified and the gates closely guarded. You would think that bringing a copy of a script round to the managers of the various theatrical troupes, as I did, would be the proper way to have your work recognized, but I am told that this route is impracticable here in China, where playwrights can only approach potential producers through the good offices of a go-between. I honestly don't know how to proceed.

Printing a copy of the script in order to capture their attention might be an option. But, to put it crassly, what happens if someone simply slips my play right into his own? I may sound ludicrously petty here, and perhaps overly generous in my self-estimation, but I could hardly be expected not to "measure the heart of the gentleman with the mind of a knave." Someone who's enamored of his own words and thoughts often tends to be possessive—which seems perfectly natural, really. I still remember the first time I saw the sea in Hong Kong: the lifeless, artificial shade of blue reminded me of the ocean on a retouched color postcard. Later, I stumbled across much the same metaphor in an English book: "You could cut out the Persian Gulf and send it home as a postcard, the blue of the water was so deep and so dull." The discovery that someone else has long ago given voice to your own words, and said them much better than you ever could, is disconcerting enough. But to discover that he didn't say it as well as you might have done is heartbreaking.

That's one aspect. What's more, plays are meant to be performed, not read. In writing a play, a dramatist must always hope that the actors will be able to breathe life into the work onstage. People always think that when fiction writers write plays, they are better read than seen. How should I overcome this presumption?

Writing essays is a relatively simple affair; one's ideas reach the reader directly through the medium of movable type. Writing drama is another matter altogether, because the original work soon becomes entangled in all sorts of complex forces that I am unable really to understand. The more I think about the complications of finding a trustworthy director and group of performers, not to mention "the proper time, the proper place, and the proper spirit," the more my head spins.

In buildings along the street, the lower stories are liable to be a little noisy. But surely that's no reason to flee upstairs?

Drama.
(1) A demon;
(2) Greta Garbo;
(3) a female martyr,
on her way either to
commit suicide or to
marry a revolutionary;
(4) a tragic heroine;
(5) heroes and beauties,
a love triangle or
quadrangle.

Good Women.
(1) Teachers and students
of a convent school;
(2) a married lady;
the pillar of society,
she herself becomes a
system, representing
rules, regulations, social
integrity, and proper
customs.

SCHOOLING AT THE SILVER PALACE

NOT LONG ago, I saw two highly educational films, *New Life* and *The Fisher Girl*.[1] (The latter does not necessarily fit neatly into the category of educational film, but it may well contribute to our understanding of the attitudes of Chinese people toward education.) Having benefited from their instruction, I cannot help writing out some of what I learned for everyone's reference.

New Life deals with the demoralization of rural innocence in the big city—a timeless phenomenon. *Three Modern Girls* and *Humanity*, two films from seven or eight years ago, also covered similar themes, and like *New Life* they showed a country boy studying in the metropolis as a typical example. Chinese films at present show a tendency to excavate favored topics from the films of the 1930s. This is not necessarily a bad thing. The 1930s was a period of intellectual vigor, despite its touchiness, its bigotry, and the annoying monotony of its grandiloquent Western-style "examination essays." The anxious and haphazard mood of that era has passed us by, but some of the more valuable of its literary and cinematic themes have survived.

Although *New Life* is designed to "expound the spirit of education and guide the young away from temptation"—to quote the advertisements—the filmmakers seemed to have been distrustful of the degree to which audiences would interest themselves in this mission. They have compromised by exaggerating the "temptations" and doing their best to simplify the "guidance." You can't really blame them, and there are precedents for such an approach. In America, religious sects known as Revivalists hold public confessionals after Sunday services in which people expound at great length on their own past sins.

The speaker describes his life of villainy and debauchery; the worse the sins, the better the story, and the clearer the contrast with one's present virtue and the happiness of having been saved. In the backward and out-of-the-way American hamlets where such practices are common, they don't have cabarets with leggy chorines; these vivid, earthy, and joyous stories of repentance are the only source of amusement.

New Life cannot pretend to that quality of vividness. It lacks a sense of reality, in part because of sheer economics. It's not that the producers weren't willing to spend enough money. The problem is that the film itself seems muddled about what things really cost. With the six hundred dollars his parents have given him for books, this unfilial son somehow contrives to live in luxury in a semidetached mansion with servants, perpetual parties, and a steady stream of girlfriends to keep him entertained. A gold-digging society girl agrees to marry him on the condition that he produce the vast sum of two thousand dollars for the marriage. These would have been fabulously optimistic calculations even by the standards of ten years ago.

The male protagonist turns over a new leaf and reforms himself; but of what exactly does his remarkable reformation consist? *New Life* makes a courageous if rather messy attempt to grapple with this question. To be fair, it is specific on this score, whereas earlier films of its ilk provide only a vague feeling of renewal not unlike that of a New Year's resolution. *New Life* introduces us to the most ideal of all modern girls (played by Wang Danfeng), who befriends the hero for the sole purpose of providing mutual assistance in the arduous course of their studies. When he wants to take the relationship a step further, she refuses his love on the grounds that the times will no longer allow for frivolities such as romance. After graduation, she moves to a school in the interior to take up a position as an extremely decorative dean of students, with a big butterfly bow in her hair. Moved by her example, the protagonist joins a group of colonists who venture forth to reclaim the barren wastes of the borderlands. This move is completely unpremeditated and seems to be prompted by momentary inspiration, a poetic longing, or some impulse bordering on escapism. Why is it that he cannot redeem his sins in the same place in which they were committed? Are there no useful tasks for a strong, capable, and well-educated young man to undertake in our immediate surroundings? To insist that he travel to a "land far, far away" seems distinctly unpragmatic.

New Life also puts forward another proposition meriting serious discussion: is elementary education for the masses a more pressing need than advanced studies for the privileged few? The protagonist's father refuses to help a neighbor's child through primary school because he needs to save every penny to be able to afford to send his own son to college. Disappointed by his son's misdemeanors, however, he turns away from his own family and sets up a school for the benefit of the children of the entire village. Here, we may note an as-yet-veiled disapproval of the modern university on the part of the filmmakers, which emerges even more clearly in an attack on the contaminating miasma of corruption enveloping such institutions.

If we want to see a treatise on the meaning of education in *The Fisher Girl*, we run into a dead end, because the film has chosen an art student as its hero. Western art in China has from the very start been a plaything of leisured dilettantes. Almost all professional painters work in traditional Chinese styles. The hero immediately alienates his audience (at least any audience with a modicum of sense) when he naively imagines it possible to earn a living for himself and his family by painting two rather awe-inspiringly towering nudes.

The maker of *The Fisher Girl* has presumably never seen a live fish, except for the kind that swims inside a bowl, but he tells the story with a rare sweetness and facility. There are some truly remarkable touches that, whether wittingly or not, illuminate the Chinese nature. For example, when the fisher girl apologizes to the art student for being unworthy of his lofty attentions, he replies, with some heat: "I don't like educated women." And yet, despite his Rousseauesque admiration for this child of nature, he cannot resist the temptation to teach her Chinese characters. In the past, Chinese scholars cultivated just such a hobby, teaching their concubines to read. Actually, to teach one's wife to read was acceptable as well, as long as she was pretty, but this sort of charming and elegant romantic occupation was normally reserved for later in one's life. In the leisurely days of retired life, a scholar could take on a "red-sleeved" young thing as a disciple to add savor to his sunset years. For these particular purposes, a regular wife would clearly be unsuitable.

Literati in ancient times only rarely had the opportunity to teach female students, which is why Yuan Mei's Suiyuan is regarded with such admiration and envy and why Zheng Kangcheng, out of extreme boredom, made his maids double as students.[2] Things are different today, of course, but several thousand years of sentimental education cannot be altered as easily as that, and we can see traces of the old ways wherever we care to look. Nowadays, Chinese people have agreed to the proposition that their women should be educated, but they prefer to educate their wives themselves, either directly or indirectly. In popular novels, a man who pays to have a poor girl go to school has irrevocably committed himself to marrying her, no matter how firmly he may insist that he only wants to help her fulfill her dreams or how loudly he emphasizes her educational potential. The "View Matrimony" advertisements in the personals often include the phrase "willing to subsidize tuition."

The protagonist of *The Fisher Girl* is only too happy to teach his charge, and she is educated purely for the pleasure of her tutor. The education the art student receives is of no use to him. He has a falling out with his father on account of the fisher girl, tries to make a living on his own, and is unable to do so. Luckily, a wealthy young woman who is enamored with him saves the day but proceeds to use a thousand and one stratagems to poison his relationship with the fisher girl. At the last moment, this enchanting buyer of souls has an attack of conscience, the two lovers are reunited, and the art student uses the wealthy woman's money to hire a fancy bridal carriage for the fisher girl. This movement from tragedy to comedy depends entirely on the not altogether reliable conscience of the rich girl—and for this reason *The Fisher Girl* turns into a tragedy on a more profound level.

PEKING OPERA THROUGH
FOREIGN EYES

To SEE China through the eyes with which foreigners watch Peking opera would be an exercise not entirely lacking in significance.[1] Bamboo poles overhead from which children's cotton-padded split pants are hung out to dry; big glass jars on store counters full of "ginseng-whisker" wine; the loudspeaker from one house broadcasting the sound of Mei Lanfang singing Peking opera; the wireless in another house hawking medicine for scabies; buying cooking wine under a shop sign that reads "The Legacy of Li Po": China is all of these things—colorful, shocking, enigmatic, absurd. Many young people love China and yet have only a vague notion of what this thing called China might be. Unconditional love is admirable, but the danger is that sooner or later, the ideal will run up against reality, and the resultant rush of cold air will gradually extinguish one's ardor. We unfortunately live among our fellow Chinese. Unlike Chinese overseas, we cannot spend our lives safely and reverently gazing toward our exalted motherland at a comfortable remove. So why not make a careful study of it instead? Why not revisit its sights through the eyes of a foreigner watching Peking opera? For it is only through surprise and wonderment that we may be able to find real understanding and a steadfast, reliable love.

Why is it that I constantly make reference to Peking opera? Because I am an enthusiastic lover of Peking opera but also a layperson when it comes to its many intricacies. Who isn't a dilettante or a dabbler when it comes to life? I single out Peking opera here because it lends itself so well to such an approach.

When the lovely ladies who have performed onstage in amateur theatricals hear that one is fond of Peking opera, they inevitably say with an understated little smile, "But Peking opera is a very complex thing, you know. Take the costumes, for instance. There's enough in the costumes alone to last a lifetime of study." Exactly my point. If the performers wore the wrong costumes, I wouldn't know the difference. If they sang out of tune, I wouldn't know the difference. All I know is how to sit in the front row and enjoy the combat scenes, the dark silk of the warrior's robes fluttering open to reveal the red lining inside, or the rosy purple silk underneath jade green pant legs, as kicks and jousts and feints swirl storms of dust across the stage. Then comes the sharp, anxious tattoo of percussion, signifying the quiet of the middle of the night, or deep thought, or even the cold sweat that pours out when one has been startled awake in the night: these are the very best sort of sound effects.

The opinions of laypeople are important. If not, why would American reporters work so hard to induce celebrities to offer their wisdom on subjects about which they know little or nothing at all? For instance, in an interview with the female protagonist in a sensational murder case, they might ask whether she is optimistic about the current world situation. In an interview with a boxing champion, they inquire as to his opinion on the reworking of Shakespeare's original scripts into dramas about contemporary life. This is a gimmick, of course, to make the reader laugh as she thinks to herself, "I know more than he does. These celebrities aren't all they're cracked up to be, after all." But there is another factor: the thoughts of laypeople can be unusually fresh and candid and are valuable for exactly that reason.

In order to avoid attacking the main subject immediately, I will take refuge in something relatively light: traditional opera as it appears in modern spoken drama. The reason for the stunning success of *Autumn Quince* in Shanghai is no doubt attributable to the ambience of Peking opera that pervades the story.[2] The unprecedented popularity of the play has given rise to five or six imitators around the city, all of which incorporate Peking-style opera into their plots. The realist new drama in China has defined itself in opposition to Peking opera from its very conception, but the very first spoken drama really to lodge itself in the hearts of the common people depends for its success on its heavy use of that same tradition. This is truly an astonishing fact.

Why is Peking opera so deep-rooted and so universally accepted by Chinese people, despite the fact that its artistic quality is less than flawless?

The most moving line in *Autumn Quince* is a quotation from a Peking opera, which was drawn in turn from a drum song:

> Wine partaken with a true companion—
> a thousand cups would not be enough
> Conversation without affection—
> half a sentence is far too much

A tired old cliché, but when it is once again rehearsed by the dispirited *Autumn Quince*, it somehow speaks of a vast and limitless sorrow. The Chinese have always been alive to the pleasure of the apt quotation or set phrase. Lovely bons mots, words of wisdom and cautionary phrases, two-thousand-year-old jokes—all circulate freely in everyday speech. These invisible tissues constitute a living past. The body of tradition is continually strengthened by its application to new people, new things, and new situations. Chinese people will never speak directly if there is a suitable quotation at hand. And when you think about it, nearly every conceivable situation has been enshrined in a cozy little phrase of its own. Writing a preface for someone else's book becomes "smearing dung on a Buddha's head." Writing a postscript is "tacking a dog's tail onto sable." Ninety percent of what passes for wit in China consists in the skillful use of set phrases. Little wonder, then, that Chinese students of Western languages invariably rely on handbooks full of idiomatic phrases, which they believe need only be linked in grammatical sequence in order to produce good essays.

Only in China does history perform itself so persistently in everyday life. (History here represents the sum of our collective memory.) If we see our use of quotations in this light, the relation of Peking opera to the society of today also takes on an epigrammatic quality.

Each of the scores of popular plays that make up the bulk of the operatic repertoire provides us with standardized and timeless narrative molds: the daughter whose father wants her to marry for money, the son who fails to live up to the family name, and the conflict between familial devotion and erotic love. *Deyi yuan* (Serendipitous marriage fate), *Longfeng chengxiang* (Auspicious dragon and lucky phoenix), and *Silang tanmu* (Fourth son visits his mother) all fit this last category, and all work strenuously to prove the old adage that "a girl's best route is to be married out."

Hongzong liema (The red-maned steed) presents the selfishness of men in exquisite detail. Xue Pinggui devotes himself to his career for eighteen years, cavalierly leaving his wife in cold storage, like a fish in an icebox. One day, he remembers her, suddenly becomes uneasy on her account, and returns home in a mad rush, riding by day and by night. Her best years have been laid waste by poverty and the loneliness of social ostracism, yet he expects the bliss of reunion to serve as sufficient compensation for her suffering. He unthinkingly puts her in an untenable position when he makes her queen of the very court presided over by the princess who helped him come to power. She must struggle with this young and powerful concubine for her very survival. Small wonder that eighteen days after having been enthroned, she dies, overwhelmed by an honor she lacks the good fortune to enjoy. Yet despite Xue Pinggui's rather inconsiderate behavior toward women, he still comes off as a good man. The charm of Peking opera lies precisely in this sort of simplicity and reserve.

Yutang chun (Spring in the jade hall) typifies the countless Chinese tales about virtuous prostitutes. For many men, a kind prostitute represents the ideal type for a wife. If she makes a living from her looks, she must be beautiful, and if she is kind, her beauty is matched by morality. The modern Chinese has abandoned many ancient ideals, but this is an exception. Not long ago a film entitled *Xianggui fengyun* (Storm in the perfumed boudoir) was quite economically promoted in the papers by its title and a single arresting phrase: "The Chaste Escort."

In *Wupen ji* (The chamber pot stratagem), the soul of a murdered man is imprisoned in an appropriately diminutive commode. It is difficult for Westerners to understand how such ridiculous, dirty, and unmentionable material can become fodder for high tragedy, unless, of course, the author of the play and his audience belong to a race of people entirely devoid of humor. This is because Chinese people treat physiological functions with frankness and without unhealthy inhibitions. That is why the torments suffered by this poor soul imprisoned in the chamber pot are greeted by audiences not with disgust or sarcasm but with horror.

"Girls like flash more than they like cash," and thus the sugar daddy in *Wulong yuan* (Black dragon courtyard) is condemned to taste the bitterness of unrequited love. The author sympathetically portrays Song Jiang, whose elevated status as the heroic leader of the one hundred and eight bandits immortalized in *Shuihu zhuan* (The water margin) does not save him from the contempt of a lady, simply because he loves her, but she does not love him.[3] The most heartrending scene in the play shows his pathetic efforts to make conversation:

MALE LEAD: "What have you got in your hand?"
FEMALE LEAD: "Your hat."
MALE LEAD: "But it's clearly a shoe. How could it be a hat?"
FEMALE LEAD: "If you already knew, why did you ask?"

A play that hardly fits within the category of Peking opera at all, verging as it does on the burlesque, is *Fang mianhua* (The cotton weaver). The popular *Xin fang mianhua* (New cotton weaver) is based on just one scene from the original. The original story tells a tale of adultery that leads to murder. The sensationally successful revival of the play draws on this gruesome subject matter to create comedy. The Chinese sense of humor is merciless.

The reasons *Xin fang mianhua* sells so many tickets are that the actors are dressed in the latest styles instead of traditional Peking opera costumes and that when the cotton-weaving girl breaks into folk songs and other ditties, the audience can join in the play and sing along, breaking down the barrier between on- and offstage and fostering an atmosphere of lively informality not unlike a performance in a school auditorium. This tremendous relief from the rigid conventions of Peking opera has taken the country by storm.

Chinese people like the law, and they like breaking the law, too, not necessarily through murder or plunder of property but by way of trivial and unmotivated violations of the rules. If a wooden sign by the side of the road reads, "Stay to the Right," they will inevitably walk on the left. The deviations of *Xin fang mianhua* from the set mold of Peking opera are in just such a spirit: less a subversion of the system itself than a playful tug at an object reverenced by all, a tug that ultimately becomes a form of recognition rather than rebellion.

Chinese people love to believe themselves wicked and powerful and derive an immense pleasure from such fictions. A man on the street chases after an overcrowded tram. Then, realizing that it probably won't stop for him anyway, he calls out imperatively, "Don't stop! Don't you dare stop!" It does not, and he laughs to himself.

I have heard that Chinese are the only people on earth who maintain a sense of order and logic when they quarrel and curse. The English don't believe in the existence of hell, but when they are cursing someone, they shout "Go to hell!" all the same. Their worst curse is to call something "bloody," but the real point of calling someone a "bloody arse," besides imputing their stupidity, is the satisfyingly vehement *sound* of the phrase. When a Chinese quarrels, he will say something very different: "You dare to curse me? Don't you recognize your own father?" The implication of an affair with his opponent's mother in some distant past imparts a tremendous sense of psychological satisfaction.

Fang mianhua succeeds because it is the first play to exploit this instinct for one-upmanship. When the weaver's husband, Zhang San, interrogates his wife about who her lover might be, she simply points at the audience itself. The husband proceeds to bow to the deeply affected theater patrons, gratefully thanking them for "looking after my wife in my absence."

In attempting to analyze Peking opera, we may be surprised that despite the fact that China is not a warlike nation, the vast majority of the plays feature martial themes. The number of plays based on the *Three Kingdoms* alone is not inconsiderable. Decisive change takes place more swiftly on the battlefield than any other place, which is why we can most easily ascertain a man's character and his attitude toward his situation in that context. The defeats suffered by the Hegemon of Chu or Ma Jun present clear and easily digestible lessons, applicable to all the spectators in the audience, be they officials, businessmen, or housewives.[4]

I don't know if anyone else is reduced to tears like I am when they see *Kongcheng ji* (The empty city stratagem). The brilliant military strategist Zhuge Liang, in whom old soldiers will always have absolute faith, is a rare paragon indeed, unparalleled in ancient times or modern, China or the West.[5] In this play, his beard has already begun to turn gray. He must cast aside the carefree life he has been leading at Sleeping Dragon Ridge to undertake a momentous mission, all on account of his lingering memories of the kindness of the late emperor, who has passed away. He thrusts himself into the heat of battle, risking his own life for the sake of Ah Dou, the unworthy heir of the emperor, but perhaps he wonders to himself all the while if it's really worth the struggle. There's a cold wisp of despair amid the clamor of the gongs of war.

The old plays that have been passed down provide us with formulas for feeling. To encapsulate the complexities of our daily lives within these formulas inevitably involves some sacrifice of complexity, but the results remain singularly gratifying. This condensation leaves the feelings stronger, surer, solidified by the weight of several thousand years of experience. Harmony between individuals and their environment is the happiest of occurrences, and a large part of what makes up that environment is the habits and customs of the masses.

The world within Peking opera is not contemporary China, nor does it bear much resemblance to ancient China in any stage of its development. Its beauty and its narrowly tidy ethical system are worlds away from reality, but they are never a form of romantic escape, either. The transition from one point of view to another is often misunderstood as escapism. A cook holds up an emptied vegetable basket to shake off the few leaves of spinach still stuck to the bottom. The leaves, a translucent green in the checkered sunlight, remind him of climbing vines on a trellis. Now, the latter is no less real or homely an object than the former, and yet the analogy is pleasing, as it calls up associations to things that mean more to us because our thoughts have dwelt on them and art has shaped those thoughts to advantage. The tiny chores in the kitchen, the immediate reality, uninteresting by itself, gains significance through its connection with a more lucid, comprehensible reality.

Characters in Peking opera speak directly and unabashedly of whatever preys on their minds. If there is no one to listen to them onstage, they speak directly to the audience. If words are not sufficient, they supplement them with gestures, costumes, the colors and patterns of their face paint. Even weeping has its own distinctive meter, resembling a string of pearls tapering into an exquisite diminuendo. On account of this surfeit of expression, those who are used to watching Peking opera find everything else pallid and lifeless by comparison. There may be just one or two actors onstage, but the volume of their presence implies a crowd.

Crowdedness is an important feature of Chinese drama and Chinese life. Chinese people are born in a crowd and die in a crowd, not unlike the French monarchs of the seventeenth and eighteenth centuries. (The last empress, Marie Antoinette, gave birth to her children in a large hall, separated from a crowd of nobles and ministers awaiting the good news only by a large screen around her bed.) For Chinese people, there is no escaping onlookers. A woman of the upper classes, if she is of a traditional bent, lives in nominal seclusion, sequestered in her boudoir, but once she wakes up in the morning she lacks even the right to close her bedroom door. In winter, a quilted curtain blocks out the wind, but the door is left wide open, inviting the scrutiny of every one in the household, great and small. To close a door in daylight hours would be to invite scandal. Even under the shelter of night, with the door closed and barred, an uninvited guest is able to see everything simply by licking the window paper and peering in through the moistened spot.

Marriage and death are above all else matters of public concern. Spectators hide under the bed in the bridal chamber, and a man breathes his last surrounded by a roomful of people waiting to hear his last words. It is not without reason that Chinese tragedies are loud, bustling, and showy. Grief in Peking opera is rendered in bright tones and vivid colors.

This lack of private life explains a certain coarseness in the Chinese temperament. "Everything can be spoken," and that which is left unspoken is almost certainly dubious or criminal in nature. Chinese people are always astonished by the ludicrously secretive attitude foreigners bring to completely inconsequential matters.

The result of this lack of privacy is that even the most subtle and intimate feelings must be justified to an ever-present crowd of onlookers. This leads in turn to a habit of making excuses. Chinese are used to making excuses not only for themselves but also *to* themselves, which means that very few individuals truly understand their own behavior. Collective life has had its impact on the Chinese psyche. There are very few genuine eccentrics among the Chinese. A few exceptionally cultivated types may affect a passion for pines and bamboos, drink themselves silly, refuse to bathe, be unable to tolerate a single speck of dust, or refrain from speaking of anything having to do with money. But all these are commonly accepted eccentricities, with plenty of precedents in the culture. In segregating themselves from one crowd, they merely join another.

Nowhere is it possible to avoid the rules. In Peking opera, it could be said that the repetition of the rules has reached its pinnacle. The highly conventionalized beauty of the movements of the actors across the stage is referred to by Westerners as dance, when in reality it represents the essence of ritual protocol. Ritual does not necessarily require a function or a meaning; often it is performed solely for the sake of performance. The custom of kowtowing in greeting has long since been eliminated. Apparently, to kowtow with style required a great deal of skill. Although I don't quite know how to do it correctly, I am quite willing to kowtow on holidays or other special occasions. Usually one's elders will only request that you pay your respects with a bow. Once when I was visiting my grandaunt's house, I went ahead and made a couple of kowtows instead, and no one tried to prevent me. In recent years, one rarely encounters people who were once accustomed to such practices. It is likely that people in the past had little sentimental feeling toward the innocuous hindrance imposed by such rituals. It is only now when the custom is about to die out entirely that it is mourned. Watching students file up to the podium to receive their diplomas at a graduation ceremony, one realizes immediately that most Chinese are not accustomed to bowing.

In the movie *Nong ben chiqing* (I'm a fool for you), Violet Koo asks for a divorce from her husband. Just as she is on the verge of leaving him forever, she offers to shake his hand. Suspecting that she has not been loyal to him, he ignores this gesture, and she slips forlornly away. In the West, a scene such as this might have rung true and tugged at the audience's heartstrings, but it simply does not play as well in China. In the West, the handshake has a history of several hundred years, such that it has become a natural form of expression that functions on an almost subconscious level. The Chinese have also learned to shake hands in social situations, but in a life-altering situation, with the most powerful of emotions in play, no Chinese would ever use a handshake to mark a parting. A handshake would be inappropriate, as awkward as an exchange of farewells, a gesture of benediction, or even a bow. Modern Chinese have no etiquette at all, except onstage. The symbolic expressionism of Peking opera is complete. It possesses the childlike intensity of a people still in its infancy. What is strange, however, is that by the time Peking opera became popular, Chinese civilization was already long past its maturity. How is it that such a coarse product of the popular imagination could have gained the respect and approbation of the elegant denizens of the ruling class in the late Qing period? The New York public takes primitivist paintings and peasant pottery to heart on the enthusiastic recommendation of the art critics. The Chinese turn toward Peking opera and away from Kun-style opera directly contradicts the judgment of almost every connoisseur.[5] Civilized people find the more sophisticated Kun style amenable to their tastes, but the newly emergent Peking opera has a childish vigor that ministers to our inner needs. The primitive in us has yet to be rooted out, perhaps because we are too tolerant as a civilization. And herein may lie the secret of our eternal youth.

ON CARROTS

ONE DAY, we had a turnip and meat broth on the dinner table, so I asked my aunt, "I suppose turnips and carrots came here from foreign countries in ancient times?" She replied, "I'm not the one to ask about such things. I don't know." She thought for a while and went on: "The first time I ever saw carrots was when I was small and I had a pet cricket we fed with them. I still remember that Granny (my paternal grandmother, that is) would always cut them in half lengthwise and then in quarters before she could put them into the cage. That was how small she had to cut them. If not for the cricket, we would never have cooked with carrots at all. Why we fed carrots to the cricket I don't understand."

I secretly jotted down this little speech, without changing even a single word and then couldn't help laughing to myself, because all I needed to do was add a title—"On Carrots"—and a stylish little essay appeared on the page before me. It may not necessarily attain the resonant simplicity of the best short essays but will nonetheless take up a column on the page of a newspaper. And its wonder lies in brevity: by the time you start reading, it's already over, which only makes you ponder its meaning all the more.

THE SAYINGS OF YANYING

MY FRIEND Yanying says: "Every butterfly is the spirit of a dead flower who has come back in search of itself."

Yanying is petite but also rather voluptuous and in constant danger of getting chubby. She never concerns herself with her weight, however, and likes to say rather philosophically: "A chestful is better than no chest at all." This is my awkward translation, via the Chinese saying describing a beautiful woman: "An armful of soft jade and warm fragrance," of her original English: "Two armfuls is better than no armful."

On the birth of quintuplets in Canada, Yanying says: "One plus one equals two, but in Canada, one plus one *can* equal five."

Yanying describes a woman's hair: "Extremely, extremely black. The black of a blind man."

Yanying flips through the pictorial magazines at the newsstand. She looks carefully through all of them, but doesn't buy a single paper when she's done. The newspaper man says sarcastically, "Thanks so much!" Yanying replies, "There's no need to be so polite."

Someone said, "I wanted to wander the world and especially to see the Sahara desert. But now there's a war on." Yanying said: "Don't worry. You can still go when they're done with the war. I imagine they won't be able to blow up the Sahara completely. I'm really quite optimistic about that."

When Yanying goes shopping, she always tries to trim a little something off the full price as she's making the purchase. Once she even tried to get a discount when we were in a Jewish shop in Hongkew. She turned her wallet inside out and said: "You see? That's all

I have. Really, it's all in here. Can you give us a twenty dollar discount? We're on our way to get a cup of tea. We came out just to go to a café. We weren't planning on doing any shopping, but when we saw what nice things you have here…"

The Jewish woman protested meekly: "Twenty dollars would hardly be enough for tea, anyway."

But the old proprietor of the store was moved by Yanying's childish air; maybe his first love had had skin of the same yellow brown hue, or maybe there had been a little sister who died before her time. He smiled sadly and surrendered: "All right then. I usually wouldn't let you get away with it, but since you're on your way to tea…" And he told her about the delicious cakes they sold at a nearby café.

Yanying says: "The moon sings out, summoning all the joy of life. A star is merely its timid echo."

There's a phrase in Chinese: "Put three stinking tanners together, and you get a Zhuge Liang." There's a similar saying in the West: "Two heads are better than one." Yanying says, "Two heads are better than one—on a pillow." She wrote this in a college essay, and the professor who graded her was a priest. Her guts are unmatched even by writers famous for being gutsy.

Yanying does actually have writerly ambitions, and she's studying Chinese quite assiduously. When she walks down the street, she will stop as soon as she sees a big shop sign or an advertising poster and begin to read the characters aloud: "'Big something Prosperity.' 'Old something something.' I know 'Watches,' and I know 'Flying,' and you say that one means 'a bird singing.' But what does 'watch flying birdsong' mean? And what does the *ca* in the Chinese word for 'café' mean?"

Chinese characters are read from right to left. This much she knows. But modern Chinese sometimes goes from left to right. Whenever she starts to read from left to right, it's actually a text that goes from right to left. Chinese characters are mysterious and inexhaustible entities, and for this reason we await the time when this woman who is able to say such clever things—and whose surprising literary sensibility goes well beyond mere cleverness—will be able to write essays for us to read in Chinese. But we will have to wait for quite some time yet.

UNPUBLISHED MANUSCRIPTS

I WRITE slowly and painstakingly. From time to time, when my editor is pressing me to finish up a piece and I still haven't anything to show him, he'll say, "If you happen to have any unpublished manuscripts lying around, you could just give me one of those, instead." After a while, I began to wonder whether I did indeed have a few old manuscripts hoarded away somewhere, resolved to mount a search, and—lo and behold—turned up quite a few. What I've done here is to provide an excerpt from each, supplemented by a brief introduction. Whoever's willing to publish them is welcome to take their pick; my only fear is that no one will ask.

The earliest manuscript is entitled "My Ideal Ideal Village," which I probably wrote when I was twelve or thirteen. There were earlier pieces, but unfortunately they have been lost. I still remember my first story, an untitled morality tale about the tragedy of an ordinary family by the name of Yun. Mr. Yun's wife was called Moon, and his sister was named Phoenix. When Mr. Yun goes away on business, Phoenix's chance to hatch a plot to do away with Moon finally arrives. That's as far as I got before I put the story aside for good. Instead, my creative fires were suddenly stoked by the notion of writing historical fiction. The story began like this: "Our story begins as the Sui dynasty fell and the Tang empire rose." I liked that era—it seemed grand and noisy and bathed in an orange red light. I remember that I began writing the story on an empty page in an old ledger book, the pages of which were very short and very wide, with a red line dividing each sheet of yellow parchment paper neatly in two. I filled up a whole page with my ink brush. As I wrote, one of my nephews, whose nickname was "Queue," sidled over to take a look. (I was only seven, but I had a lot of paternal nephews who were already in their twenties.) He said, "Oooh! You're writing a new *Romance of the Sui-Tang*!"[1] I was extremely proud of myself, but all I ever wrote in the end was that single page; somehow I lacked the determination to continue.

(It seems that I began my assaults on editors at the age of nine, but after several attempts to submit manuscripts to the local supplement of the *News* met with resounding silence, I brought the experiment to a halt. It was not until two years ago that I tried again.)

After a lay-off of a couple of years, I managed to finish my first fiction that actually had an ending when I was in grade school. As the heroine, Suzhen, and her lover go for a stroll in the public gardens, a pale and delicate hand reaches out from behind and taps her on the shoulder. The stranger turns out to be her cousin Fangting. Suzhen introduces Fangting to her boyfriend. A tragic ménage à trois ensues. Suzhen eventually drowns herself in a fit of pique. The story was written with a lead pencil on the pages of a notebook. The notebook was pored over by my classmates as they lay in bed beneath their mosquito nets, smudging the pencil marks as they turned the pages. The boyfriend in the book was called Yin Meisheng, but one of my classmates, whose last name was also Yin, said "How come he's called Yin, too?" crossed out the name, and changed it to Wang Meisheng, instead. I changed the name back later on. What with these recurrent revisions, the leaves of the notebook were torn through in a number of places.

That was what I wrote in private. In school, I also produced pedantic pieces in something akin to a new Chancellery style.[2] I still remember one cautionary line: "That intoxicating spring breeze / has turned me into a statue by your door." "My Ideal Ideal Village" is also a product of this period. It is so full of precisely the sorts of clichés of the new literature I most detest that I can hardly believe that I wrote it:

There's an exquisite dance hall on the top of the hill. After dinner, the milky white mist gradually evaporates, revealing the bright blue of southern skies. You can hear the mellifluous music descending like a peach-colored net from the heavens above, encircling the entire hill.... Here, there is the vitality of youth, the warmth of fiery red hearts. Here, there are no decadent young men and women, grown old before their time; only healthy and youthful souls possessed of the wisdom of age. The solitary silver moon wavers across an empty sky, shedding tears out of loneliness.... There is also a swimming pool, which forever resembles a kind old grandmother, her face wreathed in smiling wrinkles. When she sees little children jumping into the water like little fish, she erupts into silver splashes of delight. She is ringing with laughter. She may be old, but her heart is forever young. The children love her and hope never to disappoint her hopes for them. They try their best to become champion swimmers.... Smiling wild roses flourish by the roadside. When the wind comes, they wiggle their waists and cast flirtatious glances like models at a fashion show. A clear spring bubbles musically from between some stones, flowing, flowing, flowing all the way down the hill until it forms a pool rippling with blue light. When you are intoxicated by the flower-scented breeze, you can dally there on a little boat. No need to row; let it drift lightly across the water, as if you were afraid to wake the ripples from their sweet slumber, floating, floating, in the shade of the weeping willows ... oh what a poetic scene!

Although I didn't like Zhang Ziping, I could hardly escape employing a couple of profoundly soulful "ohs," given the tenor of the times.[3] Another equally ambitious classmate of mine shared the same surname, Zhang. She liked Zhang Ziping, but I liked Zhang Henshui, and we were constantly debating who was the better writer.[4]

Later, I wrote an episodic novel in the manner of the Mandarin Ducks and Butterflies school called *A Modern Dream of the Red Chamber*. My father helped me write appropriately traditional-style chapter headings for the table of contents. The six chapters were titled:

1. Bao-yu and Dai-yu adapt to apartment living despite trials and tribulations; Jia Lian receives an official appointment, dignifying the undignified.
2. Legal entanglements stir a tempest among family; a fashion contest occasions a squabble between maidens.
3. A playboy recants, bidding adieu to the women's apartments; feigning sincerity, a swain attends to spiritual matters.
4. Drifting hearts are anchored by conjugal passion; a couple is driven by cold fate down the road to the netherworld.
5. Awaiting news that never comes, intimate friends shed tears in vain; charmed by light playing across the waves, a pair of lovers enjoys the pleasures of spring.
6. Braving traps laid across the road, a tenderfoot steps into dangerous territory; embarking on a journey with a song, a wanderer is saddened upon waking from a dream.

The beginning of the novel describes how Bao-yu receives a photograph sent to him by Fu Qiufang:

Bao-yu grinned: "Aroma, perhaps you should have a look and decide for yourself. Is she prettier, or . . . is Cousin Lin prettier?"

Aroma fixed him with a withering glare: "Hmmph! I'm going to go tell Miss Lin. How could you possibly compare her with random girls from outside the family. . . . And don't forget. Yesterday the mistress said that your father is coming in on the express train from Nanjing tonight and that you must at all costs go to meet him so that he isn't provoked again."

On Jia Lian receiving an official appointment:

The room was packed full of people, and even the concubines, Aunt Zhao and Aunt Zhou, had hurried over from the other residence. Aunt Zhao was holding on to Xi-feng's sleeve: "Congratulations! This is truly wonderful!" . . . Xi-feng, her face wreathed in smiles, grasped hold of Bao-yu, saying, "Why don't you go over and congratulate your cousin Lian? Your father has arranged for him to be promoted to bureau chief in the Ministry of Railways."… Bao-yu squeezed his way through the crowd, encountering as he did Grandmother Jia, who was sprawled across an "Empress Yang" divan, while Faithful sat beside her on a little stool, lighting her opium lamp, and Amber leaned across the cushions, massaging her legs…. Jia Lian was so exultant that his usual westernized manners were left entirely by the wayside. He retreated a step, lowered his arms respectfully to his sides, made a deep obeisance to Jia Zhen, and cried out in ringing tones: "Thank you, Uncle, for this promotion!"

Xi-feng sets out wine to toast Jia Lian in their own rooms:

She presided over the occasion but looked over at Patience and smiled: "Why don't you join all the fun tonight? No need to observe the proper etiquette. Sit down and enjoy yourself!"

…The three passed the wine cup from hand to hand in celebration…. Jia Lian said, "We've had to tighten our belts the last two years, but it will all be fine now."

Xi-feng fixed him with a look: "They say that 'cash in hand bites its owner.' It looks like you had better start looking for a couple of fresh new concubines."

Jia Lian burst into guffaws: "Rest assured, darling. With a couple of women as lovely as you and Patience by my side, why would I need to look anywhere else?"

Xi-feng sneered: "Surely you exaggerate our beauty. You haven't been able to take your mind off that woman who lives in Drenched Blossoms Townhouse Village for one moment, so don't feed me any of your false piety! I can see right through you."

Jia Lian hurried to his own defense: "Ever since you went and kicked up a fuss at the Yous' place, I've heeded your warnings and never gone back again. Patience can attest to that."

"But how many other little whores besides her are you keeping in the brothels? Tomorrow, I'm going to make inquiries, and once I have a complete census, I'll settle my accounts with you." Patience, seeing that they were moving into dangerous territory, tried to change the subject and restore the peace.

Jia Zhen arrives with a letter from Miss You saying she has engaged a lawyer to sue Jia Lian for seducing and subsequently abandoning her. She has decided to blackmail him because he has recently "made a name for himself in officialdom and would not want his reputation besmirched." Jia Lian is unable to come up with the money. "It looks as though the only recourse is to try to touch Jia Zhen for the funds. After all, he's played his own part in all this. I'm fairly sure that he won't want to refuse me."

Because he's afraid the debt will go unpaid, Jia Zhen transfers his wife's own money to Jia Lian and invents a story that he's borrowed it from another friend.

What comes next is a description of the First Lady Jia Yuanchun's New Life Movement fashion show, the elopement of Qin Zhong and Sapientia, how Parfumée and Lotus join a song-and-dance troupe after having been ejected from the Jia household, how they become objects of desire for Jia Zhen, his son, and Bao-yu alike, plus the kidnapping of Qiao-jie, as well as Bao-yu's demand that he be allowed to go abroad with Dai-yu. When this request is denied, he leaves home in protest, and only then do Grandmother Jia and Lady Wang finally cave in and give their consent to the arrangement:

Aroma instructed Bao-yu to go to Bao-chai's apartment to say his farewells, but Bao-yu demurred, "Lately, Auntie Xue always sees to it that I feel uncomfortable in her presence." With a twinge of regret, he asked Aroma, "Has Cousin Bao said anything? Does she blame me for what's happened?" Aroma replied, "How should I know how things stand between the two of you?" Bao-yu ... heaved a long sigh.

On the eve of their departure, Bao-yu and Dai-yu quarrel once again, this time so seriously that they sever ties with one another completely. Before they are able make amends, Bao-yu has already left for abroad, alone.

This was, of course, popular fiction. But I wrote some relatively high-minded pieces as well. Just before I graduated from middle school, I published two serious short stories in our school magazine, written in the prevailing new literary mode, and entitled "Ox" and "Farewell, My Concubine," respectively.

One might say that "Ox" is a perfect example of how your average literary youth, born and bred in the big city, attempts to write about rural areas. An admirable effort, and yet every time I reread it, I can't help losing patience with myself:

Luxing sucked on his water pipe as he stood, hands resting on his hips, by the doorway. The rain had only just cleared, and the thatched roof glistened with dripping beads of water. The muddy pond below was overflowing with greenish water. In the middle of the pond were a few sparse foxtails, moving along with the currents of the water, pale chestnut-colored fringes softly swaying. The wind blowing toward him was still cold enough to chill his nostrils but seemed more redolent of grass than it had been in the winter.

Luxing tapped the stem of pipe against the door frame, tightened the sash around his waist, and moved toward the cowshed. In the shed, the wan sunlight that had only just come out after the rain was shining through the slats of the walls, casting rectangles of light and shade across the muddy ground. Two timid and scrawny chickens, shaking their bedraggled wings, moved back and forth with their beaks to the ground in search of morsels to eat. Inside the shed, the water troughs, empty and coated with dust, lay silently waiting. They were covered with a thin layer of paper, atop which sat dried vegetables. In the corner, there were still some bits and pieces of

UNPUBLISHED MANUSCRIPTS · 135

straw. To one side, the slats were worn smooth and shiny. That was where the ox, after he had eaten his fill, always used to rub his neck to scratch an itch. Luxing softly laid his hand against the worn-out slats, feeling the rough wood under his fingers, as bitterness rose in his throat, tickled his nose, and the tears welled up in his eyes.

Luxing, having sold his ox, can't plow his fields when spring arrives. He wants to give his two chickens to a neighbor in return for the use of a single ox. At first, Luxing's wife opposes the plan: "Heavens! First it was the ox... my ox... led away in the prime of his life, and then the silver hairpin... and now it's these two chickens' turn. What kind of man are you? All you seem to know how to do is dispose of my things."

In the end, he does end up borrowing a bull, but it has a bad temper and bucks under his supervision. When Luxing bears down with the whip, the bull charges him, piercing his chest with its horn, and this is how he meets his end:

Once again it was dusk, and Luxing's woman, wearing the rough burlap of mourning, escorted a wooden coffin carried by two men out of the house. She pressed her face against the cold coffin, rubbing her disheveled hair against the lacquer, still only half dry, that had been used to seal it. Tears filled her meekly trembling big brown eyes, and she softly uttered in a quavering voice: "First... first it was my ox... my big strong ox, fit to eat and fit to work... led away in the prime of his life... then the silver hairpin... almost a tael of silver as my dowry... shiny silver hairpin... and then it was my chickens... and now... now they're taking you away from me, too..." She cried in broken sobs, for she knew that everything she had once loved or pitied had grown wings and flown away, disappearing into the damp, chilly evening wind.

A yellow moon slanted against the chimneys, blackened by the haze of kitchen smoke, morning glory flowers put forth their purple trumpetlike blossoms atop disorderly grave mounds, and foxtails rustled as their chestnut brown fringes swayed in the wind. The road of life that lay before Luxing's wife was a long night, a long night without the sound of the chickens clucking and the sway of Luxing's giant shadow in the flickering lamplight. What a long and lonely night it would be!

When I saw Li Shifang perform the play *Farewell, My Concubine* (*Bawang bieji*) last year, I was quite struck by it and felt that I should rewrite it as a short story.[5] But I wasn't able to do it, because I had already written a story on the same theme in the past and was haunted by sentences from the original that I had once found quite moving and later realized were bloodcurdlingly bad. That first "Farewell, My Concubine" had very little Chinese flavor. It was in that sense much like one of our contemporary costume dramas. Xiang Yu was the treasonous king and general of the domains to the east of the river. Concubine Yu was a faithful but altogether pallid presence who was loyal to the king. Once the king had conquered the world, even if he did in fact make her his consort, her future would by no means be assured. For the moment, he was her sun and she his moon, reflecting his light. Yet if he were to establish a grand imperial palace, there would be countless shooting stars orbiting around him. And this is why she secretly hoped that the war would go on forever. One night when the army was trapped at Hai, just as the night sentries were making their final patrol, she heard the sound of an anthem of Chu called "Lamenting the Great Wall" coming from the enemy camp. She hurried back to the tent to report what she had heard to the king but could not bear to wake him from his slumber.

He was one of those rare mortals who was forever young: although there were gray strands among the locks of hair dangling from his forehead and the knife of time had carved deep furrows in his brow, his slumbering face still possessed something of the candor and stubbornness of a child.

The king soon hears himself surrounded on all sides by the enemy's song and realizes that Liu Bang has already won the kingdom of Chu for himself:

Concubine Yu's heart ached when she saw King Xiang's stubbornly set lips turn white. His eyes put forth a cold, glassy light. The expression of those eyes as they stared into the foreground was so frightening that she covered them with the wide expanse of her sleeve. She could feel the rapid flickering of his eyelashes on the palm of her hand, and she also felt a string of cold teardrops roll from her palm down to the crook of her arm. This was the first time she knew that this heroic traitor was indeed capable of shedding tears.

He brushed away her hand and, with heavy steps, staggered back toward the tent. She followed him inside. He sat bent at the waist, head buried in his hands. The candle had burnt down almost completely and the soft light of dawn had already begun to steal in through the curtains of the tent.

"Give me some wine." He raised his eyes toward her.

As he lifted the glowing amber goblet in one hand, he placed the palm of his other hand on his knee and smiled. "Yu, we're finished. It looks like we will be caught like beasts in a trap. But we don't want to be the hunted. No, it's far better to be the hunters. Today! Today will be our very last hunting trip. I want to carve a path of blood through the armor of the Han army! Ha! That Liu Bang! Does he really think that he's got me trapped forever inside his cage? I've been given one last chance to enjoy the thrill of the hunt, and my arrows just may pierce his heart before I'm through, just as they would skewer a rare purple sable. Concubine Yu, put on your Persian armor. You must follow me to the very last. We shall die astride our horses."

But Concubine Yu does not want to go, for she fears that his concentration will waver because of her presence. He says:

"Oh? Then I will leave you in the rear, and when you are discovered by the Han army, you will be given as a battle prize to Liu Bang."

Concubine Yu smiled. She swiftly removed a little dagger from its sheath and, with a single motion, plunged it deep into her own chest. Xiang Yu rushed to catch her, holding her at her waist. Her hand was wrapped tightly around the gilt handle of the dagger. Xiang Yu lowered his large eyes, which burned with light and brimmed with tears as they gazed toward her. Her eyes widened and—as if unable to bear the intensity of the sun—closed once more. Xiang Yu pressed his ear to her trembling lips and listened as she uttered something he could not understand:

"I like this ending better."

After her body had gradually gone cold, King Xiang pulled the dagger from her heart and wiped the bloodstains on his armor. Then, gritting his teeth, he shouted with the hoarse cries of a wild boar, "Lieutenant! Lieutenant! Blow the horn! Ready the cavalry! We're charging down the hill!"

This last scene is perhaps a bit too much like a Hollywood movie.

Later on, I went to Hong Kong for college and didn't write anything in Chinese for three whole years. I even wrote all my correspondence in English so that I could practice, which was indeed quite helpful. Now I am writing in Chinese again, without any restraint or limitation whatsoever. It's certainly a good thing to stop writing in Chinese for a while. Picking up a pen to write after three or five years, I may feel as though I've made some little progress—one never knows.

WHAT ARE WE TO WRITE?

A FRIEND of mine asked, "Can you write stories about the proletariat?" I thought it over and replied, "No. Except perhaps about amahs, because I know a little something about them." Later, I looked into the matter and discovered that amahs don't count as proletarians, anyway. It's a good thing that I'm not planning to change my style, since it would only result in disappointment.

The discussions taking place among writers as to our present course and our path forward seem to me an unimaginable liberty—as if there were any choice in the matter. No doubt the garden of literature is broad and inclusive: when visitors buy their tickets and enter its precincts, they can have their pictures taken on the Nine-Bend bridge, swarm over to the zoo, or roam as they wish across the grounds. *Their* freedom of movement is truly enviable. But I believe that writers themselves should be like trees in the garden, growing naturally within its confines, with their roots extending deep into the ground below. As they grow, their viewpoint will begin to grow wider, and as their field of vision expands, there is no reason why they shouldn't be able to develop in new directions, for when the wind blows, their seeds will disperse far into the distance, engendering still more trees. But that is the most difficult task of all.

When I was first learning how to write, I believed that I could write whatever I pleased: historical fiction, proletarian fiction, modernist "new sensation" fiction, even the relatively vulgar genre of "family ethics fiction," not to mention social exposé or martial arts novels or decadent stories of romance and seduction. The sky really was the limit. But later I felt more and more constrained. Here is an example. I have at present enough material assembled for two stories. Not only do I have outlines of the plots and all the characters; even the dialogue has already been prepared in advance. But the stories are set in the interior, and that is why I cannot write them, at least for the time being. And even if I could go there, it wouldn't really be any use. If I were to take a hurried look around, I would be no better than a news reporter on assignment. Perhaps it's true that first impressions are the most important. But while a foreigner might well take away extremely vivid impressions from a visit to a "swallow's nest," his perspective won't necessarily reveal very much about the psychology of those who frequent it.[1]

"Observing the flowers from astride a horse" will only take you so far. But even if you were to live someplace for a few months, searching high and low for dollops of local color, you might well fail to achieve your objective. True immersion in the atmosphere of life usually takes place spontaneously. It isn't something that can be forced or willed into being. All a writer can strive for is to live with integrity. A real writer can only really write about what he himself thinks. He will write about what he can write; what a writer should or should not write is ultimately beside the point.

Then why do we often feel that we need to change the direction of our literary work? The answer is that a writer will often make the same technical mistakes over and over again and come to abhor the constant repetition. If there is no way to treat the same material with different techniques, might there be a way to apply one's old techniques to new material? This second option is almost impossible to achieve, because of the limits of individual experience. How many people are like Gorky or Shi Hui, wandering the world throughout their lives and seasoned in any number of different professions?[2] Perhaps in the end these anxieties about what and how to write are merely superfluous. As long as one's subject matter isn't too specialized, one can write about common experiences—love and marriage, birth, growing up, growing old, getting sick, and dying—from any number of disparate angles and never lack for material. If there came a day when an author could no longer write anything about such things, I imagine it would be because he had nothing left to say, even for himself. And even if he came across some brand-new subject, he would still only be able to produce clichés.

MAKING PEOPLE

I HAVE always felt close to people older than myself, looked down a little bit on people more or less my own age, and felt both esteem and terror when confronted with little children, from whom I deliberately maintain a respectful distance. This is not because I "fear being eclipsed by younger generations," as the old saying goes. I imagine that, once they grow up, most of them will be quite ordinary and no better, in all likelihood, than my own generation.

Children are little packets of new energy dispatched from the wellsprings of life. That is why they are to be respected and feared.

Children aren't as muddleheaded as we imagine them to be. Most parents don't understand their children, while most children are able to see right through their parents and understand exactly what sort of people they are. I remember how as a child I longed to reveal all that I knew, just so that I could shock and dismay my elders.

The distinguishing feature of youth is the ability to forget, for as soon as we pass beyond childhood, we completely forget how children think, and it is only as we grow old that we once again grow closer to them. It's the time in between that usually throws up the biggest barriers, so that as adults we lose contact with children almost entirely. This is also precisely the time in our lives, of course, when we actually go about *having* children.

No wonder those who have children keep on having them. They see children as amusing little blockheads, lovable and laughable encumbrances. They fail to see what is so very frightening about children's eyes—such earnest eyes, the eyes of the angels on Judgment Day.

Without any real credentials, we blithely make eyes such as these, their little minds capable of criticism and judgment, their bodies capable of experiencing the most exquisite pain as well as pleasure. Without credentials, we make people, and stumbling between hunger and satiety, between knowledge and ignorance, we raise them to adulthood. Making people is quite a dangerous occupation. Mothers and fathers are not gods, but they are forced into occupying a position of divinity. And even if you play that divine role with great care, even if you prepare meticulously for the arrival of your child, there is no way to guarantee what sort of person the child will eventually become. If conditions do not favor a child even before he is born, then he can hardly be expected to succeed later in life. Such are the operations of fate.

Of course, the more arduous the situation, the more apparent will become the tremendous love parents bear for their children. Either the parent or the child must be sacrificed to circumstances, and it is from this hard truth that we have derived the moral virtue of self-abnegation.

The self-sacrificing love of a mother is indeed a virtue, but a virtue only within a moral code that has been passed down to us by our animal forebears. Since even domestic animals seem to share this virtue, there's no particular reason to be proud of ourselves on this account. Instinctual love of this sort is merely an animal virtue, not a quality that separates us from the beasts. What does distinguish mankind from the beasts are our higher degree of consciousness and higher powers of comprehension. While this approach to the question may appear excessively logical, overly dispassionate, or lacking in humanity, real humanity lies in a refusal to accept merely animal virtues as an ethical standard for human beings.

Animals possess instinctive compassion but also instinctive cruelty, and this is why generation after generation can and does survive the bloody, competitive struggle for survival. Nature is a mysterious and magnificent thing, but we cannot "rest content in nature." Nature's ways are shockingly wasteful. A fish will produce several million eggs, most of which will be swallowed by other creatures of the sea, only to yield a few surviving spawn that might eventually grow into fish.

Why should we expend our flesh and blood in such a profligate manner? Civilized people are extremely expensive creatures, requiring enormous sums of money to be fed, raised, and educated. Our energy is limited. Our time on this planet is limited. And there are so many things that we can and should do while we are here. What on earth could induce us to produce these useless creatures, destined as they are for the evolutionary scrap heap, in such profuse quantities?

It is in our nature to want humanity to thrive and proliferate, to reproduce and to continue reproducing. We ourselves are destined to die, but our progeny will spread across the earth. But what unhappy progeny are these, what hateful seeds!

BEATING PEOPLE

On the bund, I saw a policeman beating someone for no reason save his own momentary whim. The person being beaten was a fifteen- or sixteen-year-old boy, neatly attired in a padded cotton robe and vest, with a sash around his waist. I could not see very clearly what the policeman was using to beat him, but it looked like the knotted rope attached to the end of his baton. There was a whistling sound as he bore down, striking again and again until the boy was forced back against a wall. The boy certainly could have tried to make a run for it, but he did not run, gazing instead at the policeman with a furrowed brow and squinting eyes, like a peasant in the fields who cannot quite force open his eyes against the glare of the sun. There was something like a little smile on his face. Everything had happened much too suddenly. Often, people without any acting experience cannot adjust their expressions with the necessary quickness and dexterity.

I almost never have feelings of righteous indignation. If I do not want to see something, I have a talent for not seeing it. This time, though, I kept turning back to look, with a suffocating feeling in my chest, and, with each blow, my heart seemed to recoil. When the policeman was done beating the boy, he strode in my direction, and I fixed him with a fierce and cutting stare, hoping that looks could kill and that I would be able thereby to give adequate expression to my contempt and fury, my utter abhorrence for such a leprous character. But what he noticed was only that someone had taken notice of him, and, with an exultant air, he adjusted the leather belt cinched around his waist. He was a northerner with a long face and a full mouth, and not unattractive.

He swaggered over to the entrance of the public toilet and grabbed hold of a destitute-looking man in a long robe. He refrained from beating him immediately, preferring instead to glare menacingly as he brandished his baton in one hand. Despite his surprise and fear, the man was still able to crack a joke in his local dialect: "Is it because I was about to shit in the pit, sir?"

Perhaps it was because I've never undergone any proper ideological training that the notion of class warfare never once crossed my mind, even at a time like this. In the fury of the moment, all I wanted was to become a government official or the First Lady. That way, I could march over and slap the policeman across the face without so much as a by-your-leave.

If this story had taken place in the fictional world of the early Republican-period writer Li Hanqiu, a Western missionary with justice on his side would have sallied forth at just this moment, or, better yet, the mistress of the police chief (who would inevitably be revealed as the bosom friend of the heroine and the hero's sweetheart from bygone days).[1] Once in a while, a touch of naiveté goes a long way, but that kind of systematic naiveté ultimately leaves a lot to be desired.

Petty Figures.

(1) She knows how to abuse her children and her servants;
(2) she knows how to dress up for a dance;
(3) he knows how to force his attentions on a woman;
(4) she knows how to save money;
(5) she knows how to act like a lady;
(6) she knows how to hunt for a man;
(7) he knows all sorts of ways of being vicious;
(8) he knows how to be delighted with himself;
(9) she sees through everything;
(10) "But, seriously, we really ought to take this point into consideration . . ."

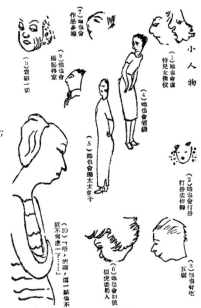

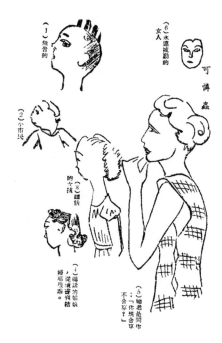

Pathetic Beings.

(1) Helpless;
(2) petty urbanite;
(3) an obedient girl;
(4) an obedient girl will always be good and obey, from her schooling to her marriage;
(5) she always asks you, "Do you think it's a good deal?"
(6) a woman who's forever passive.

POETRY AND NONSENSE

SUMMER days roast, one after another, strung together by a white hot thread, slender and nearly burnt through, connected only by the shrill cries of the cicadas: *ji ya, ji ya, ji* ...

This month, since I've been ill, I've managed to save substantial sums of money that would normally have been used for groceries and carfare, and suddenly I feel rather well-off. I'm suffering from a less than refined malady—stomachaches so nasty that I roll across the straw mat on my bed, moaning in pain—but it is summer, and I'm idling away at home, unable to tackle anything more weighty than a few pieces on Cézanne's paintings, some books I've read, and Chinese religion, all admittedly rather elegant topics. I have decided that this should be my "month of elegance," and, continuing in this cultivated vein, I've started to discuss poetry as well.

I made my aunt read a famous Japanese poem, translated by Zhou Zuoren into Chinese, that goes like this: "Summer nights / like bitter bamboo/ slender stalked and close jointed / in but a moment / comes the dawn."[1] My aunt, a typical amateur intellectual, looked it over, shook her head, and said, "I don't get it." After another moment's thought, she added, "Since he's so famous, there must be something to it, no? But who knows? Once someone has reached a certain level of celebrity, they seem to have earned the right to talk nonsense."

I was reminded of Lu Yishi.[2] The first poem of his that I ever read was "Sanbu de yu" (Fish on a stroll), published in a monthly literary digest. That particular poem was not exactly nonsense, admittedly, but it was rather overdone. When the tabloids began to make fun of him on a daily basis, I laughed right along, for quite a few days on end. On this front, I can be just as merciless as the tabloids, if not more so. For instance, when I read that Gu Mingdao had died, I was delighted, for the simple reason that his fiction was so badly written.[3] In truth, I never knew him, and if I had, I'm certain that there would be reasons to hold him in great esteem, because he was a model of what a writer ought to be and experienced all the trials and tribulations that writers have been known to suffer throughout history. Besides, he has passed away, so to speak ill of him seems quite unpardonable. And yet I cannot help remembering when *Mingyue tianya* (Bright moon horizon) was being serialized in the *Xinwen bao* (Daily news). I was terribly annoyed by both Sun Jiaguang, the paragon of progressive youth in the story, and the girl he was helping through school, Mei Yuezhu. Whenever Sun visited her at home, her mother would heap the table with fish and meat to express her gratitude, an extra expense that must have exceeded by many times over the cost of her daughter's tuition. Mrs. Mei would then recount the honorable conduct of her late husband and go on to detail his many misfortunes, the minute circumstances of which appeared daily in the paper for two weeks running. And I had no choice but to read on, precisely because the novel was divided into daily installments and exercised thereby a most exasperating kind of appeal. I had a cousin who was also a reader of the *Daily News*. Whenever we got together, we would roundly criticize *Mingri tianya*, prattling on about its deficiencies even as our eyes continued to scan across the pages.

There really isn't anything extraordinary about Gu Mingdao's fiction. What is extraordinary is that the mass public is able to stand such colorless idiocy. The popular success of *Autumn Quince* at least is justifiable.[4]

To speak of Lu Yishi in the same breath as the Mandarin Ducks and Butterflies fiction that he despises with such passion would no doubt infuriate him. What I am trying to make clear is that I cannot forgive Gu Mingdao for his fiction just because he is dead. Nor can

I excuse Lu Yishi for some of his later works simply because he wrote some good poetry in the past. After reading "Bangwan de jia" (Home at dusk), however, I changed my mind. Not only "Sanbu de yu," I think, but even the immaturity, venality, and pretension of his other works can be forgiven solely on account of this one poem. It has an integrity that demands that I quote an entire stanza:

> Home at dusk is the color of dark clouds
> wind comes to the little courtyard
> finished counting the returning crows
> the children's eyes grow lonely
>
> at dinner in my wife's small talk
> events of several years past disperse like mist
> and in the blandness of the vegetable broth
> I taste something of the desolation of living

All of Lu Yishi's best poems possess this same purity, sadly lucid, sparing in their use of color, like ink paintings of bamboo. The field of vision is small, but because it's not bound to a distinct time or place, it gains an eternal, universal quality. For instance:

> once more the flurries of February snow
> somber house bathes in spring chill
> ah, warmth that once was, now distant
> my wife's eyes are forlorn

And then there are these lines from "Chuangxia yin" (Poem by the window):

> But to speak of my
> green, green
> love, mirror calm
> yet so very distant

a distance that
for sparrows and young crows
would be absurd

This poem is relatively long, with variations of tone that are extremely charming and supple. In "Eryue de chuang" (A window in February), there is an altogether more subtle and ambiguous feeling, a feeling unique to modern man:

The lazy westward-drifting clouds make one melancholy
trailing sorrow-laden eagles in their drawn-out wake
slowly as an unthinkable sail
as each unthinkable day
sails past my February window

To have found in one volume just a few such stanzas is already immensely gratifying. China's new poetry—starting from Hu Shi, on to Liu Bannong and Xu Zhimo, and then even Zhu Xiang—seems to have been heading toward a dead end.[5] It will no longer do to speak of our concerns in the words of the Tang dynasty, because all those words have already been said. Even when we try to express ourselves in our own language, however, something is still amiss; all in all, an exasperating state of affairs. Yet there are still some unexpectedly good poems. This stanza I came across in Ni Hongyi's "Chongfeng" (Reunion) is really quite good:

The purple carnation you called the flower of momentary
    love
three years ago
the colors of summer fell limp
in the dead city
you suffered a sleepless night
colors of night surged and ebbed
words like a night train

you said
by my future grave will be night-blooming jasmine
I said why not plant a "love for a moment"?

Phrases like "momentary love" and "fell limp" sound extremely forced, but they are employed as a means of poetic economy, imparting a sense of solidity and compression, rather than a life-or-death desire to "never cease writing words that startle," as Du Fu would have it. I especially like "words like a night train"; the metaphor sounds out intermittently, distant and bleak.

Or, later:

you were sacrificed at the altar of chastity before our
    generation
fatigued by the noise and the clamor
you will not see what comes later
your face obscured in silence

This last phrase is cast in the visionary mode of modern painting. I know very little about the person depicted in the poem, yet I feel that the picture looks just right: with gentle despair, she sinks slowly into the shadows, stretching her malleable white arms in an arc.

The last line of the poem is purely impressionistic, and the author himself has said that he fears it will not be understood:

you wholly possess dark-hued green

Having seen her, we may perhaps come to understand that within this limitless "dark-hued green" are concealed tranquil wounds. And yet there is a momentary uncertainty. For she is not so much a withered flower fallen from a branch as a plucked blossom embroidered on ancient silk, broken but very beautiful, broken yet necessary nonetheless.

And thus living in China has something lovable about it: amid dirt and chaos and grief, one discovers everywhere precious things,

things that bring joy for an afternoon, a day, a lifetime. I hear the roads in Germany are so squeaky clean that you can use them as a mirror, that they are wide, ruler straight, tidy to a fault, and planted all along their length with towering trees. And yet I suspect that walking along such a road day after day would drive one mad. Then there is Canada, a country that in the majority of people's minds seems to lack any distinguishing characteristics whatsoever: a formless and desolate land. And yet my aunt says it is the best place in the world, with a cool climate, blue skies, emerald-colored grass, creamy white Western-style houses with red roofs as far as one can see, each with a freshly scrubbed look and boasting its own garden. If she could choose, she would live the rest of her life there. If I were to choose, I could not bear to leave China: I'm homesick even before I leave home.

WITH THE WOMEN ON THE TRAM

EVERY word of what follows is true, without the slightest tailoring or embellishment, and cannot be considered fiction.[1]

There were two women dressed in Western style sitting on this side of the tram, probably of mixed race or else Portuguese, who looked like they were typists working for a foreign firm. The women speaking was a bit plump, with a three-inch-wide black patent leather belt cinched around her waist and a round belly below. She had slender eyebrows, bags under her eyes, and because her forehead was rather prominent, her face seemed to be divided into two distinct halves. She said, "And so I haven't spoken to him for a whole week. If he says 'hello,' I say 'hello.'" She arched her eyebrows coldly, and the upper half of her face ascended along with them. "You know how stubborn I can be. When I know I'm in the right I'm always stubborn."

On the other side of the tram sat another woman speaking of some other "him," only her "him" was not a lover but a son. She was a middle-aged married woman, who looked like the proprietress of a little shop. Her hair was combed back in a lustrous black bun, and a pair of fashionable red lacquer earrings dangled from her ears. The young man listening to her speak must have been her nephew. With each sentence, he nodded his head in sympathy, and then the woman would nod again for emphasis. She said: "I wanted to update my wardrobe, but he wouldn't let me. So I told him he wouldn't be getting any spending money from me. The other day we were on the tram, and I told him to buy us tickets. And what do you think he said? 'Sure, I'll buy you tickets if you give me ten dollars!' Awful, isn't he?"

At first, it seemed that the "he" in question was a worthless husband, but as she went on it became clear that "he" was really her son. Evidently, he had perpetrated some other enormity to offend his mother: "His father insisted that he get down on his knees. 'Get down on your knees, get down!' But he refused to give in. 'Why should I?' So his father said to him: 'You are going to get down on your knees and beg for her forgiveness! Go on! Get down!' It took a long time, but after a while he just couldn't fight anymore: 'All right, all right. I'll do it.' Which is when I said, 'I don't want him to. I don't want him to do it.' And all the others were saying: 'He's all grown up now. It'd be too humiliating for him to get down on his knees. Why don't you just have him bring you a cup of tea and say something like "Mama, please don't be angry with me anymore."' And so he ended up bringing me a cup of tea, and when he came up to me, I couldn't help laughing out loud . . ."

The women on the tram filled me with sorrow. Women—women whose lives are consumed in talking about men, thinking about men, resenting men, now and forever.

WHISPERS

In the depths of night, I hear whispers as the moon sets like a golden basin.

DO WORDS spoken at that hour of night seem especially intimate, even when they're not? I don't mean to pretend that any of the things I am about to say are solemn secrets. But since my editor is forcing me to finish this essay quickly, my words may not have been selected as carefully as they might. What I write here need not be thought about too intently, because these are the sorts of things that are always there, part of the backdrop of the subconscious. So pretend, if you will, that you heard these words whispered endlessly into your ear on a night when the moon slowly sets like a golden basin.

This morning, the landlord sent someone up to measure the length of the hot water pipes for the radiator, in all likelihood so he could take them apart and sell them as scrap. My aunt could not help feeling a kind of retroactive attachment and heaved a sigh for the vulgar notions people have when they think shortsightedly and merely for the moment: these are chaotic times.

People living in chaotic times get by however they can, without a real home to call their own. And yet I maintain an abiding attachment to my aunt's place. My mother and my aunt lived together for many years, and although they moved several times and my mother is no longer in Shanghai, leaving my aunt behind, her house has always presented itself to me as an exquisitely complete system, one that I must not allow to be dismantled in any way. The day before yesterday, I broke a glass tabletop that cost six hundred yuan to replace, and I was already just about bankrupt, yet I still rushed to call the carpenter to come and fix it.

Lately, for some unknown reason, I've been unusually prone to breaking things. (Things, that is, besides cups, plates, bowls, and soup spoons, which don't count. If my aunt happens to break a teacup, I always delightedly announce that "Now it's finally Auntie's turn to break something!") The most recent incident happened when I was in a rush to go out to the balcony to take in the wash and tried to push open the glass doors, which refused to budge. I put my knee against the door and gave it a shove, and with a sudden shattering sound, the pane fell to pieces. There was only a small cut on my knee, but the blood ran down my leg all the way to the top of my foot, and when I covered the wound in red iodine solution, it dripped down my leg along with the blood, so I ended up looking as if I had been at the receiving end of Big Knife Wang Wu's proverbial knife. When I showed my aunt, she hurriedly bent down to inspect the wound, and having assured herself that it was far from fatal, began to ask with genuine concern about the window glass, which I ended up replacing.

My home at present is basically complete to the very last detail, and yet all I do is crash back and forth across it, breaking things as I go. And since a real home should always fit, growing up along with its occupant, I'm reminded of homes I have had in the past.

My first home was in Tianjin. I was born in Shanghai, but we moved to northern China when I was two years old. We went to Beijing as well, but all I remember of that time is being carried hither and thither by a servant as I held on to the loose skin around her neck with my hand. As she grew older, the skin gradually began to sag, and it felt different each time I reached my hand under her chin. I had a terrible temper as a child, and when I got impatient I would grab her so hard that there was blood on her face. Her last name was He, and she was called He Gan, which sounds like "what to do?" I don't know which local dialect we were using, but we always ended up calling the old servants "What to Do." He Gan sounds a bit like one of those fashionable pen names, like He Ruo (What Is It Like?), He Zhi (Where to Go?), and He Xin (What Heart?).

I have a copy of George Bernard Shaw's *Heartbreak House* that my father bought around that time. He inscribed his name in English on a blank flyleaf:

Timothy C. Chang
No. 61, 32nd Street
Tientsin, North China
1926

I have always found solemnly noting one's name and address, and the date on a book quite dreary, even superfluous. But when I came across these lines, the discovery pleased me, because they exude the desultory atmosphere of a spring day, like our house in Tianjin.

There was a swing set in the courtyard. Once, one of the maids—a tall woman whom I called "Scar Girl" because she had a scar on her forehead—swung herself up to the very top and flipped over. We had chickens in the back court. On a summer afternoon, I sat on a bench in the courtyard, dressed in red pants and a short silk blouse printed with little red peaches on a white background, finishing up a bowl of pale green herbal tonic, which was slightly astringent but also a touch sweet, and reading aloud from a book of riddles: "A little dog that takes a bite with every step." The answer to the riddle was "scissors." There was also a book of collected children's songs, including a tune that extolled a life of scholarly seclusion spent somewhere between the country and the city. I only remember one line—"With peach branches and peach leaves as our consorts"—which doesn't sound very much like the sort of thing children would enjoy singing.

In the corner of the courtyard, there was a big gray stone tablet. One of the servants, who was full of ambition and knew how to read and write, always used to practice writing big characters on it by dipping a traditional writing brush in water and running the tip across the stone. He was thin and rather elegant, and he used to tell me stories from the *Romance of the Three Kingdoms*.[1] I liked him. I gave him an unaccountably strange-sounding nickname: Brush Thing. Brush Thing's two younger brothers were thus Brush Two and Brush Three. Brush Thing's wife was Bride of Brush Thing, or Brush Bride for short. Brush Bride had a ruddy, oval face the shape of a goose egg, with liquid eyes, and loved the story of how "Meng Lijun masqueraded as a boy to win glory in the official examinations"[2] She was a lovable creature but also someone whose waters ran deep. Scar Girl later married Brush Three and was forced to endure a lot of bullying from Brush Bride. Of course, I understood very little of all this at the time. All I knew then was what a lovable and appealing family they were. They were from Nanjing, and I have had a sense of the pleasantly bright and bountiful life of the common people of that city ever since—a feeling that doubtless has no grounding in reality. Much later, they left our family to open a grocery store, and another maid brought me and my little brother to their shop, so that we could give them some extra business. We did our best by picking out a few cheaply made hot water bottles decorated with floral motifs and drank a cup of tea in their upstairs room. That visit also left me with a feeling for the pleasant bounty of glass jars stuffed full of candy. In the end, though, their family wound up losing all the money they had invested in the shop and fell into dire economic straits. And Brush Thing's mother always blamed her two daughters-in-law for not providing the family with a male heir, an accusation Brush Bride secretly rebutted by pointing out that her mother-in-law had made the two couples sleep in the same room—even if there were curtains hung over each of the beds.

The woman who took care of my little brother was called Zhang Gan. She had bound feet, she was nimble and eager, and she always gained the upper hand no matter where she went. The woman who took care of me, He Gan, discouraged on account of having been put in charge of a girl child instead of a boy, deferred to her in all matters. I could not abide Zhang Gan's chauvinism and her contempt for girls, so I always picked fights with her, and each time she would say: "With a temper like yours, you'll end up a spinster! I hope you get married off somewhere far, far away; even your brother wouldn't want you to come home!" And she knew how to predict my future simply by looking at the way I positioned my fingers when I held my chopsticks: "You hold your chopsticks close. That means you'll be married far away." I quickly shifted my fingers farther up the chopsticks. "What about if I hold them farther away?" She said, "Of course, if you hold them like that, you'll be married even farther from home."

That infuriated me even more. From very early on, Zhang Gan made me aware of the inequality between men and women, and because of that awareness, I was determined to sharpen my wits and surpass my little brother.

Not that my little brother was very formidable. He was quite sickly, and his diet was severely restricted as a result, which made him extremely greedy. If he saw someone's mouth moving, he would demand that they open up and let him see what was inside. Sick in bed, he would noisily demand to be given some pine brittle, a treat made of powdered pine nuts and flakes of rock sugar. Someone once mixed a little gold thread syrup (a bitter herbal medicine) with the rock sugar to discourage him from eating it. He burst into tears, stuck his little fist entirely into his mouth, and kept right on eating. And so they rubbed some of the bitter syrup on his fist, and his sobs grew even louder and more inconsolable. But he continued to suck on his fist.

The pine brittle was kept in a little decorative tin with gold-colored handles. Next to this tin was a yellowish orange ceramic container in the shape of a flat peach, which contained prickly-heat powder. The white afternoon sun used to shine across the surface of that antique dressing table, rubbed pale and smooth by the years. Once Zhang Gan bought a persimmon and put it away in the drawer because it still wasn't ripe enough to eat. A couple of days later, I opened the drawer to take a look. I began to suspect that Zhang Gan had forgotten all about the persimmon's existence, and yet I could not bring myself to ask her about it, out of a perverse kind of pride. After many more days, the persimmon had rotted into a puddle. I felt terrible pangs of regret about the whole affair, which is why I remember it to this day.

This earliest home lacked that someone known as my mother, although we hardly felt that as a loss, because she had been missing from our lives from very early on. When she was there, I remember that the servants would bring me to her bed every morning. It was a big brass bed. I would crawl across the checkerboard of her indigo cotton quilt, uncomprehendingly reciting the Tang dynasty poems she was teaching me to memorize. She was always grumpy upon awakening and would have to play with me for a long time before she could begin to perk up. I first began learning Chinese characters lying on the edge of that bed. Every afternoon, I was given two pieces of mung bean cake as a reward for having learned two characters.

Later, when my father took on a concubine outside the house, he wanted to bring me along to his other place for a visit. He carried me to the back gate. I absolutely refused to go along and held on to the door as if my life depended on it, flailing wildly at him with my legs. He was so angry that he flipped me over, gave me a spanking, picked me up, and carried me out the gate. When we arrived, I complacently consumed a not inconsiderable amount of candy. His other apartment had mahogany furniture and little silver saucers with tiny feet that sat atop a mica tabletop edged with carved floral motifs. His mistress was very skilled at making small talk with me.

On the day she boarded the boat to go overseas with my aunt, my mother lay on the bamboo bed sobbing. She was wearing a green blouse and a green skirt with little shiny sequins that trembled along with her body. The servants came into the room several times to tell her that it was time to leave, but she seemed not to have heard them, and they dared not speak again. They pushed me toward her and told me what to say: "Auntie, it's getting late." (I was technically in my father's brother's custody, which is why I had to use "Aunt" and "Uncle" to address my own parents.) She ignored me and continued to sob. Sprawled across the bed, she looked like the sea reflected on the window glass of a ship's cabin: a slender strip of green, full of the endless turbulence and unfathomable sorrow of the ocean.

I stood in front of the wicker bed watching, at a loss for words, for no one had told me what else I was supposed to say. Fortunately, another servant finally led me away.

After my mother left, my father's concubine moved in. The house became extremely lively, with frequent banquets during which the guests would be entertained by hired courtesans. I would hide behind the curtains and steal glances at these goings-on, gazing with particularly rapt attention at two sisters of sixteen or seventeen reclining on the sofa, their hair done up identically in bangs, sporting matching jade green Chinese-style jackets, leaning snow-pale across one another, like Siamese twins.

My father's concubine disliked my little brother and as a result went out of her way to show me her favor. She would bring me to the Catherine Ballroom every night to watch the dancers. I would sit in a chair at the table, confronted by the creamy white icing piled eyebrow high atop my piece of cake. And yet I would eat the whole piece of cake and then gradually doze off in the red dusky light, sleeping there until three or four in the morning, when one of the maids would carry me home on her back.

The family hired a teacher for my brother and me on the traditional model of home schooling in the Chinese classics. We read and recited texts all day long, rocking our bodies back and forth as we chanted by a window until dusk. When we read the line "The Great King serves Xunyu," I changed it to "The Great King craves smoked fish [xunyu]" in my head so that I could memorize it. At that time, I suffered quite often for my failures to learn my lessons by heart. Perhaps it was because I had cried early in the morning on the first day of the New Year and was thus condemned to cry all year long. On New Year's Eve, I had instructed the maid to wake me bright and early the next morning so that I could watch the festivities. Who would have guessed that, fearing I would be overtired from staying up the night before, they would let me sleep a few extra hours? By the time I awoke, all the firecrackers were already spent. I felt as if all things wonderful and boisterous were gone forever, had bypassed me entirely. I lay down on the bed and cried, and then I cried some more, refusing to sit up until they pulled me onto a wicker chair. Someone slipped a pair of ceremonial "New Year's shoes" on my feet, and still I cried—because even a new pair of shoes could not help me catch up with the new year.

My father's concubine lived downstairs in a dimly lit, cluttered, and cavernous room that I was only rarely allowed to enter. I would stand by my father's opium couch reciting my lessons. My father's concubine knew how to read and would lash out impulsively at her nephew as he was taught to recite lines like "The fish in the pool swim to and fro." These blows were so fierce that her nephew's eyes were often swollen shut. Nor was my father exempt from these beatings. She once cracked his head open with a spittoon. That was the incident that ultimately drove someone in the clan to speak up and send her packing. I sat on the ledge of the second-story window and watched as two carriages slowly moved away from the front gate, laden with silver and household goods. The servants said among themselves, "So much the better that she's gone."

The year I turned eight I came to Shanghai by boat, crossing "darkling waves and green swells" that really were as black as lacquer and as green as jade, and though I had yet to read any literary odes to the sea, I was thrilled by the sensation it gave me. I would fall asleep in the cabin reading for the umpteenth time my copy of *Journey to the West*, in which one finds only high peaks and the hot red sand of the desert.[3]

When we arrived in Shanghai and rode into town in a buggy, I felt delightfully opulent in my vest-coat of foreign cloth across whose pink background fluttered a host of embroidered blue butterflies. We stayed in a very small *shikumen* house with red-stained walls.[4] For me, even the walls were an enveloping crimson pleasure.

But it was then that my father injected himself with an overdose of morphine and very nearly died. He sat on the balcony, a wet towel over his head, gazing fixedly forward as thick white ropes of rain fell from the eaves in front of him. I could not tell what he was muttering to himself over the roar of the rain, and I was very frightened.

The maid told me that I ought to be very happy because my mother was coming home. The day she was due to return, I noisily demanded that they let me wear what I thought of as my most impishly stylish red jacket. But the first words to emerge from her mouth when she saw me were, "How could you let her wear such a tiny little jacket?" And very soon after, an entirely new wardrobe was made for me, and everything else was different as well. My father bitterly repented of his past mistakes and was sent to the hospital. We moved into a Western-style garden villa, with a dog, flower beds, children's books full of fairy tales, and an abrupt infusion into our home of lovely and elegant relatives and friends. My mother sat with a plump auntie on the piano bench, imitating the love scene in a movie. Sitting on the floor watching, I burst into peals of laughter and rolled back and forth across a wolfskin blanket.

I wrote a letter to an old classmate in Tianjin describing our new house, filling three whole pages with illustrative diagrams and sketches. There was no reply: who wouldn't be annoyed by such raw and un-cultivated braggadocio? I was of the firm opinion that everything about our house stood at the very summit of beauty. In retrospect, a blue sofa set matched with an old rose red carpet can hardly be said to be the most harmonious combination, but I liked it then, and I also liked Great Britain, because the characters for "England" made me think of little red houses underneath a blue sky, while "France" was a blue-green shade of drizzle, like the porcelain tiles in the bath-room, redolent of the aroma of shampoo. My mother told me later that England was dreary and rainy and that France was sunny and bright, but I have always been completely unable to revise these first impressions.

My mother also told me that in drawing pictures one should always avoid using red in the background, because the background must be kept at a distance from the rest of the image, and red seems to leap right out of the picture and into your eyes. The walls of the bedroom I shared with my little brother, though, were painted just the sort of orangey red that refuses to keep its distance. I had chosen the color, and when I drew pictures, I still liked to color the walls behind all the little people red, because things looked warmer and cozier and more intimate that way.

Besides drawing, I played piano and learned English. That was probably the only time in my life when I luxuriated in the stylish ways of a pampered foreign girl. Not only that: in those days I was flush with a superabundance of sentiment. Coming across a dried flower pressed between the leaves of a book, I listened to my mother tell a story about how it came to be preserved there, and tears ran down my face. When my mother saw that I was crying, she said to my little brother, "Look at your sister! She knows that there are better things to cry about than candy." I was so pleased by these words of praise that my tears immediately ran dry—which posed quite an embarrassing dilemma.

At that time, *Xiaoshuo yuebao* (Short story monthly) was serializing Lao She's novel of Chinese emigrés in London, *Erma* (The two Mas). We received the latest issue every month by post. My mother would sit on the Western-style toilet seat laughing and reading aloud, while I leaned against the door frame laughing along with her. To this day, I still like *Erma*, even though Lao She's later novels *Lihun* (Divorce) and *Huoche* (Train) are much better.

After my father recovered from his illness, he underwent yet another change of heart and began to withhold living expenses from my mother, forcing her to supplement her fixed allowance with her own funds until she had spent every last penny. After a while, she would be too broke to leave him, if she had desired to do so. They would fight with such fierce intensity that the servants were frightened into removing the children from the scene of battle and instructing us to behave and not pay any mind to things that didn't concern us. At such times, my little brother and I would sit quietly on the terrace on our little tricycles, without making a sound. It was late spring, and the terrace was shaded by a green bamboo trellis, striping the ground with sunlight.

My parents eventually agreed to a divorce. My auntie, who was in fact father's younger sister, had never been able to get along with her brother, so she moved out with my mother. My father moved to a house in a narrow Shanghai-style alley. (My father never cared much for the arts of attire, eating, or residing. He cared only for driving, and his car was the only thing on which he could bear spending any money.) Although my opinion was never solicited as to the merits of the divorce, I was entirely in favor of it, despite the melancholy knowledge that I would be unable to continue living in my blue-and-red home. Fortunately, the agreement stipulated that I could still see my mother on a regular basis. It was in her new apartment that I saw a built-in porcelain bathtub and gas stove for the first time, which made me very happy and came as something of a consolation.

Not long after, my mother decided to move to France. I was then at a boarding school. When she came to say good-bye, I expressed no regret at her departure, and she seemed quite cheerful as well. That last good-bye was so smooth, so unruffled, so free of any entangling incident that I knew she was thinking to herself "how cold and un-feeling the younger generation has become." I stood in the distance, watching as she made her exit through the school gate, gazing past a giant cedar tree in the courtyard. Even after the red iron gate shut behind her, I remained unmoved. But I gradually came to the realization that scenes such as these called for tears, and so the tears came. I began to sob loudly in the cold wind just so that I could see myself cry.

My mother was gone, but something of her atmosphere lingered in my aunt's house: an exquisitely carved table with an interlocking "puzzle-piece" mosaic on top, gentle pastel colors, wonderful people whose lives were beyond my ken constantly bustling in and out the front door. All the best things I knew, be they spiritual or material, were contained in those rooms. And that is why spiritual and mate-rial virtues have always seemed intermeshed for me, unlike the aver-age young person, who sees them as diametrically opposed and is thus prone to moments of pained conflict that culminate in one inevitably being sacrificed at the expense of another.

On the other side was my father's house. I looked down on every-thing there: opium, the old tutor who taught my little brother to write his "Discourse on the First Emperor of the Han Dynasty," old-style linked-chapter fiction, a languorous, faded, dust-laden way of life. Like a Persian worshipping at the altar of Zoroaster, I forcibly divided the world into two halves: bright and dark, good and evil, god and the devil. Whatever belonged to my father's side was bad, even if I sometimes liked it. I liked the sunlight filtering through clouds of opium smoke, hovering like a fog over an untidy room strewn with stacks of tabloids. (Even now, great big stacks of tabloids give me the sensation of having come home.) I liked reading the paper and joking with my father about family affairs. I knew he was lonely. When he was lonely, he liked me. My father's room was a perpetual afternoon, and when I sat there for a long time, I would always feel that I was sinking deeper and deeper into it.

On the positive side, I was full of vast ambitions and expansive plans. After high school, I would go to England to study at the university. There was one period during which I determined that I was going to learn how to make animated movies as a means of introducing Chinese painting to the United States. I wanted to make an even bigger splash than Lin Yutang.[5] I wanted to wear only the most exquisite and elegant clothing, to roam the world, to have my own house in Shanghai, to live a crisp and unfettered existence.

But something all too solid and all too real came along instead. My father decided to remarry. My aunt first told me the news as we sat one summer night on the balcony. I cried, because I had read so many novels about stepmothers and had never thought that it would happen to me. I had only one desperate thought: I must not, at any cost, let this come to pass. If that woman had been leaning against the iron railing of the balcony, I would certainly have pitched her over the side and put an end to the matter once and for all.

My new stepmother was also an opium smoker. After the marriage, we moved to a Western-style house in the style of the early Republic, which had originally been our own family property. In fact, I had been born in that house. The rooms had too many family memories, like stacks of indistinct photographic prints clouding the very air around us. The sunny corners of the house set one dozing, and the shady spots had the desolate chill of an ancient tomb. The dark, green-tinted heart of the house was wakeful, a strange world unto itself. And at the border where light and shade met, you could see the sun outside, hear the tinkle of the tram bells, and even hear the song "Oh, Susanna" played over and over from a discount fabric shop nearby. In this cacophony of sound, one could doze off but not quite fall asleep.

Living at school, I was allowed to come home only infrequently. Although I saw the tortures my little brother and He Gan were undergoing and felt their injustice, I politely made the best of things since it was so rare that I could come home at all. My father was thrilled by my compositions and even encouraged me to study poetry. All told, I wrote three seven-character quatrains in the classical style, the second of which was an ode to summer rain. I thought it was a good poem because it had been covered with approving circles and underlinings by the brush of my tutor:

> A booming like the ancient drums of Jie
> bids the flowers to open
> Cupping the rain, a lotus leaf
> puts forth its first bloom

The third poem sang the praises of the woman warrior Hua Mulan, but it was so bad that I lost interest in continuing my study of poetry.

The year I graduated from middle school, my mother came back. Although I myself was unaware of any changes, my father did not fail to note that my attitude toward him had indeed changed. And for him this was an unbearable slight: I had lived with him for so many years, he was the one who had supported me, he had provided me with an education, and yet my heart remained tied to the other side. I made matters all the worse by delivering a speech proclaiming my determination to study abroad—a halting, altogether inept speech. His temper flared. He announced that I had been manipulated by interested parties. My stepmother launched into a tirade directed at my mother: "She's got her divorce, yet she still wants to meddle in our family affairs. If she can't let well enough alone, why doesn't she just come back to live with us again? Too bad she's a little too late! She'll have to be content as a concubine this time."

My problems had to be set aside for the moment when the Japanese attacked Shanghai in 1937. Our house was near the Soochow Creek, and I could not sleep at night because of the noise of artillery fire, so I went to stay at my mother's house for a couple of weeks. The day I got back, my stepmother asked me, "How could you have left without even letting me know?" I said that I had told my father. She said, "Oh? You told your father! But you didn't pay the least attention to me!" And she slapped me across the face. I instinctively raised my hand to strike back but was dragged away by two of the servant women. My stepmother ran screaming shrilly up the stairs, "She hit me! She hit me!" At that moment, everything around me suddenly took on an exceptional clarity: the dimly lit dining room with its shuttered windows, the dishes that had just been laid on the table, the goldfish bowl without any goldfish, slender trails of orange algae sticking out from inside the porcelain. My father's slippered feet came slapping down the stairs, he grabbed hold of me, and, in a hail of feet and fists, shouted: "So you hit people now? If you can hit her, I can hit you! Today's the day I'm going to beat you to death if it's the last thing I do!" I felt my head flattened to one side and then to the other, more times than I could count, and my ears went deaf from the blows. I slumped to the ground and lay flat on the floor, yet he still held me fast by the hair and let fly with a series of kicks. Someone finally dragged me away. I remembered very clearly something my mother had once said—"If ever by any chance he hits you, whatever you do, don't hit back. Because if you do, you'll always be made to be in the wrong"—so I had no thought of resistance. He went back upstairs. I stood up, went to the bathroom, and looked at the cuts and livid finger-shaped welts on my face. I decided to report what had happened to the police, but when I reached the front gate, the guard grabbed hold of me with these words, "The gate is locked. The key's with the master." I tried my best to make a scene, screaming and slamming at the iron gate with my feet in hopes that I could catch the attention of the local beat cops outside, but to no avail. It is actually quite difficult to make a scene. I went back inside, and my father boiled over again, launching a flower vase at my head that flew slightly wide of the mark and showered the room with ceramic shards. After he had left, He Gan sobbed, "How could you have let things come to such a pass?" It was only then that I felt the resentment and injustice of it all bubble up inside me, and I burst into a wail. I sobbed in He Gan's arms for a long time. She blamed me entirely for what had happened, for the simple reason that she cared for me and was frightened that the consequences of having offended my father would spell a very miserable fate indeed. Her terror made her cold and hard-hearted. I cried all alone for a whole day in one of the empty rooms downstairs and fell asleep on an old-fashioned red lacquer wood bed.

The next day, my aunt came to play the peacemaker. As soon as my stepmother saw that she had arrived, she sneered, "So you're here to take away the opium?" Before my aunt had even said a word in reply, my father leapt up from his opium couch and struck her right across the face with a blow that sent her to the hospital, although she never reported it to the police, if only for the sake of the family name.

My father proclaimed that he would kill me with one shot from his pistol. I was locked for the time being inside the empty room downstairs, and my existence in the house where I was born suddenly became strange and unfamiliar, like a wall in the moonlight whose whiteness only stands out against the blackest of shadows, its contours flattened and demented.

Beverly Nichols has some lines in a poem that speaks to the somber half-light of dementia: "in your heart / the moonlight sleeps." When I read those lines, I am reminded of the blue moonlight shining on the floor of our house, of the hushed threat of a murder about to take place.

Even if I knew somehow that my father would never really kill me, I also realized that were I to remain imprisoned for a few years, the person who would eventually emerge would no longer be me. I aged several years in the course of a few weeks. I clasped my hands so tightly around the railings of the balcony that I might have squeezed water from wood. Above my head, the blue sky was brilliant. The sky at that time was suffused with sound, because the air was full of airplanes. I hoped that they would drop a bomb directly on our house, for I would have been willing to die along with all the rest of them.

He Gan was afraid I would try to run away. She ordered me again and again not to "go through that door, because once you leave, you'll never be able to come back again." Even so, I pondered my plans for escape long and hard. Adventures like *The Three Musketeers* and *The Count of Monte Cristo* seemed the likeliest sources for escape plans, but what I remembered best was how in the novel *Jiuwei gui* (The nine tails of the turtle), Zhang Qiugu's friend's lover uses a sheet to make a rope and then climbs out a window to freedom.[6] But my window did not open onto the street. The only way out would be to climb over the wall that enclosed the garden. There was a goose coop next to the wall that would aid me in my ascent, but in the quiet of night, it would hardly do to set a few geese squawking in alarm.

The courtyard was also full of large, quacking white geese who liked nothing so much as chasing and pecking at all comers. There was only one tree, a magnificent white magnolia with huge flowers that looked like over-sized dirty handkerchiefs or great clumps of wastepaper, forgotten and neglected, littering the ground the better part of the year. There have never been such forlorn, dispirited flowers.

Just as I was planning my exit route, I came down with a case of gastroenteritis that very nearly killed me. My father did not call a doctor, and there was no medicine for me, either. For half a year, I lay sick in bed, staring at the light blue autumn skies and the stony gray deer antlers protruding from the gatehouse, the rows of little bodhisattva statues arrayed across the courtyard. I could not tell in which age or dynasty I was living. I was born in this house in a hazy dream state. Would I just as hazily die there as well, only to be buried in the courtyard outside?

As I lay thinking these thoughts, I listened with all my might to each and every opening or closing of the front gate, to the two metallic squeaks that rang out each time the guard pulled the rusty iron bolt that fastened the door open and shut, and to the booming sound of the iron gate shuddering on its hinges. I heard the sound in my sleep, even in my dreams, along with the crunch of footsteps on the black gravel path that led through the garden and to the gate. Was it possible that because of my illness they would let down their guard? Could I slip down the path and out the gate unheard?

As soon as my legs were strong enough to support me, if only by leaning against a wall, I began to plot my escape. First, I coaxed He Gan into telling me what time the two guards changed shifts. On that wintry night, I crouched against the window holding a telescope, watching to see if the black gravel path was clear. I edged along the wall, step by step, until I reached the front gate, pulled out the bolt, opened the door, deposited my telescope in the milk delivery box, and slipped out—it was really and truly the sidewalk that I had reached! There was no wind, just the bitter cold of the wrong side of the lunar calendar. There was nothing under the streetlamps save chill gray pavement, but how adorable the world outside appeared to me at that moment! I walked with hasty steps along the side of the road, and each smack of my feet on the ground was a kiss. Not far from my house, I began to bargain with a rickshaw puller about the price of a ride—how happy I was that I had not lost my knack for haggling! I must have been temporarily insane, for I could well have been caught and brought back inside at any moment. It was only later that I came to appreciate the hilarity of this adventure of mine.

I heard later that He Gan suffered a good deal on account of her suspected complicity in my escape. My stepmother gave all my things away and acted thenceforth as if I were dead. That was how the home I had once lived in came to an end.

I fled to my mother's house, and that very summer, my little brother followed in my footsteps, carrying a pair of basketball shoes wrapped in newspaper, and proclaiming that he would never go back. My mother explained to him that her economic might was insufficient to the task, that she could only take on the expenses of one child at a time, which was why he could not stay with her. He cried, and I sat to one side and cried, too. Later, he did in fact go back, taking his basketball shoes with him.

He Gan secretly spirited some of my childhood toys to me as souvenirs. Among them was a carved ivory fan with pale green ostrich plumes, which, because it was so old, would shed its feathers whenever I waved it back and forth, choking the air with dust and bringing tears to my eyes. To this day, I get that same feeling when I think of the day my little brother came to visit.

I immersed myself in books in preparation for the entrance exam to the University of London. I had grown used to being alone at my father's house, which produced in me an abrupt desire to grow up and be responsible for myself. To play the sheltered daughter in straitened circumstances seemed a terrible burden. At the same time, I could see that my mother had sacrificed quite a lot for me and that she doubted whether I was worth the sacrifice. I shared her doubts. I often went all alone to the top of the apartment building to take a solitary walk around the roof. The white stucco Spanish walls cut sharp lines across the blue of the sky, shearing the world in two. I would lift my face to the fierce sun above, standing exposed before the sky and its judgment and, like every confused adolescent, hang suspended between overweening pride and intense self-loathing.

It was from that time onward that my mother's house was no longer full of tenderness.

I passed my entrance examination, but because of the war I was unable to go to England and ended up being diverted to Hong Kong instead. Three years later, once more on account of the war, I returned to Shanghai without having finished my degree. My apartment was still there, just as I had left it, and even though I no longer believed in it as absolutely as I once had, it is precious to me still. I live now among old dreams, even as I dream new ones.

Having arrived at this point in the essay, the breeze at my back blows a bit more chill, so I stand by the glass doors and gaze out from the balcony at a drizzle of yellow moonlight.

Night in ancient times was punctuated by the beating of drums. Now, we have the wooden clappers of wonton vendors. For a thousand years, the dreams of countless multitudes have been measured out by the same beat—tock, tock, tock, tock: what lovable yet miserable times.

UNFORGETTABLE PAINTINGS

THERE are some paintings I will never be able to forget, but only one of them is famous, Gauguin's *Nevermore.* A Hawaiian woman lies naked on a couch, quietly listening to the conversation of a man and a woman as they walk past her door.[1] The rosy sunset glow of springtime in the background seems to spray skyward like mist, giving a feeling of transcendence to the scene, and yet for this robust woman, who looks about thirty years old, everything is over and done. The woman's face is coarse, with narrow slitted eyes, and she cups her cheek in her hand, sending her gaze slanting upward in a slyly flirtatious gesture so reminiscent of many common Shanghainese woman that it strikes us as quite familiar. Her body is the golden brown of hardwood. The dark brown of the sofa, though, is rendered in a shade more like ancient bronze, and little white flowers are visible on the sofa cover, semitranslucent like mother-of-pearl. Inlaid on this dark bronze background is the atmosphere outside: colored glass, blue sky, red and blue trees, a pair of lovers, a big clumsy bird from a children's fairy tale perched on a stone railing. Glass, bronze, and wood: these three textures seem to encompass the different worlds that we can touch with our hands, in a way that is as tangible as the woman herself. She must have loved with every fiber of her being and now "Nevermore." Although she sleeps on a civilized sofa, her head nestled on a ruffled pillow embroidered with lemon-yellow flowers, there is still a primal sadness here. It is nothing like our own society, where a lovelorn woman no longer in her prime will almost certainly be confronted with countless little indignities and hardships that shred her self-respect to pieces. This woman is not prone to the same sedimented sadness, because she retains a sense of clarity and resignation. On her golden brown face, there's still a trace of an irrelevant smile, as if a mirror had cast on her face a fugitive fragment of the sunlight.

A painting called *Thanksgiving* by a not-so-very-famous American woman artist, on the other hand, belongs absolutely within the purview of modern civilization. It depicts a family busily embroiled in Thanksgiving festivities. The turkey is removed from an electric stove, the table covered with a tablecloth, under which mischievous children play. The rosy-cheeked housewife in a flowery dress is carrying an armful of plates and glasses out to the dining room. The kitchen floor is composed of big gray and green tiles, and across this gray and green expanse many others bustle back and forth in gusts of activity. This is very likely a comfortably middle-class family in a small American city, just back from church and ready to thank the Lord in the manner of their pioneering forefathers for another year of prosperity. They're hungry, and so they busy themselves preparing what will be an exceptionally hearty midafternoon meal. And while this is the very picture of an active and happy family, something is different from before, and, for some unknown reason, things aren't quite so simple as they used to be. Although these people are eating and drinking and talking and laughing, they look as if they're wearing shoes and socks that are wet from walking in the rain: damp, and cold, and sticky. Their movements, enthusiastic and agile as they seem, have an acrid quality, redolent of iron, calling to mind the spine of a streetcar moving swiftly down the tracks on a rainy day: dark as lacquer, water spattered, a faded, steely blue.

A painting called *Tomorrow and Tomorrow*, also American, portrays a prostitute who has rented a room on the upper floors of a tall building, from the balcony of which many other skyscrapers are visible. She stands with her back to us, one hand resting against the door, gazing out. Blond hair falls to her shoulders, and her silk bathrobe is the reddish purple color of last year's bloodstains, the color of sin but also its proxy, for here there is only a flat exhaustion. Tomorrow and tomorrow again: silk stockings slipping down into a swollen pile around the ankles; the corner of a white iron bed frame, mussed pillows, slept-in sheets; and beyond the balcony the dark yet luminous shapes of the skyscrapers, piled like time itself, weighing more heavily with each passing day.

There is no more profound painting of a prostitute than this. I also remember a painting on a similar theme by Lin Fengmian.[2] It used to be that the only Chinese painter in the Western mode whose work I liked was Lin Fengmian. His paintings of Annamese and Burmese women in their sapphire blue tunics have an extremely dexterous formal beauty. But the one painting that left an especially lingering impression on me isn't brightly colored at all. It depicts a young woman in a small Chinese town, clad all in black, walking alongside an earthen city wall, followed by a woman who is clearly her madam. Because the painting is composed primarily of pale washes, there is a feeling of rain in the air despite the fact that it is not raining, and one feels the warmth of their bodies through the damp cold all the more viscerally as a result. The woman isn't especially fashionable, and her face is unformed, but one has the distinct sensation that she represents a certain sense of possibility for the common man, an expectation not unlike the vague loss and longing Meng Lijun felt for the fiancé she had not yet seen.[3] This image by Lin Fengmian paints the prostitute through the eyes of the ordinary male, like the kind of Mandarin Duck and Butterfly fiction that never fails, even in its most vulgar and sentimental moments, to maintain a bashful propriety, without any ill will whatsoever. But there is no malice here. The attitude of the average woman toward the figure of the prostitute is far more complex. Besides feeling contempt and condescension, some envy her, especially upper-class women with too much time on their hands and too little companionship, whose inclination is to picture such a life as a romantic idyll. Women such as these would have to be sold into service at a third-rate brothel before they could truly understand the bittersweet savor of such an existence.

There is a Japanese *bijin ga* called *The Twelve Hours in the Pleasure Quarters of the Yoshiwara* that portrays the life of a geisha over the course of twenty-four hours.[4] The solicitous respect and gravity of the attitude the painter adopts toward his subject is difficult for artists here to understand. To be sure, China has had its share of famous courtesans, women such as Su Xiaoxiao and Dong Xiaowan, who distinguished themselves from the ordinary run of painted faces and went on to great distinction. But in China, it is a question of individual talent, while in Japan this phenomenon has already become a *system* (in Japan, *anything* can become a system). Geisha are rigorously trained and rule-bound sweethearts for the masses, and even the most trivial of their movements carries the weight of a tradition that brooks not the slightest deviation. Of the twelve pictures, I only recall the one that depicts life after midnight, when the geisha is changing into the wooden clogs that she wears in her own room. With one hand, she holds the front of her skimpy robe to prevent it from slipping off her shoulders and, with the other, grasps a stick of incense, from which a few slender wisps of smoke drift into the air. There is a maid in attendance, kneeling to one side, who is painted to look much smaller than her mistress. The geisha stands in place, seemingly far too tall. Her drooping neck is too slender and too long. Even the little white foot making its way toward the wooden clog is disproportionately small. And yet she knows full well that she is loved, even if she finds herself alone at midnight. And because she is secure in that knowledge, the night is all the more serene, all the more ageless.[5]

The sole explanation I can offer for this idealization of prostitutes is the emphasis the Japanese place on training. Geishas are trained with exceeding care and thoroughness, which means that they come to approximate most closely a certain standard of feminine grace and beauty. This is the only scenario, in any case, that can explain how a geisha comes to stand in for the holy Madonna in Junichiro Tanizaki's novel *Kami to Hito to no Aida* (Between gods and mortals).[6]

As for the European Virgin Mary, in the days before the cinema, she was the one and only sweetheart of the masses, and all the great artists throughout the ages tried their hand at painting her portrait. Among these paintings is a work entitled *Our Lady of the Immaculate Womb*. It seems that the "oomph girl" of old is much the same as a "womb girl" today. We civilized moderns, however, are much more repressed than our forebears. Who now would dare to trade openly on the commercial appeal of an immaculate womb?

The Madonnas of various European countries represent divergent standards of beauty. There is the Dutch version, with her long, wispy blond hair and long, cold, and sculpted countenance, tinged with gold and possessing a jadelike pallor, not unlike Marlene Dietrich. Or the Italian, who resides in the countryside and looks like a fruit vendor, with her blue-black eyebrows, abundant flesh, and abundant charm. The Madonnas of Germany seem to have been beaten into submission by their men: their pale, startled blue eyes project precisely the animated yet delicate beauty so beloved by the Germans. Yet what each of these religious artists wants to evoke is the same: an innocent country girl, extremely humble and modest, on whom fate has bestowed a solemn duty and, consequently, a new nobility. She holds her princely son in both arms, offering him up to all the world to see, for he will one day save the world with his own blood. There is no easy way for painters to represent the mighty wisdom of this child, so he is often portrayed as a wrinkled and wizened old creature. Sometimes, he is bundled in swaddling clothes, and she is unwrapping a corner as if opening a gift box containing a very expensive present. Sometimes, she plays with him or gazes gently toward him as he nestles in her arms. But these gestures always seem to take place to the silent accompaniment of countless spectators watching the play from outside the picture frame.

That is perhaps why I prefer Japanese paintings of the Old Maid of the Mountains and Kintaro to Madonnas. They are based on a folktale, but I am still not sure whether the Old Maid is Kintaro's mother or not. Kintaro is a hero of some sort, and he may have been raised by mountain spirits. The Old Maid of the Mountains has wild, black hair, a long, fleshy face, bewitching eyes, and a bleak smile that lends a dreamy, faraway cast to her expression. Her head is lowered, and her hair flies violently to one side, tossed by a wind so fierce that it threatens to knock down all the trees in the forest. Perhaps on account of the oblique angle, her breasts seem to start just below her neck and sag far below, like the proverbial sacks of flour. The crab-faced little Kintaro is curled up above her breast, staring wide-eyed, with a strange look on his face, occasionally reaching out with one hand to squeeze her nipples mischievously. She doesn't seem to mind in the least. She merely smiles bleakly as she attempts to divert him with a toy drum painted with little flowers that she holds in one hand. It's hard to say whether the look in her eyes is seductive, modest, or indulgent, or whether the willful cruelty and imperiousness of the dark little boy at her breast contain the seeds of a greater wisdom. This is a picture that says something fundamental about mothers and sons and, by extension, about men and women and their relations with one another. And since there is only one man and one woman here, with no one to watch the drama unfold, it has an elemental honesty, like a picture from the beginning of time.

Which reminds me once again of Raphael's most famous image of the Virgin, the Sistine Madonna, who cradles the child in her arms as she stands atop a mass of clouds, angels at her feet and a kneeling retainer by her side. The most endearing quality of this Madonna is her expression, which is suspended between fright and reserve by the sudden appearance of the celestial effulgence that surrounds her. A village maid, common as dirt, is abruptly elevated to the status of queen and selected precisely on account of her innocence and her lack of distinction. And yet, once she has been apotheosized, she needs to maintain the illusion that she is still ordinary—which is why the role requires playacting. This is not unlike the phenomenon in America whereby big companies choose a typical "average guy" to promote their products. The average guy likes to smoke X brand cigarettes, uses X brand razor blades, wears an X brand raincoat, approves of Roosevelt, and is against women wearing short shorts. Exposed to the eyes of the world, how long can the average guy stay average? This normalcy has a kind of abnormality about it, while the bewitched and bewitching appearance of the Japanese Maid of the Mountain seems that much more human and endearing.

Of the dreamlike paintings of the surrealists, the one that has left the deepest impression on me is an untitled picture of a woman sleeping in the desert. She has the broad, brown face of an Egyptian, slender, even dainty, hands and feet, and she is wearing a simple, sacklike robe, striped red on a white background. She is surrounded on all sides by endless sands; above the sand is the sky, which despite the lateness of the hour remains a pale blue, infused with a sand-swept golden luminescence. A yellow lion approaches to sniff at her body. There is a milky white bottle next to her head. One can only surmise that she has collapsed from exhaustion on her way to find water. A strip of sand, a strip of sky, and, lying inert between them, a body burdened by the weight of nature, in a state of deep, pure slumber, untroubled by dreams, nuzzled by a lion.

Another painting, called *The Virgins of Night*, has a similarly fresh way of invoking the atmosphere of terror. Four giant female figures, with Jewish features and long hair, stand looking at one another with their protruding eyes. They appear to be discussing something. Each of the round white stones at their feet shines in the moonlight. There is a brick wall in the distance, with a vaulted door through which the tiny black shadow of a man can be seen. He is in a sort of trance, for this is his dream.

When Chinese people paint with oil, they seem to be at an advantage, precisely because they are Chinese and thus able to excuse their disrespect for the basic principles of Western painting by incorporating traditional Chinese techniques into their artwork. Without such trickery, they often find themselves hampered by the scholastic traditions of the West. I recently encountered the work of Mr. Hu Jinren, which is an exception to the rule. What surprised me most was his painting of white magnolia blossoms, silvery white in an earthen vase, with long rounded petals, translucent, but fleshy at the same time, stretching in this direction and that, as if they positively needed to indulge themselves in the luxury of blooming. These are lustful flowers, flowers determined to obtain what they desire. Their lust is tempered by joy and can be forgiven for that reason, like youth. Among the magnolias is a spray of winter jasmine that explodes into little gold flowers like a string of firecrackers. Even the little tea table is painted with real feeling: one can almost sense the calm forbearance of this courteous brown rectangle confronted by the clamor of color above its head.

There is another painting, slightly larger but also of white magnolias, slender and luminous, like jade or perhaps crystal, reminiscent of the cool savor of the little jade fish that the imperial concubine Yang Guifei is said to have held in her mouth whenever she suffered from a toothache. The forceful contours of a profusion of jasmine blooms intrude boldly into the scene, with a self-assurance about their own destiny that is at once graceful and domineering.

The background of both these paintings is the bluish purple you see on the backs of matchboxes. Seldom does one see this color used so effectively. In a painting called *Dusk in Spring*, the dark afternoon sky is the same stifling blue. In the park, surrounded by masses of green trees, two women walk swiftly down a little path, pursued by some unknown terror and heading toward some even more frightening place. Their retreating figures seem swollen, their big backsides move with an emphatic swing, and somehow the vulgarity only compounds the sense of impending terror.

Civilized people, tame and docile as they are, sometimes encounter a chilling sense of desolation, even when they abide by the rules. *The Mountains in Autumn* places another sort of terror on view: against a pallid blue sky and a low yellow sunset, two tall, emaciated trees are foregrounded, their soft, slender branches swimming through the air like a coil of tangled eels. Two women, their shoulders hunched and bodies huddled together against the cold, rush through a dusk that signals the early advent of winter.

In *Summer by the Lakeshore*, a woman sits by the water, underneath white clouds set in a blue sky. The wind ruffles a milky green tree, the noise of cicadas resounds through the air—the tableau is complete, but it seems there ought to be something else. Maybe a café with a bandstand shadowed underneath the trees, from which drifts a rendition of a popular song only freshly arrived in the provinces, its grainy sound merging with the lapping of the water and the buzz of the cicadas, vulgar in its insistence on being heard.

There is a pile of charcoal briquettes next to the feet of the protagonist of *The Old Serving Woman*. She bends over, stretching her hand toward the fire, a white towel folded across her knees that only emphasizes her timeworn and battered hands. She wears a knit cap, and her enormous figure almost completely encircles the tiny little fire. She smiles to herself, queen of all she surveys. This is clearly the moment she enjoys most of all, which makes the picture so much the more miserable.

There is a still life with a scattered group of objects against a light brownish purple backdrop: a clean white bottle, a knife, water chestnuts, mushrooms, lavender, a dishcloth. One seldom comes across such a deliberately cluttered composition in an oil painting. Only in the seventeenth century, after Chinese silks and porcelains had first arrived in the West, did English court painters begin to emulate Chinese New Year's paintings, in which various votive objects are arrayed in rows across a white background. Perhaps the Chinese flavor of this painting is neither intentional nor unintended. Its saturated squares of purple are so fresh and so luxuriant that one begins to imagine eating breakfast on a brilliant morning in the land of milk and honey.

There is also *Autumn in the Nanjing Mountains*. A small road unfolds like a silvery creek. Two white trees are crowned by trembling yellow branches. It seems that the sun has only just risen. A little farther off stand two more trees, one blue, the other brown, rendered with careless strokes that might resemble Chinese brushwork if not for their formlessness. The man gazing at the scenery seems to have come from very far away; he has yet to catch his breath, so that even the vague blue contours of the mountains are still rippling in the distance. There is a sense of the sudden and the incomplete, as if the scene were merely a distant dream, conjured from a rooster's crow and the chill of a sleeping mat.

UNDER AN UMBRELLA

IT'S POURING. Some people are carrying umbrellas and some people are not. Those who don't have an umbrella press against those who do, squeezing beneath the edges of passing umbrellas to avoid the rain, which provides some shelter. But the water cascading from the umbrellas turns out to be worse than the rain itself and the people squeezed between umbrellas are soaked to the skin.

This is a parable, of course, the moral of which is perfectly clear: when poor folks associate with the rich, they usually get soaked. I thought of it one rainy day but never wrote it down, because it sounds too much like the style of the tabloid "tea talks" of Mr. Nachang.[1]

ON DANCE

CHINA is a land without dance. Perhaps it existed in the past: I have seen it in costume dramas on historical themes in which elegant and accommodating silken sleeves are unhurriedly extended in courteous arcs, first to the left and then to the right. Dancing girls in ancient times were apparently possessed of the wise and saintly demeanor of our sages, as monotonous as that might seem. Yet there is also the line from the Tang poem, "we danced down the moon in the heart of the willow tower," which seems to imply a relatively pungent kind of gesture, capable of sweeping the moon from the sky.[1] Those days are distant from us now, however, and we cannot investigate the actual steps of dances like Big Dangle Hands and Little Dangle Hands, much less reconstruct them from nothing. Although song and dance were always mentioned in the same breath during the Ming and Qing dynasties, all that remains of the dances of that era are some of the characteristic movements and gestures of the Chinese opera. Even in the days when there was dance, people merely watched the performance, rather than actually participating in it. And so, in recent years, although countless people are working hard and on the move, there is no movement for the sake of movement, and nothing that might allow one to feel the soaring joy of limbs in flowing motion. (Except perhaps in private places, which is why erotic paintings are so popular.) Such a vast and magnificent country, and yet its landscape lacks even the prospect of hands clapping in celebration. Stasis has prevailed here for thousands of years, for countless generations—fearful to think of it! This is why the waists and buttocks of Chinese women are especially low-slung; seen from behind, Chinese women look like they are sitting, even when they're standing up.

Yet social dancing has become quite common among the Chinese in recent years. Some feel that it is improper, while others defend it as a form of art and decry the salacious minds of those who find it sexually suggestive. The truth is that your average social dance is in fact inevitably bound up with sexuality. How else can we explain the fact that the sight of two women dancing together tends to strike us as rather dull?

Dance.

To dress in a presentable manner, congregate in a decent place, see others of one's own kind and be seen by them in turn: this is the essence of social interaction. If you talk too much at such gatherings, there is always the worry that your shortcomings will be exposed. And if you keep within the confines of small talk such as the "weather is blah blah blah," finding sufficient chatter to fill in the blanks of the "blah blah blah" is in fact an onerous chore. In order to avoid exchanges of a similarly thoughtful nature, one must come up with various substitutes for conversation, such as games that allow one to converse with one's hands. Dancing is a conversation between feet, and its superiority to either mah-jongg or poker lies in the fact that it is the most elementary and the most harmless means of mixing between the sexes. But if there is an artistic aspect to dance, it exists only by way of negative example: people who can dance well lack the horrendous clumsiness of those who cannot and don't step on their partners' toes. That is all. It is because we insist on seeing an artful image in everything that our civilization has become so anemic.

Old-fashioned dancing in the West has yet to go that route and retains a profound sense of intimacy and feeling. There is a passage in a story by Chekhov that is the best piece of writing I have yet to encounter on dance:

> She went on to dance the Mazurka with a tall military officer, whose movements were very slow, like a corpse with clothes on, his chest and neck shrunken, his feet stepping wearily across the floor. He was able to dance only with great effort, while she incited him with her loveliness and the bareness of her neck, titillating him; her eyes caught flirtatious fire, she moved with passion, while he became more and more indifferent and held his hands out to her as stiffly as a king.
>
> The onlookers burst out into a cheer: "Bravo! Bravo!"
>
> But slowly the tall military officer grew more excited; his steps had more life, and, overcome by her beauty, he danced with extraordinary liveliness and grace, while she merely swayed her shoulders to and fro, glancing slyly in his direction, as if she were now the queen and he her vassal.[2]

These days the tango shares something of this atmosphere, but it is not quite the same. The tango comes from Spain.[3] Spain is a poor country that, upon the discovery of their colonies in the Americas, was suddenly awash in wealth, wealth dazzling to the point of absurdity, arriving home from abroad in boatload after boatload of gold and precious stones. Yet this wealth was exhausted all too soon, and inevitably the glorious past became little more than a burdensome memory: black gauze veils and inlaid tortoiseshell combs worn by women, the little gold lamé jackets above wide crimson sashes worn by men, poison, daggers, roses showered on heroic bullfighting matadors—there is no romance here, only the rules of romance. Like a black cloth covered with shining gilt, this cruel and extravagant people got too rich too fast, and thus their wealth was always merely fantasmatic, a macabre and almost nightmarish episode, and the poverty they endured thereafter came to seem all the more inexplicable, doubling their sense of despair. Their dance has an intoxicated desolation, an emptiness at its heart; wine alone is no longer enough to make them drunk. Their movements are mostly mere formalities and careful flourishes. There is a dutiful playing out of this protocol of attack and retreat: a step conceded and a step taken, a position held and then released, in a protracted seesaw struggle, a polite promiscuity.

We moderns dislike this effusive quality, which is why the tango is not terribly popular here. In the dancehalls, one sometimes sees it performed by professionals, but only as window dressing.

At one time in the U.S., the entire country was mad about dancing the jitterbug (the word means something like our "sleeping insects awakened by spring").[4] Everyone would move in a line like kindergarteners doing drills in a playground: a few steps forward, one hand lifted in the air, then a great shout: "Hey!" With each shout, excitement would rise to a fever pitch, and they would abandon themselves to kicking their legs, dancing until they were so exhausted that they could dance no more. Jaded social flowers, businessmen, and housewives alike found a kind of liberation in the dance, a return to the fountain of youth. But simple-mindedness is not necessarily the same as childishness. The way children dance has very little in common with the jitterbug; in fact, it more closely resembles the free movement advocated by Isadora Duncan, which even when it has a pattern, retains a leisurely and unhurried feel.

There is a mad kind of dance in India that is different from the jitterbug in that the dancers shake violently on bended knees, seemingly shrunken to half their normal height. And yet their legs somehow manage to shimmy back and forth, as if they are dancing on a hot stove and can't bear to stand still. The music they dance to is the same, constantly tickling the ears with a high-pitched, shrill concatenation of sound. The singer seems to be trying to hold hot soup in his mouth as he sings, and his voice quavers constantly as a result. The virtue of a dance such as this is that it could be no other way: so perfectly is it in harmony with their habitat that it smacks of the eternal. The first creatures to come into being arose from the swamps. In that epoch, the swamp was everywhere, hot and damp the whole year round, treeless, choked with the giant fronds of water weeds. The sun poured mercilessly down on the black surface of the water, and the little creatures at the bottom grew restless, set into a violent yet formless commotion, like vaporizing air. Filth is always a result of some sort of blockage, of partial death; places as full of vitality as the primeval swamp cannot be filthy. This Indian dance is much the same.

Even when civilized people want to be primitive, they cannot, for they have no fear of the primitive, and no respect for it either. They believe that when they have grown weary they can escape, seeking refuge among children and savages, but such an escape is impossible; only in ignorance can they find repose.

When I was in college in Hong Kong, a flock of little girls from a convent school came to live in our dormitory for the summer. The dining hall was suffused with the sour aroma of sweaty white uniforms and the damp smell of canvas shoes. Outside the dining hall was a garden laid out across the slope of a hill, traversed by cement pathways and enclosed inside iron railings. Beyond the railings, all there was to see most of the time was mist or misty rain and, beyond the mist, blue-green hills by the sea. When I was little, I ate from a little plate edged with gold, the center of which depicted just such a bay, surrounded by hills, complete with green water, and boats, and people. Gradually, everything but the blue-green of the hills was worn away. I remembered that little plate and a pair of red ivory chopsticks that went with it very clearly, and although these little girls annoyed me no end, I still felt an indifferent sort of sadness when I saw the difficulties they faced. They spent their days screaming and making a commotion just like any other children, but the moment they were called to order, they would disappear. It was as if they had been wiped clean from the face of the earth. And yet they refused to be wiped entirely clean, because the black-and-white tile floor of the empty dining hall was crisscrossed by the scuff marks of their rubber soles, and the damp stink of their canvas shoes still lingered in the air. They had a gramophone, too, which played the same record all day long, featuring the bright little voice of a girl singing:

> My Mother said
> I never should
> play with the
> Gypsies in the wood.

Whatever made them happy was not allowed, not allowed, nothing was ever allowed. With the doors of the dining hall thrown open and the gramophone blaring, rain would come in a sudden downpour, pattering across the cement paths, each drop a black mark. A Russian girl named Natalia sang along with the record, "My mother told me / I can't go anymore," arms stretched in the air, swaying back and forth in the music and the rain. The others all laughed and shouted, "Natalia! Wiggle your ears for us," because Natalia knew how to wiggle her ears. She and her sister, Maria, were orphans who had been adopted by an American lady and raised by her until they were five or six years old. When the adults moved back to the States, they left the children at the convent in Hong Kong. They had enjoyed a comfortable life at the home of their American foster parents and did not understand why they were now relegated to a miserable charitable institution where they were told to keep quiet, made to drink water from cups that smelt fishy and eat bread swabbed with a thin layer of pale red jam, forced to memorize passages from the Bible, and told to kneel down and pray before and after each and every lesson. Natalia had a long, pale face, and when she smiled, her lazy green eyes narrowed with a weary look. Like many lower-class Russians, she was warm-hearted and generous but also slovenly and was rewarded for these traits with beatings. Her older sister, Maria, was more sophisticated in the ways of the world and knew how to get on with her superiors, although you could sometimes see a flash of dull disdain in her big blue eyes. Maria had a pretty face that jumped right out at you, and it was said that when she had first arrived with a full head of golden curls that cascaded all the way down to her ankles, the nuns in the convent had promptly cut it all off because it would have been too much trouble to wash and comb.

On one occasion, a thief snuck into the dormitory. The next morning, when it was discovered what had happened, the girls ran breathlessly up and down the stairs in their excitement. This was more joy and freedom than they had enjoyed all summer long. They surged through the door of my room, brimming with expectation: "Miss Eileen, did *you* lose anything?" It was if they expected to see my room emptied. I could only somewhat sheepishly reply that I hadn't lost a thing.

There was also a Thai girl among them named Madeleine whose family lived in Bangkok. She could dance the traditional sacrificial dance of Thailand, with her slender brown wrists dangling behind her back as if they had somehow been disconnected from her arms. Thai temple dancers are usually just about her age, twelve or thirteen, with white powder slathered across their sharp yellow faces. Their faces look lifeless because of the powder, but each part of the body below—waist, legs, hands, and arms—seems to have a wholly independent life of its own, flipping upside down, twisting entirely around, coming to life in impossible ways, all in honor of the particular deity being propitiated by the dance. But the gilded brilliance of the deities of her home country were far away, and all Madeleine could do was take care of herself as best she could by becoming a sly little sycophant.

Apart from the little girls in the dormitory, there were also some of my own college classmates, including a few overseas Chinese girls from Malaya who had been educated for the most part in convent schools. Jintao (Golden Peach), who had a brown complexion and buckteeth, was spoiled in that regard. She had only been subjected to six months of Catholic schooling and had been spared thereby the usual consequences. Jintao showed everyone how the Malayans dance: boys and girls line up opposite one another and then undulate their bodies, choosing either to take mincing steps forward or just wiggle in place. The girls, who hold billowing handkerchiefs in their hands, wave them through the air, chanting: "Shayang ah! shayang ah!" "Shayang" is the word for one's lover, and it is the monotony of the song that makes it all the more lulling and lovely. The girls in Malaya wear either Western fashions or Chinese-style jackets over silk pants. Only on grand public occasions do they wear the cheongsam. In the town where Jintao grew up, there was only one cinema. Jintao and all the other daughters of wealthy families would congregate there every night. If, on any given evening, she saw that one of her friends had come dressed in Western style, she would run home without any further ado to change into a similar ensemble, returning just in time for the beginning of the picture show. The Malaya in which she lived was a domesticated little world, a tableau of civilization embroidered atop a sweltering background of savagery, a floral-print cotton quilt big enough to cover your head but not your feet.

There was an eighteen- or nineteen-year-old Malayan Chinese girl from another town called Yuenü (Moon Girl) who was really quite lovely: a round, pure, pale face, large almond eyes, and a slim yet voluptuous figure. She had only recently arrived in Hong Kong when I first saw her. She was just coming out of the dormitory bathroom after taking a shower, smelling of prickly heat powder and wearing white floral-print pajamas. A silver cross dangled in front of her chest, and she smiled and made a polite little curtsy. She said, "It's great here! At the convent where I went to school before, everyone had to bathe together in a big cement pool, and they gave us big white smocks to wear in the pool, which looked like ..." She covered her face, and broke into peals of laughter, and was seemingly at a loss as to how to describe them: "... You've never seen anything like it. There was a big seam at the back, and they were as wide as a mosquito net. You'd stand in the water and then secretly lift the edge above your knees so

192 · WRITTEN ON WATER

that you could rub some soap underneath. It was really..." There was often a bashful, almost pained expression on her face as she spoke, and her limpid phoenix-shaped eyes would redden slightly at the edges. She went on to speak of the convent. The garden was full of coconut trees whose slender trunks shot seven or eight yards straight up into the air. The Malayan children would wrap themselves around the trunks and shimmy up to the top, gathering the fruit just like monkeys. As she told me about the trees and the children, that same bashful and somewhat pained look of disbelief drifted across her face.

Her father was a merchant who had made his fortune only after a great deal of difficulty and built himself a big new house. But almost as soon as he had moved in the whole family, he fell for a woman of ill repute and squandered his life savings.

"When we see her coming toward us on the street, we spit on the ground. Everyone knows that she does sorcery."

"Maybe. But she wouldn't necessarily need to know sorcery to do what she did," I suggested.

"No! It's sorcery for sure! It's not just that she's over thirty. She's not even pretty, either!"

"But even if she were already in her thirties and not very good-looking, she might..."

"No! It was sorcery for sure. Otherwise, how could my father have been so completely bewitched? Why would he come home from her just to beat and abuse his own family? Once when I still little he even grabbed me by my braid and knocked my head against the wall."

Of the Malays, who were also said to be proficient in sorcery, she knew only evil things: "The Malays are terrible. When you're riding your bike to school, they love to run after you and knock you down."

Her elder brother was going to school at Hong Kong University and hoped that he could one day arrange for Yuenü to enter the university as well. When the war broke out, he asked that my friend Yanying and I take special care of her, because "Yuenü is a very innocent girl." She was in fact terrified by the prospect of being raped and thought about it so much that her face was pale and puffy with worry. And yet when things were at their worst and no one else dared to show their faces outdoors, it was Yuenü who went out on the balcony to watch as column after column of troops marched just below. Then she cried out in alarm and called for all the other girls to come out and see what was happening.

Her mind was like a locked little room, with whitewashed walls stained with mildew, a vacant room at an inn on a cloudy day. Overseas Chinese have no spiritual home to which they can return. She was a simple-minded person living in a not-at-all-simple world, lacking any kind of cultivation, any tradition to which she might belong, and bereft of any dance she could call her own. Yuenü knew how to dance socially but would consent only to dance with either her father or her older brother.

Among the fashionable young ladies of Shanghai, ballet is considered an extremely high-class art form. Not a few of my friends have told me: "And the colors! You should go see the ballet, if only for the colors of the costumes and the backgrounds. Such brilliant colors. You're sure to love it!" But I did not like the colors, because they were in such perfect accord with my expectations. A thieves' lair in the depths of the forest, flooded with blue light; a pirate wearing a bright red bandanna; a damsel in distress decked out in a white gown; the bewitching wife of a Muslim prince, her silken blouse flashing with snakeskin sequins. None of these images were nearly as intimate or as memorable as the pictures on collectible cigarette cards, which, although cheaply made, still belong to us. "Spring Beauties in the Inner Palace" is one such tableau. As the curtain rises, a panoply of dancing girls hold a variety of poses, frozen in place, arrayed across a resplendent background. In that moment, they resemble an illustration from a medieval monk's hand-copied book, a precious illuminated manuscript, with flesh-pink people arrayed against a delicately incised background of gold, further embellished with bright red and powdery blue filigree. Another moment passes, the dancing girls begin to move, and the picture is transformed once again into a mere cigarette card. That is what I like so much about Chinese cigarette cards: they have about them a threadbare sort of luxury. The images are full of gilded beauties of every size and shape, like the famed Qiao sisters of the

Three Kingdoms era, their faces caked with powder as they pose on clean, shiny tile floors next to vermilion lacquered columns, brocade hangings, and pearl-strung curtains. And yet this material abundance seems always to betray its origins in the minds of people living in the maw of poverty, which lends its own special kind of novelty. I like anticlimax. The creation of a lush ambience, followed by its sudden dissolution, lets one feel all the more acutely the humanity of legendary characters forced by circumstance into tears of anguish. But I cannot forgive the anticlimactic quality of ballet. Even from the back rows of the theater, I can see the grotesquely well-developed sinews and rounded thighs of the Russian dancers. Their hard and seemingly swollen white flesh makes me feel anxious for them. One false move as their feet hit the floor, and surely they'll come tumbling down with a resounding thud?

The ballet *Il Corsaro* is based on Lord Byron's epic poem. To tell this story by way of movement seems particularly appropriate, for Byron's poem is full of howling winds and surging waves. But these operatic movements—rendered in a deliberately clear and comprehensible manner, yet lacking for that same reason any basis in the feeling of folk tradition—fall flat. The kidnapped maiden seems like a bird in a cage, flailing wildly back and forth in the excess of her despair. Her body is always expressive, and each expression of emotion is scrupulously appropriate—and bland to the point that it smacks of nothing real. Reality is often inappropriate. This truth is laid bare by the portion of *Dream of the Red Chamber* completed by Gao E. Compared with the rest of the novel, it seems terribly barren, not because the Jia family has been demoralized by its decline but because Gao E writes poorly. The problem is not, in other words, that Gao E's denouement doesn't make sense. It *does* make sense. What it lacks is sensibility; the feelings he portrays are merely sentiments, without a sense of verisimilitude.

The hero and heroine of *Il Corsaro* go through a series of tribulations. The heroine is given to the king, and the queen, fearing that she will be replaced in his royal affections, chases her and her secret lover from the palace. Unfortunately, their boat capsizes in the ensuing storm. The final scene is very brief: one is confronted by a mechanical stage set, all crashing waves and clouds scudding toward the horizon, indicating the forward motion of the boat. The boat is packed with people, and even as they desperately confront the mortal danger in which they find themselves, there is somehow still enough time for a few dramatic gestures, performed on point, before they sink to their deaths. Such a hastily concluded tragedy strikes one as amusing more than anything else. The use of mechanized scenery almost always seems a bit contrived, with the possible exception of certain vaudeville comedies. When you are used to seeing storms and sinking ships, combat and conflagrations, on the movie screen, staged depictions lack the requisite realism. But that lack is precisely what Chinese audiences enjoy about such performances. The Chinese drama *Haizang* (Burial at sea) takes a page from the same playbook, except, in this version, the boat does not capsize. Instead, from among the crowds on deck, a pair of star-crossed souls leap to their deaths, landing on the stage below with a thud, only to be engulfed in "seas" that rage up to their waists. A few seconds later, they slump to the floor and out of view. The boat continues to row on ahead, and the audience, stirred to its very core, stands up and goes home to bed. I've been told that, without such scenes, it becomes difficult to send the audience packing. In the absence of a grand finale, the patrons will linger in the theater, waiting for the play to end.

I have seen Indian dance only once. The dancer, Indira Devi, actually wasn't Indian at all. She came from a small central European country—I'm not sure which one—but underwent rigorous training in India and has performed to great acclaim all over the world. The performance I saw was somewhat unorthodox in that the stage was too small and there was only an old stage curtain for a backdrop, but despite all that, this tiny woman sat on the stage with her palms clasped together, legs coiled under her body, feet wrapped around her knees, the folds of her robe quietly draped across the ground, resembling some sort of deity. For a long time, she did not move. Indian saris look a little like ancient Greek togas, but this woman lacked not only the grace of Greek statuary but also its classical proportions: her head was too big, her eyes were too large, and her hard, wrinkled mouth seemed to show her age. Even so, it would be hard to tell her exact age; for all we knew, she might have sat on that stage for several thousand years. Gazing at that face left you with a cold sense of terror, which reminded me of George Bernard Shaw's play *Back to Methuselah*, in which he posits that mankind will one day evolve to the point that babies will be delivered not from the womb but from the male testes. Childhood as a stage of human development will have been eliminated, and people will emerge from an egg as fully grown young men and women. These young men and women dance and play and make love and paint pictures and make sculptures for four whole years, until they grow so weary of material beauty that they venture forth on their own and contemplate the difficult depths of cosmic principle. In this way, they go on to live one hundred million years as purely sentient beings, having cast their bodies aside to weather the wind and sun alone. The men become indistinguishable from the women: dark, rail thin, loincloths hanging limply from their waists. The young men and women who have yet to turn four regard these creatures as oddities and refer to them as "the ancients." They are divided into two categories, male and female, but it hardly seems to matter. The research of the ancients into the principles of scientific knowledge have attained such an exalted level that they are able to transform their own bodies at will. If they choose to grow eight arms, they may do so; if they need to climb down a mountain, they simply lie flat on the ground, transform themselves into liquid, and flow downhill. And, indeed, that was the impression imparted by some of the more dynamic portions of Indira's performance. She would hold out one hand, with two of her fingers clasped together and the others fanning out in an altogether different direction, and proceed to alter the configurations of her fingers with incredible rapidity, until one could be forgiven for thinking that she had really grown eight arms. Apparently, each of these gestures has a mysterious symbolic meaning in traditional Brahmanism, but, as far as I could see, what was really being expressed was her superhuman mastery over her own body.

For her second number, Indira Devi changed into a lighter-colored shawl. She clapped her hands as she emerged, kicking open the red-and-yellow lining of her pleated skirt with each stride forward, the golden bracelets on her arms jangling against each other, entirely erasing the unfortunate impression she had given earlier of advanced age. With a flash of her big round eyes, she suddenly transformed herself into a beautiful maiden in ancient India, exultantly describing to anyone who would listen the beauty of her new lover: how tall he stands, how wide his shoulders, the shape of his eyes, his nose, his mouth, the mirror charm dangling from his neck, the sword hanging from his belt, how he looks when he smiles and when he's angry, and yet nothing seems to describe him exactly right, no matter how hard she tries to capture him in words. Look for yourself, then! He's on his way—he's coming now! She runs repeatedly to one side to see if he has arrived; she climbs a tree to gaze into the distance; she drizzles well water across her face, using a hairpin dipped in a dark decoction made of liquid bronze to lengthen her eyelashes...

Indira Devi also performed a piece she herself had choreographed called *Mother*, which, because of its pretense to realism, was very well received, although I myself found it quite annoying. A mother who has lost her child walks grief-stricken by a religious shrine, where she kneels to pray. She falls into a reverie, dreamily swinging her empty bassinet from side to side. Finally, she grows angry and pushes the shrine to the ground with a crash. Shocked by her own heresy, she quickly kneels back down and begs the forgiveness of the gods. There's nothing wrong with the subject matter, which describes the disease and disaster plaguing India as well as the stubborn superstitions of its women in a deeply tragic, if overly narrow, manner. But all that is really described here is motherly love: a "motherly love" that ought to come in quotation marks. Motherly love is a big topic and, like any other big topic, has long since been overwritten by too many clichés. The people who advocate motherly love the most loudly are men: men who have been sons and who can never be mothers. Women, if they praise motherly love at all, do so only because they understand that they possess nothing else that will earn the respect of men, that they must play this role to the exclusion of all others. There are some emotions that, performed over and over again, come to seem like nothing more than performance—and no emotion more so than motherly love.

Whenever the Takarazuka Song and Dance Troupe is mentioned, one immediately thinks of the chorines featured in their advertisements, clad in short pants, wearing little heart-shaped hats worn at a rakish tilt. Truth be told, Takarazuka's Western-style dancing is quite limited in scope. There is always the same chorus line, standing erect with their arms linked together. They look to the right in perfect unison, bend their knees, and kick their legs up and down until, at the sound of a cymbal, their heads suddenly switch direction, and they repeat the same steps a second time before changing their costumes and coming out for an identical encore. I am told that the reason they perform this Western-style routine so frequently here is that Chinese audiences are unduly enamored of it. The only dance of theirs that I really like is entirely of their own making. The entire troupe takes the stage wearing lovely, brightly colored kimonos. They line up in single file, each dancer's hands resting on the back of the dancer in front of her, and then shuffle quickly across the stage, moving in lockstep as they rock their heads from side to side, their necks seemingly only loosely attached to the rest of their bodies, like bobble-head toys or dolls made of silk gauze. Likening real women to toys is perhaps insulting, but these toys seem to think they're fun, and they bob their heads from side to side with all the delight and wondrous sense of discovery with which a child bends one of her own toes back and forth.

For Japanese people, Japan is like a toy box with cardboard partitions. You clear a space and put the miniature teakettles and little toy soldiers inside, each in its own appointed enclosure. An individualist would naturally have trouble endorsing that sort of environment, but the fact is that the vast majority of people fit very nicely into their partitions, because very few of them really stand out. Even many of those who are considered exceptional, or at least consider themselves exceptional, are in fact quite unexceptional. The stylization of society, unlike its mechanization, is a natural process and has its benefits. Which leads me to the little figures who serve as embellishments to Japanese landscape paintings. They never resemble the ethereal sages and wizened old men leaning on walking sticks who populate Chinese paintings. They are, instead, everyday folks: those women walking across a bridge are probably on their way to pick up the kids from school. The colors in these pictures are solid and deep: blue pools and green willows, a pale ink-washed sky, tranquil times and complacent weather. And because of this complacency, everyone minds his own business. The women marry and serve their husbands and children, each wearing her hair in the same fashion as the rest and mouthing the same polite phrases. There is an oppressive quality to all of this, a light melancholy that has become one of the signal characteristics of Japanese art.

There's another Takarazuka dance number that left a deep impression on me called *The Lions and the Butterflies*. The lion onstage is played by a dancer, so there is naturally no pretense of realism. Chinese dancing lions and stone statues of lions look less like lions than Pekingese dogs because of their bulging eyes. That's why I have always suspected that the only lions Chinese people ever saw were sent to the court as tribute and were never examined with anything more than a cursory glance. And Chinese people seem to love to create strange beasts such as kirins and the like. If humanity must have its own creations, why not just make more houses, and pottery, and fabrics? Making beasts, in the end, doesn't seem to be our forte. The lion in the Japanese dance, in any case, was content to stand just like a man, except that he wore a mask. Brightly colored whiskers dangled down from his white face, and his head was fringed by a vermilion mane. A great unkempt red tail hung from behind, wagging back and forth whenever he was excited. As *The Lions and the Butterflies* begins, we are deep in the mountains. A group of butterflies dances through the air, while two lions sit quietly in their midst. With the crash of a cymbal, the lions suddenly rise to their feet, red tails swishing back and forth so vividly that you really feel you are in the presence of lions. The butterflies scatter in all directions, and the whole scene is like a vision glimpsed from the edge of a dream, filling you with a gorgeous, make-believe fright.

This kind of fright plays on the deepest childhood fears. The Japanese really understand children best, perhaps because they are children themselves. Their finest moments come in the course of talking to children. The attitude Chinese people take toward children is almost never right. The already slightly antiquated way of dealing with children among Westerners is through a polite and measured distance, as if parents and children have come together simply in order to fulfill a duty. With tepid decorum, parents will teach their children to say: "May I please have one more piece?" or "May I please take my teddy bear to bed with me?" The new way, on the other hand, dictates that parents read extensively in childhood psychology before they have even married. The more they research the topic, the more confused they become, and the result is a tendency toward overindulgence. They will plead with their children ("Darling, *please* don't destroy papa's book"), kiss them good morning, kiss them good night, kiss them before they go off to school, and kiss them after they are finished with their lessons. The children's rhyme goes "What are little girls made of? Sugar and spice and everything nice." But the world of the child is not all sweetness and delicacy and light, like the atmosphere of the popular song: "Come, children, clasp your hands together..." There is a revolutionary art school in the United States that encourages children to paint as they like. One of the most memorable paintings was of a bad child with glasses and rotten teeth. Another painting was of a reddish purple sunset by a lake, across which flitted two shadowy phantoms with bulbous and distended heads. Another truly frightening work was composed entirely of little handprints heaped atop one another.

There's a fairy in the Japanese movie *Ligong gesheng* (Songs in the fox fairy palace) who is the incarnation of an ancient white magnolia tree. She wears flowing white robes, parts her hair in the middle, and has a small, almost oval-shaped face. Her voice is extremely high-pitched, thin, and monotonous, and during her longest monologue, the sound sent chills running up and down my spine. At least you could tell that she was a fairy and not a ghost. Nor did she seem like a movie star, unlike the fairy in the cartoon version of *Snow White*, who looks like she should be starring in a commercial for raisins. Although a film like *Ligong gesheng* and Disney cartoons such as *Snow White* and *The Adventures of Pinocchio* are all fanciful and supernatural tales for children, I always feel that the Disney pictures are like an adult shamelessly stooping over to ingratiate himself with a child, whereas there was no trace of such pandering in the Japanese film.

For a time I went to see Japanese movies quite frequently. The two films with which I was most satisfied were *Ligong gesheng* (originally called *Kogoden* [The fairy palace] in Japanese) and *Wu cheng mishi* (The secret of the city of dance; *Nami no Odori* [Nami's dance] in Japanese). A Japanese acquaintance sneered when I mentioned these two titles; the former, he laughed, was made for children, and the latter for ignorant and uneducated young girls. But I remain unashamed. The virtue of *The Secret of the City of Dance* has nothing to do with its legendary story of love and hate. Certainly, aspects of the story are quite moving. When the father is compelled to sell the already engaged daughter to a powerful man as a concubine, he kneels stiffly in front of the ancestral tablet, holding back the tears in his eyes as he explains his plight with a trembling voice. His daughter kneels behind him, bowed and motionless. In that cold little hall, partitioned off with white rice-paper screens, one can feel the persistent grip of ancestral feeling. When the fiancé returns to take his revenge, an old servant takes the girl to see him, but she suddenly stops halfway, lowers her head, and turns in the opposite direction. Distressed, the servant calls out to her, "Miss! Miss!" But the girl merely continues to pace back and forth with her head bowed down. The servant urges her, "But he's waiting for you there." Only after several entreaties is the servant able to convince the girl to go reluctantly ahead. The fiancé, waiting for her on a sandy stretch of beach, has undergone countless trials and adventures in order to be by her side, and yet not one tender word falls from their lips when they finally meet. He merely walks to one side, wrapped in a mantle of self-absorption, passionately exclaiming that he "never dreamed that a day like this would arrive." She follows quietly behind him through the silvery gray mist of the seaside. Suddenly, he spins around to face her, and she, too, turns on her heel and walks swiftly back toward whence she came, head still bowed, as he follows in the distance. There was just such an endless scene of romantic entanglement in a recent Chinese play, in which one lover walks away and the other follows closely behind, both immersed in silence. Or perhaps it was two heroic fighters, one male and one female, marching forward with icy resolve. The cowardly villain, frightened out of his wits, takes an initial step backward, and when the heroes continue their triumphal progress unfazed, he backpedals in a manner resembling a dance.

At the center of *The Secret of the City of Dance* is a dance festival. The old and young of the whole town come out to dance in the dazzlingly white sunshine, waving their arms, tapping their feet, and performing all manner of kicks and pirouettes as they chant: "Today is the festival of dance! Whoever doesn't dance is a dunce!" Perhaps the film was overexposed: the entire scene looks washed out. One can vaguely discern the joyous motion of heads and arms and limbs and bodies clad in floral-print blouses and checked cotton cloth, the glossy black of the women's hair, the bobbing gray hair of the elderly dancers, but everything is pallid, lacking in local color, less distinctly Japanese than merely human. Inside the throng, the hero grabs hold of his enemy, lifting him by his collar, and recites a litany of his many crimes. He seems to mouth phrases like "at last, you've fallen into my hands" several times in Japanese, so that the whole process takes far too much time. The dancers, not content to serve merely as a backdrop for these proceedings, act in a manner entirely unlike anything you'd see in a Hollywood musical (in which dancers are a forest of jade pale thighs entirely at the director's beck and call), surging across the frame and entirely engulfing both the hero and his mortal enemy. All you can see is dancing, dancing, dazzling white gyrations under a dazzlingly white sun. When the camera finally finds its way back to the hero, he is still talking with the villain, and then, somehow, the villain lies slain at his feet. To conclude such a legendary story with a scene like this is so disappointing that it seems almost funny—blame it on the dance.

ON PAINTING

ON THE wall of the classroom in my old school there hung a repro-
duction of the Mona Lisa, the famous painting of the Italian Renaissance. Our teacher told us, "Notice the strange smile on her face."
And it was truly a disquieting smile, lovely yet ambiguous. It looked
as if it might disappear at any moment, and even though the smile
remained in place as I carefully examined the painting, I was left all
the same with an unaccountable sensation of loss. Our teacher told
us that when the master was working on this painting, he had exerted
himself to the utmost searching for rare and exotic objects from across
the globe to place in front of this woman, all in order to get her to
smile that particular smile. I didn't like this explanation. Green
tortoises, mummy's feet, or mechanical toys: none of these would
necessarily elicit a smile like that. To make someone smile that particular smile would surely be more difficult. Or perhaps easier than
one might think. When a woman remembers a gesture or a little
habitual motion that her lover tends to make, there is a childishness
to her expression, lovable and at the same time pitiful, for she is suddenly suffused by a tender lenience that radiates outward, casting her
past and her future in its shade. And at that moment, there might
well be a smile as evanescent as this one in her eyes.

It has been determined that the model for the Mona Lisa was a
young married woman. Perhaps it was something clever her youngest
child had said that morning—such a knowing little boy, and only
four this August—that made her want to grin, but she restrained
herself in the presence of the painter, because noble women are never
supposed to show their teeth when they smile.

In any case, a nineteenth-century British man of letters—was it Walter de la Mare? I can't remember anymore—wrote an essay about the Mona Lisa that spoke of her ghostly wisdom, like the mysteries of aquatic life in the depths of the sea. I have nothing against wanting to write poetry when confronted by a painting—great art should call forth the creativity of each person who witnesses it, providing more than merely passive enjoyment—but I despise his view of the Mona Lisa because of the way it limits interpretation. If one had read the essay first and only then viewed the painting, one would not be able to help looking for the shadows of schools of fish in her eyes. Such a gorgeous (if somewhat strained) analogy might seem to add to our experience of the work but serves in the end to impoverish the meaning of the painting itself.

In our Chinese textbooks, we read a piece called "A Record of Painting" that quite tersely calculates how many horses in a certain painting were standing and how many reclining. The colophons on Chinese paintings should be viewed as calligraphic characters that, when executed well, sometimes really do complement the structure of the painting and, intentionally or not, serve as a counterbalance to the painting itself. This counterbalancing effect is the hallmark of Chinese painting. The words themselves, however, never have much to contribute to the image; no matter how exquisite the writings might be or how carefully they are chosen, once they have been transposed to the painting, they immediately lose their relevance.

And thus, as I prepare to write this essay on some paintings I have seen, I am all too aware of the fact that I must infringe the very rules I have been at pains to establish, for it is very difficult indeed to talk about paintings without actually *describing* them. Any attempt to describe a good painting will inevitably have its limits, but I wonder if it is really necessary to concern myself with these questions before I have even begun to write. Isn't it quite natural, after all, for one friend to say to another when they meet: "The moon's been so beautiful the past couple nights. Have you seen it?"

I recently obtained an illustrated volume of the paintings of Cézanne and have had the opportunity to examine his work quite carefully. I had always been aware of Cézanne's role as a progenitor of modern painting, but I was more interested in the work of later disciples such as Gauguin, Van Gogh, Matisse, and Picasso, each of whom grasped hold of different aspects of his work and developed them to their logical conclusion. As a result, their work seemed more tendentious, more immediately distinctive, and thus more accessible. And the only impression I had of the abundant possibilities and broad significance of Cézanne's work was a still life poorly reproduced in a magazine, which portrayed a few grayish apples laid on a tablecloth, behind which stood an array of wine bottles. From the arrangement of the apples, I should have been able to see the way he had gone beyond line to a new discovery of blocks, but I had yet to understand his technique fully.

The book I have now before me is called *Cézanne and His Times.* It is written in Japanese, so I can't even get the names of all of the paintings straight. Of his early portraiture, a few paintings are worth noting for their contrasts with one another. One painting from 1860 portrays a man with full eyebrows and large eyes who looks like a poet surrounded by mist and fog. Only his face and the whiteness of his collar emerge from the somber gold surface of the painting. I am not fond of the romantic tradition: its atmospheric suggestions of mysteries left complacently unexplained strike me as tantamount to flicking on a light switch so as to shine artificial moonlight on whatever comes in view, fabricating a scene of hazy blue beauty, intermingled with dark shadows, through which one might hear the excited calls of insects and the startled croaking of frogs.

If we turn to another painting, from 1863, we see a similar estrangement, a discomfort with the real, which manages this time to avoid the cut-rate poetic posturing of the first painting. Here, we see a little person with a large head, already well into middle age, with his long light-colored curls parted in the middle in the style of the day. He sits on a high-backed chair, his wandering eyes expressing a world-weariness born of age and experience, with a slightly mocking, supercilious composure in the hint of a smile underneath his prominent triangle-shaped beard. What is discomfiting about the painting, however, is that the proportions of the figure are so wrong. His legs are too short, his arms are too short, but the large hands dangling at his sides are very long, and the bony white joints of his fingers set against the floral-print fabric of the chair produce a subtle, civilized sense of terror.

The monk in a portrait painted in 1864 is hirsute, with black bushy eyebrows, a white robe, a white cassock, and a cross hanging from his neck. He crosses his arms across his chest. He has large hands. The surfaces of his face and his hands are extremely rough; one can discern where the skin has cracked and puckered from the cold. The whole painting is done in pure tones of gray and grayish-white, but there is nothing wretched about the extreme cold; there is only the fundamental quality of struggle between man and the elements around him.

In Cézanne's hands, the clichéd themes of European religious painting ever since the Renaissance are transformed. His *Madonna Clasping the Dead Jesus to Her Bosom* is truly astounding. His Madonna is a common woman, poor but clean, who has made her living as a seamstress, doing piecework, soul gone gray, hair gone gray, the petty frustrations of forty or fifty years of suffering contained in her hooked nose and tightly compressed lips. Nor does she actually clasp the baby Jesus in her arms. Her back is turned to him as she attends to some other matter. We can smell her poverty seeping from between the folds of her dark robes. Someone else is holding Jesus, a big, stout man who looks like a butcher, his arms as thick as stone columns, the blinding whiteness of his bald head melding with the dark face below. At first glance, he is a frightening figure, but on closer examination it is clear that his cruelty has its roots in other sorrows, and that he, too, is deserving of sympathy. What is particularly strange is the figure of Jesus himself. His complexion is dark, his muscles are beautifully defined, and his expression is serene. He stretches his legs such that his body extends across the entire width of the painting. His role in the painting appears to be purely aesthetic, lacking any other significance.

In *The Walkers*, one man is a little taller, wearing a gentlemanly stovepipe hat, the other somewhat shorter and more like a military man, wearing a felt cap with a folded bill and tall leather boots, walking stick in hand. In the heat of the afternoon, grass and trees and pale-colored houses have all been steamed into a misty white haze. Inside their shirts, the smell of old and new sweat intermingles, but the neckties of these walkers are neat and tidy, and they good-naturedly stroll arm in arm directly toward us, pitifully immaculate in their distress.

The backs of the two stylish young men in *Country Landscape* convey a similar feeling of sad triviality. The subject of this painting, however, is two women in the latest fashions. This sort of composition is usually a cliché of portraiture in the academic style: aristocratic women, elaborately made up, festooned with strings of pearls and precious jewels, stand proudly like little white mountains against a backdrop decorated by a forest and a castle, which may very well be their own family's fief. The women in this painting, though, are resolutely realistic. The brunette sits with her palm resting on her cheek. She has a low forehead; she is strong, with a worldliness of the smartest sort. The blonde is somewhat more contrived in her nobility. Her slender body is held at an angle so as to exhibit the long feather-like flourish of the train of her dress. Her face is partly hidden behind her leather muff, and the expression in her washed-out eyes is ambiguously lyrical. To place these two women in such a barren landscape, with a huge flag waving in the wind in the distance behind them, is an idiosyncratic gesture, to say the least, so much so that one is reminded of the more recent surrealists: a painting of a tree in which a sofa sits in the uppermost branches, and the country sun shines across the patchy floral upholstery, as desolate as a dream. Cézanne did not develop such images to their fullest potential, and this is why one grows so fond of the forthrightness of his painting.

Shepherd's Song portrays a group of men and women by the water, kneeling, reclining, sitting, their white flesh and white clothes flowing like music across the painting, describing the arclike shape of the letter *U*. By one corner of the arc, a nude woman cradles the back of her neck in her own outstretched arms. The flesh of her body seems to undulate, and the surface of the painting is bathed in the languor of a strangely irregular light.

A painting called *Olympia* is surely based on Greek mythology. I do not know the original story, but I am taken by the woman in the center. She sleeps curled up into a ball, and although her legs are swollen and distended, one is still able to see that her flesh is young and firm.

I don't like *The Temptation of St. Anthony*, perhaps because Cézanne was too partial to the subject matter, which he painted twice. The earlier version is dark and cluttered—St. Anthony has women's breasts, and the woman who appears to him in a dreamlike state resembles a horse—while the later version is diluted and confusing.

A Summer's Day captures the eternal yet fleeting feeling of sun shining on one's body. A little boy stands by the water with arms akimbo and legs spread apart, looking radiantly happy, the shape of his body from behind resembling that of a toad. The woman with a little parasol under the burning sun is a bit ludicrous. There are more holidaymakers on the other side of the water, where a grove of trees floats above the landscape in a cloud of green and the pale blue sky shelters clouds that hover above the lily pads, despite the withering extremity of the heat. The canvas sail of a little boat flashes in the white-hot glare, and its sailors and deckhands are burnt black by the sun.

If one places portraits of two different children next to one another, the contrast between their personalities can sometimes be quite shocking. One child cups his face in his hand, and his prominent forehead radiates intelligence, skepticism, mischief, and cunning. This is humanity putting its best foot forward into the arena of struggle. Still, children are children. A patch of the white shirt he is wearing peeks out from underneath his over-sized overcoat. It is such a small, white thing, this shirt, so vulnerable and easily destroyed. When he reaches a certain age, that which is insubordinate in him will be made to toe the line. But there are also those who toe the line from the start, such as the boy in the second portrait, who is bright and correct and civilized, and as gentle as a bowl of porridge. He looks directly at the viewer with his great big eyes. It is not that there's no hint of mischief or evil in those eyes. It is merely that those hints can be completely ignored, because they are of no use. There is no ambition here, no resolve, only deceit and a crooked face.

In terms of technique, the first picture has already been simplified to the extent possible, but in order to capture the complex layering of the boy's spirit, a welter of brushstrokes has been added atop the blocks of color. The picture of the second boy from seven years later is composed entirely of flat blocks of color, but the flatness here has a rich substance of its own.

There was a man named Chocquet (according to the Japanese transliteration) who must have been Cézanne's friend and whose portrait appears twice in this volume. The first time that we see him, he already looks old and senile. His lips seem to tremble, and he sits with his legs crossed, one hand resting on the chair back, fingers splayed. From his head to his shoes and socks, a look of querulous distrust conveys his cowardice, his reproachfulness, his pettiness. It is clear that this is a man who has been through everything and learned nothing thereby. He's at loose ends but at the same time believes himself rich with the fruit of his experience, of which bounty he is only too happy to share in the form of lectures delivered beneath a triumphal arch consecrated to the virtues of old age. The satire here is not entirely lacking in sympathy for its subject. But in a painting from nine years later, this sympathy has expanded into an exquisite tenderness. This time, he sits outdoors against a backdrop of dense foliage, and although his hair is still gray and his figure similarly gaunt, he looks much younger. The terror of his own incomprehension has given way to a sense of perplexity that, because it encompasses everything around him, is much more serene. In his lowered eyes, we can see sentimentality, grief, retirement. His sunken mouth carries a little smile; perhaps he's spending a pleasant summer morning in the garden. There is love in every single brushstroke, for this man, and for his stubborn affection for life.

Those who are interested in the exaggerated and distorted line of modern art would do well to look closely at his over-sized, obliquely angled hands.

Over the course of several portraits of the artist's wife, we can also detect some significant psychological developments. The first example uses the traditional image of a pair of lovers as its theme, but when we look ahead to the later paintings, it is clear that the woman portrayed here is strikingly similar to the artist's wife. This is clearly a depiction of the painter's own love story. The background is romantic. Tall reeds of some sort grow by the side of a lake. The limpid sunlight shines across the woman's white bonnet, with something of the freshness of a line from an old Chinese poem: "tender reeds in the distance green / white dew lends a frosty sheen."[1] The woman lays her hand on the man's bare arm, just below his shoulder. She is a shallow woman at bottom, who finds virtue in obeying the rules, yet in the moment that she is illuminated by the sunlight of love, she becomes more generous of spirit, smarter, more confident in her knowledge of the world, and all of this moves her so much that tears shine in her eyes. The painter desires her to be transformed in this way, and thus he paints her just so, while he represents himself as an entirely passive, subordinate, and characterless young man, sitting with his head bowed at her feet, accepting her kindness, his body seemingly shrunken to one size smaller than hers.

In this, her very first appearance in Cézanne's work, she is depicted with a squarish face and slightly protruding eyes. She seems a mild young woman who has undergone the rigors of a strict bourgeois upbringing. This is why she remains exceedingly reserved throughout. Yet entranced by his own romantic ideals, Cézanne has sanctified their relationship through his art.

Her second appearance in his work comes as a real shock. It must be quite a few years later. She sits on a sprawling old velvet sofa the color of dark clouds, her head bent to her sewing, with prominent circles under her eyes, a sharper nose, and a squarer chin. She is strong-willed: her hair is pulled back into an unshakable iron bun, and her upper body is sheathed in what looks likes galvanized sheet metal. The door to the room is visible just behind her, a hard rectangle, locked. There is flowered paper pasted on the wall, and each flower resembles a little iron cross. Can it be easy for a poor artist's wife patiently and smilingly to maintain such iron-clad wifely virtue? What a frightening thing life can be!

When Cézanne goes on to paint his wife five years later, he captures her in a tender moment. Her hair is loose, and she is wearing what appears to be a nightgown, made of satin, its soft and luminous flow of wide vertical stripes seemingly unable to prop up her body. She holds her head to one side, lost in her own thoughts, and reminiscence makes her young—although a young woman's eyes could not contain the depths of sadness in these eyes. She is someone who has suffered for her ideals, only to discover much later that very little remains of them. Even their remnants are distant and indistinct, and yet, because she has suffered, they seem all the more appealing, like a simple melody floating through the air from afar, mingling with the breath of the earth and the seasons.

This aspect of her, however, is only fleeting. In another portrait, her hair appears to have been clipped short like a boy's, and even her face resembles that of a boy who has been weathered by a storm, aged before his time. Her chin extends forward from the picture frame, and her sharp semiprofile resembles a rust-blackened blade that's just cut through an apple and is sticky with its sour juice. Yet she smiles, and in her eyes is a bleak courage—a courage that would seem solemn, if she had been able to manage something heroic rather than merely bleak.

The next picture is even more unhappy. The painter's wife sits in her husband's atelier, a brilliantly colored floral-print window shade slanting above her head. Sunlight and shadow play across the wall, but the light here does not belong to her. She is merely the woman from the kitchen. She wears greasy, somberly colored clothes. The object she is clasping in her hand might be a handkerchief, except the way she holds it suggests that it is more likely a dishcloth. She was probably busy using it when he called her in to serve as a model, and much as one would placate a child, she has decided to stay for a moment to humor him. She has been smiling all these years, and now the time has come for the painter to acknowledge the truth: it is an exhausted, insipid, and sloppy smile. On that long-suffering face, there is very little left of the feminine. One eyebrow is raised, perhaps parodying her disappointment, and the parody itself is actually a gesture of tenderness, of the sort that's only possible through a long and familiar intimacy. You need to look carefully before you can see it.

Cézanne's final portrait of his wife is lively and distinct. She sits in a flower garden illuminated by the sun, with luxuriant foliage and the white, swirling dust of late spring and early summer on the road behind her. She is wearing her best Sunday gown, tightly encircled by a whalebone corset. She has recovered the slim figure of her youth, and when she stretches out her arms, her wrists look firm and lovely. And yet the spring scene in the background has nothing to do with her. The painter's circumstances have improved, the hard times are behind them, but having been formed by precisely those hardships, she is no longer able to live her life in peace. The happiness on her face is a happiness devoid of content. If one were to remove that brilliant backdrop, the happiness on her face would seem strangely hollow, even idiotic.

Having seen Mrs. Cézanne's wifely virtues, it's something of relief to see a selfish woman. His subject in *Woman in Bonnet and Leather Shawl* has a long pallid face and a long nose, and her eyes possess a chilly allure. She retains the rancorous air of a city slicker who has ended up in the countryside. She could be a gentry woman, or she might be a con artist with pretensions to gentility.

In a very few brushstrokes, the painting entitled *Statue* manages to express that solidity and hardness that is the special quality of stone. This is the most statuelike object I have ever seen reproduced in a book of paintings. I don't know whether the painting was intended as some sort of parody. It looks to me as if it may well have been: this all-too-typical image of a child, with prominent and plump cheeks, round belly, and contoured limbs, is supposed to convey divine health and vitality but ends up smacking of greed, impudence, and an excessive fondness for wine and women, instead. In the end, this Cupid resembles neither a god nor a child.

In addition to these, there is a large group of paintings that take groups of bathers emerging from the water as their theme. Each of these paintings is set on a shore beside a wood. There are a few men who look mostly alike, but the focus is on a number of women and the difficult task of capturing their gestures and the figural beauty of their bodies. This is especially true of the last such picture, *Women Bathers*, in which the depiction of the human form has gradually grown more and more abstract, prefiguring the cubism of the century to come.

There are two paintings sketching Mardi Gras that seem to be about the naked pursuit of love between men and women during the wild jubilance of the carnival. The atmosphere is frenzied, and the brushwork is frenzied as well, and what I took away from these paintings was merely that the women's midsections were invariably bigger than those of the men.

The Last Day of Mardi Gras, however, is a masterpiece. Two vagabonds, dressed up as harlequins, are on their way back from the celebration. One holds a walking stick, and the other is unsteady on his feet, his waist bent and one hand propped on his knee, holding himself in a slyly jocose posture. They seem to be walking downhill. All the lines in the painting are slanted, and the atmosphere is suggestive of the repose that comes in the wake of desire fulfilled. Mardi Gras is an ancient custom, which has long since fallen into disfavor, but the faces of these two men are as common as could be. They are giddy with a simple sort of self-confidence, drunk with their own inconsequential cleverness, betrayed by their own lack of feeling, and lack of interest.

Boy with Skull presents a student on the cusp of maturity seated next to a table, his knees pressed against the legs of the table, as if they can no longer fit underneath, as if everything has somehow gone out of proportion. His face is truly that of a student: mischievous, inquisitive, full of fantasy, impatient of others. One can almost feel the pressure exerted on his legs by the wave-shaped edges of the cheap wooden table at which he sits. On the table, there are books, a ruler, and a skull sitting atop some papers. The skeletons used for the study of anatomy possess a real intimacy, because they are merely ordinary; one's student's days are especially ordinary, like the smell of feet perspiring inside a pair of basketball shoes.

A portrait of old age is found in *Woman in a Straw Hat*. Her head is bowed as she counts the beads on her rosary, and under the brim of her hat is revealed a foxlike face whose humanity has been diminished by half, leaving only cupidity. She lacks the energy for stealing, larceny, or the hoarding of goods, and this lethargy leaves her uneasy. She bends over her rosary, praying not for serenity or for heavenly ideals but only to be allowed to continue to murmur over the hard little beads, to count and catalog more of the objects that lie within her purview. She will not be with her beads for much longer, and she can do nothing more than pass them back and forth across her mouth until they are slick with the smell of her spittle.

Cézanne's own old age was not like that at all. In his very last self-portrait, he wears a hunting cap at a rakish tilt, like a man about town. He has grown a white beard, and his slender, raised eyebrows give him the crafty look of a man who's seen through it all. The smile in his eyes is exceedingly endearing, as if to say: I know—even after I'm gone, spring will come again. Old age is not lovable in and of itself, but there are many lovable old people.

Of the landscape paintings, I am fondest of his *Broken House*. This is a white house sitting beneath the afternoon sun, with a blackened window that looks like a solitary eye peering out from a face. There is a great big crack running from the roof all the way down to the ground, so that the house looks as if it's laughing itself to pieces. The little path that leads to the house is already barely visible through the undergrowth, and the house is surrounded on all sides by weeds, which look extremely soft and pale under the sun, forming a blurry expanse. The suffocating color of the sun reminds one of the lines of a poem: "On the ancient road to Chang'an, no sound and no dust, no sound and no dust / through fading sunset in the west wind appear the towers of the Han imperial tombs." Here, however, there is no magnificent past to mourn, only bourgeois desolation, emptiness within emptiness.

ON THE SECOND EDITION OF *ROMANCES*

I ALWAYS used to think to myself: when my book has been published, I want to make the rounds of the newsstands, and I want the cover of my book, in my favorite blue-green hue, to open a little nocturnal blue window on the shelf, through which people can see the moon and all the excitement of the evening. I'm going to ask the news vendor, feigning nonchalance, "How's it selling? Too expensive, isn't it? Would anyone really buy it at that price?" Ah! Make yourself famous as early as you can! If success comes too late, the pleasure of it isn't as intense. The first time I published a couple of pieces in the school magazine, I was deliriously happy, poring over the pages again and again, as if seeing the words for the first time. But nowadays, I'm not so easily excited. Which is why I have to push myself even harder: Hurry! Hurry! Otherwise it will be too late! Too late!

Even if I were able to wait, the times rush impatiently forward—already in the midst of destruction, with a still-greater destruction yet to come. There will come a day when our civilization, whether sublime or frivolous, will be a thing of the past. If the word I use the most in my writing is "desolation," that is because this troubling premonition underlies all my thinking.

I've been meaning to go see the kind of *bengbeng* opera that's already fallen out of fashion in Shanghai but could never find the right person to go along with me.[1] I'm too embarrassed to admit that I'm interested in such a rubbishy, lowbrow sort of thing. It was only recently that I finally came across a married lady whose family didn't dare accompany her to see Zhu Baoxia in the midst of the summer heat, so we went together.[2] As soon as the *huqin* player began to tune up,

I listened with a strange twinge of sorrow to the high winds and distant skies of the melody, intertwined with the squeak of strings. "Heaven and earth dark and brown, cosmos vast without bounds," the wind blowing through the northern passes, howlingly pursued by the emptiness in its wake, with nowhere to stop and rest.[3] A man in a great blue robe beats the rhythm out on a bamboo clapper, with a ruthless hand: "Kua! Kua! Kua!" He moves to the front of the stage, very close to the audience, deliberately drowning out the singer: "Kua! Kuu-wa! Kuu-wa!" His blows rain mercilessly down. I'm sitting in the second row, and I'm so overwhelmed that my head swims, and so much of the stuff in my brain is beaten out that I'm left only with what's most primitive. In the poor cave dwellings of the northwest, people can only live the most rudimentary of lives, and even that is no easy matter. The people in the play contend at the top of their lungs with the caustic wind of the *huqin* and the iron beat of the mallet. The northern girl playing Li Sanniang, her skin dark and without a trace of powder, with two ink-black streaks for eyebrows, buckets dangling from her carrying poles as she makes her way to the well, laments the bitterness of her fate: "Though I can't compare with Wang Sanjie . . ." She keeps her eyes fixed on the ground as she loudly and gravely declaims each word. When she is drawing water from the well, along comes "a dashing young commanding officer on horseback," who turns out to be her son, with whom she is unknowingly reunited. This little general later begins to suspect that this poor country woman is indeed his mother and questions her about her family background: "What was your father's name? Who was your mother? What about your older brother?" She answers each question, her "I's" sounding like "Ah's," until she's even explained her sister-in-law's background: "Ah have a sister-in-law called Zhang." Living in cave dwellings, surrounded by violent dust storms and perpetual dusk, one's existence is restricted to simple facts: who is your father, who is your mother, your brother, your sister-in-law? There's very little to remember, so nothing's ever forgotten.

Before the main play, there was also a short comic sketch about a woman who manages to kill her own husband. Two huge streaks of rouge drooped down across this lascivious woman's broad cheeks. Even the sides of her nose were covered with rouge, so that only a narrow strip of powdery white nose remained. This contrivance— aimed toward creating the impression of a high, narrow, and aquiline Greek nose—just didn't fit the width of her face. Her teary eyes seemed to be located on the side of her face, like an animal's. She had a gold tooth, two long, greasy braids dangling almost to her ankles, and from under the sleeves of her pink blouse, you could catch a glimpse of her plump, copper-colored wrists. Her husband's aggrieved spirit lodges a complaint with the authorities, appearing as a gust of wind. An officer in a palanquin, having heard him out, reports: "There's an apparition blocking the road." The magistrate asks, "Is it a male apparition or a female apparition?" After a careful inspection, the answer comes back: "The apparition is male." The magistrate orders the officer, "Follow that apparition, and make no mistake about it." He follows the wind to a fresh tomb, where the young widow is arrested. She kneels in front of the officer as she explains how it came to be that her husband came home to her one night, fell suddenly ill, and died. She tries a hundred different circumlocutions in order to get her meaning across. And still he doesn't understand. She sings: "Your honor! Did you ever see a stove without a fire? Did you ever see a chimney without smoke?" The audience cheers.

Women who manage to get the upper hand in barren and backward country aren't actually much like the wild roses most people imagine them to be, with dark, flashing eyes, even stronger than a man, brandishing a horsewhip in one hand and willing to use it at the slightest provocation. That's just an image city dwellers have made up to satisfy their need for titillation. In the barren wastes of the future, among the broken tiles and rubble of the ruins, the only sort of woman left will be like the singers in *bengbeng* opera, who are always able to find a way to survive safe and sound, no matter in which era and no matter in what kind of society; their home is everywhere.

That is why I felt such great sorrow.

Perhaps it's because of H. G. Wells's prognostications that I often think of things like this. I used to think they lay very far in the future, but now they don't seem so very distant at all. And yet it's autumn now, as clear as water and as bright as a mirror, and I should be happy. For the second edition of the book, I've used Yanying's design for the cover, which resembles the cloud tendrils coiled atop ancient brocade or a noisy cascade of sea spray softly falling from a dark and massive wave. If you look carefully, they're mostly made of little interlocking jade rings, in twos and threes, inseparably linked. There are a few single rings, like little moons, sufficient unto themselves. Others are in pairs, standing mildly next to one another, although what's done is done, and the scene has already changed: there's no reason they cannot stand in as symbols for the connections between the characters in the book.

Yanying only did a draft sketch. Struck by the strength and beauty of her line, I was more than happy to trace methodically over her lines to make a copy. Life's a little like that as well, no? It possesses the pattern, and we only get a copy. And so they have a saying in the West: "Let life come to you." That sort of submission resembles very little the uncomprehending, wretched, unsightly, and clumsy submission of the characters in my fiction, yet it is just as desolate.

ON MUSIC

I DON'T like music very much. Colors and smells often make me happy, but music is always sad. Even so-called light music is the same: its bounce seems superficial, a little artificial. But colors: indoors in summertime with the curtains down, old pajamas neatly folded and piled on bamboo mats. An azure blue summer top, and sea-green silk pants. Next to one another, the blue and the green have a layered, delicate beauty. Not a beauty that necessarily reminds you of anything. But in the dimness of the room, they carve out a space and quietly pervade it with a sort of joy. I sit to one side, catch sight of them without having intended to look, and they make me happy for a long while.

There was another time when I had put a new air-raid cover over the bathroom light. The dim greenish light shone coldly onto the surface of the bathtub, green seeping into the white, black seeping into the green, laminating the tub with a glossy coat of color, simplifying everything. Gazing into the bathroom from outside the door, it looked exactly like a modernist painting, an altogether new and different dimension. It seemed to me that one could never pass into that alien dimension, but somehow I managed to go in anyway. It was as if I had accomplished an impossible feat. I felt happy and a little scared all at the same time, and just a little numb, as if I had been shocked by electricity, and I came out almost as soon as I had gone in.

In short, colors are only desolate when they lose their luster, but when they can attract your attention, they are always something to be celebrated, because they make the world seem that much more real.

Smells are the same way. I like a lot of the smells that other people don't like: the slight scent of mildew in the mist, dust moistened by the rain, scallions and garlic, cheap perfume. Take gas, for instance. Some people feel dizzy when they smell gas, but I like to sit next to the driver on purpose or stand behind cars so that when the engine starts with a chug, I can smell the exhaust from the tailpipe. When we used to wash clothes with a little butane once a year, the room would fill with its bright, steely, stainless aroma. My mother never wanted me to help her, because I would work as slowly as I could so that as much butane as possible would evaporate into the air.

When milk burns or matches burn down, the smoky smell makes me hungry. The smell of oil-based paint, precisely because it seems so aggressively brand-new, is like celebrating New Year's in a new house: sterile, fresh, jubilant. When ham or salted meat or peanut oil have sat for a long time and start to turn, there's a kind of greasy smell that I like a lot, too, because it makes the oil smell even oilier, ripe to bursting, almost rotten, like the "rice spoiling in the granaries" of ancient times. During the Battle of Hong Kong, all the food we ate was cooked in coconut oil and smelled strongly of soap. At first, it was hard to accustom oneself to the smell, and it made you want to vomit, but later I realized that soap has a certain cold fragrance all its own. During the war, there wasn't any toothpaste, but I didn't mind brushing my teeth with the coarse, fatty soap you usually use to wash clothes.

Smells are always ephemeral, coincidental. Even if it was possible to smell one thing for a long time, you wouldn't be able to stand it. In that sense, smells are only a minor diversion. Colors are right there in front of you, which is why they make one feel at ease. Perhaps the joy of colors and smells has something to do with this quality. Music is different. Music is always on its way somewhere else, and no one can determine exactly where. Once it gets there, it's already gone, and all that is left is to search for it. Music leaves you alone and at a loss.

The violin is the worst. I'm frightened of the way it always flows away like water, taking all the things in life you would like to grasp hold of and cherish along with it. The Chinese two-stringed violin is much better, because as bleak as it sounds, when it reaches some sort of conclusion it always "comes around again to the beginning," as northerners like to say, circling and perambulating its way back to the world as we mortals know it.

When someone plays the violin, there is always a moment of high musical drama and innumerable melodramatic twists and turns, all of which are much too clearly intended to elicit the audience's tears. The violin is the tragedienne of musical instruments. I think a play should have a female lead, a foil, and a female supporting role. There's no need for a tragic part, a femme fatale, or a commentator (in the "civilized plays" of the early Republic, there was always an old commentator on hand to supply a political message).

Nor do I like violin and piano duets or even small groups of instrumentalists centered around the piano and the violin. There's nothing there to hold on to; everything's in bits and pieces, and the awkward way in which the separate parts come together makes you feel uneasy. It all turns out a little like those Chinese paintings that several people work on together. Someone paints a beautiful woman, someone else adds some flowers, and yet another person paints in the pavilions and scenery behind her, but often the picture as a whole lacks any particular atmosphere, and nothing approaching harmony emerges from the effort.

A full-scale orchestra is another thing altogether. It comes at you with all the grand bombast of a May Fourth Movement, transforming each individual's voice into something altogether different from what it was in the beginning. The whistling and scraping on all sides become your own voice, and you are shocked by the depth, volume, and resonance of the sound you are making. It's a little like the moment after you wake up in the morning: someone calls your name, and, unsure whether the voice is someone else's or your own, you feel a vague kind of terror.

And since writing orchestral music is so very complex and composers have to undergo such arduous training, they often end up drowning in lessons and are unable to extricate themselves from their influence. That's why orchestral music is so often afflicted by too much formalism. Why do they always have to keep coming back to the same old bag of tricks? The orchestra will suddenly grow tense; with heads bowed and teeth clenched, they enter the penultimate phase of the battle, urged on by the timpani, which pounds out its drumbeat over and over, determining the orchestra's destiny: to overwhelm and annihilate the audience completely. And all the audience can do is put up silent resistance to the orchestra's attack. Most of them are from the upper classes and schooled in the ways of classical music. They've sat through countless concerts before, and they know full well from previous experience that this music, too, shall pass.

I am Chinese, so I know how to appreciate noise and clatter. Chinese drums and gongs descend heedlessly on your head with an ear-splitting clatter, all at once, and I can take as much noise as they can dish out. But an orchestral assault is mounted slowly, painstakingly, allowing time for each weapon—tubas and trumpets, pianos and violins—to be set in place for one ambush after another: that kind of premeditated conspiracy frightens me.

I came into contact with music for the first time when I was eight or nine years old. My mother and my aunt had just come back to China. My aunt practiced piano every day, extending her tiny hands toward the keyboard, her wrists tightly encircled by the narrow sleeves of her knitted blouse, its bright red weave shot through with silver threads. Flowers were usually blooming in the glass vase atop the piano. What emerged from the piano was another world, and yet it wasn't another world at all, just the world in the mirror that hung on the wall across from the piano, reflecting the civilized elegance of an apartment equipped with hot running water.

Sometimes, my mother would stand behind my aunt, one hand resting on her shoulder, singing scales: "La, la, la, la." My mother was learning to sing purely because her lungs were so weak and the doctor had told her that singing would be good for her health. No matter what song she sang, it always sounded a little like she was reciting poetry (she was in the habit of chanting lines from Tang dynasty poems in her drawling Hunanese accent). And her intonation was always one half-pitch lower than that of the piano, but she would just smile apologetically and offer charming excuses for being out of tune. Her clothes were the soft crimson color of fallen autumn leaves, and a corsage of crimson flowers would hang from her shoulder, forever threatening to drift down to the floor.

I would always stand to one side and listen, less because I liked the piano music than because I enjoyed the atmosphere. I would exclaim with real feeling: "I'm so envious! I only wish I could play that well!" And thus the adults came to believe that I was a child who was unusually sensitive to music, and since it would not do to bury this rare talent, they immediately started me on piano lessons. Mother told me, "Since you are starting off on a lifelong pursuit, you need to learn first of all how to take loving care of your instrument." Each of the piano keys was as white as snow, and I was not allowed to touch them without first having washed my hands. Every day, I would wipe the dust from the piano with a square of parrot-green felt cloth.

When my mother first took me to a concert, she warned me over and over before we even arrived, "Whatever happens, don't make a sound, and don't say a thing. Don't let them say Chinese people don't know how to behave properly." And indeed I sat silently, without so much as moving a muscle, and did not fall asleep. During the ten-minute intermission, my mother and my aunt whispered to each other about a red-haired woman: "Red hair is so awkward! It really limits the kinds of things you can wear. Reds and yellows clash. That just leaves green. When someone with red hair wears green, now that's something..." In the dimly lit auditorium, I combed the crowd in vain for a glimpse of this red-haired woman. And as we rode back in the car after the concert, I wondered the whole way home whether it was really possible for someone to have bright red hair? It was all terribly perplexing.

After that, I never once took it upon myself to go see a concert. In fact, I wouldn't even consider sitting in the park on a summer night and listening for free to the orchestral music coming from the bandstand in the distance.

My piano teacher was a Russian woman whose wide, prominent cheekbones were covered with golden peach fuzz. She would always lavish me with praise, her excitable blue eyes filling with tears as she held my head in her hands and kissed me. I would smile politely, note exactly where her kisses had landed, and, after a discreet interval, wipe them away with a handkerchief. My family's old maid would accompany me over to my teacher's house. I still didn't really know English, and yet I somehow managed to talk with her quite a lot, and even the old servant sometimes joined in our conversations. One weekend, when she had just come back from swimming at Gaoqiao, she proudly and happily opened her collar to show us the pink sunburnt skin on her back. Although it had already been a day since she had returned, I thought I could still smell a powerful aroma of sunshine and sweat coming from her body. The walls of her parlor were hung with lusterless, old brown carpets and fitted with green painted screen doors. Each time we entered or exited, her husband would very politely hold the door open. I was always very reserved and never actually looked at him, so that after several years I still had no idea of what he was like, merely a vague impression of a face that seemed never to have seen the sun. His wife made a living teaching piano, but he didn't do anything at all.

Still later, when I started going to school, I had a piano teacher who would always get angry with me, flinging sheet music onto the floor in exasperation and bringing her hand down on the backs of my hands so hard that they slammed into the keyboard cover and my joints ached. The more she hit me, the lazier I grew. I lost all interest in the piano, and whenever I was supposed to be practicing, I would sit on the floor behind the piano and read novels instead. After the piano teacher got married, her temper improved considerably. Her face powder didn't so much float above her skin; it seemed to protrude an inch beyond it. Wrapped loosely in this voluminous layer of white powder, she would manage to smile in my direction and say, "Good morning!" But I was still afraid of her, and before each class, I would stand by the door to the music room and wait for the bell to ring, trembling and wanting to go to the bathroom instead.

The several years I had spent learning the piano were like investing money to open a shop. It would have seemed a shame to give it up without any return on the investment, so I kept at it for quite a while longer, until I finally had to quit. At the time, I was living at boarding school and often had to pass by the music building, which was made up of lots of little rooms filled with lots of people prodding and plucking at their instruments. The sounds of all the various instruments seemed to sway and scatter forlornly on the ground, like rain at the dawn of a day that seems as if the sun will never rise. With an almost unbearable emptiness, the sounds strike hollowly against the aluminum siding of the Western-style building. When some student happened to step on the piano pedal, the scattered instruments would merge together for an instant, but that was merely like the wind whipping the rain into a fine mist. Once the wind had passed, the pitter-patter of scattered notes would start to drip down once more.

Playing an instrument is like being in a skyscraper. You run up the back stairs reserved for servants and coolies and salespeople. The gray cement steps and black iron handrails are enclosed by gray cement walls, and the landings are piled with Western-style red metal buckets and garbage that is cold and gray and doesn't smell because it's winter. You don't see a single other person on your whole way up; all you can do is keep moving into the teeth of the dark, cruel winds of the tower.

Later, when I had left the misery of learning piano well behind me, I did listen to some orchestral music (but mostly on a gramophone, because records are mercifully short), but I always disliked the rousing declamatory style and overly self-important manner of that sort of music. I much prefer the courtly music of the eighteenth century. Those exquisite little minuets dance gingerly on cloven hoofs, as if they're afraid to break something underfoot. In fact, the Europeans of that era were fascinated by Chinese porcelain. Even the furniture in their houses was made of porcelain; dainty little porcelain chairs were embossed with gold on a white background. My favorite classical composer isn't a romantic like Beethoven or Chopin but Bach, who came a little earlier. Bach's compositions are not as finely woven as courtly music. They have neither churchly airs nor heroic gestures. The world inside the music is heavy, even cumbersome, but it fits comfortably in one's hand and pleases the heart: a clock hangs from the wall inside a wooden house, ticking as its pendulum sways back and forth; people drink sheep's milk from wooden bowls; women curtsy as they take their leave; thoughtful cows and sheep move across green fields under unthinking white clouds; ponderous joy sets the gilded bell of matrimony to ringing. Just like the line in Browning's poem: "God is in his heaven— / All's right with the world."

Operatic sorts of things can be precious, but that's the extent of their appeal. The stories in opera are usually quite puerile. Jealousy, for instance, is the most primitive of emotions, and, in opera, even the simplest kind of jealousy is blown a thousand times out of proportion by its luxuriant expression in music of the utmost sophistication and complexity. And precisely because of this discrepancy, the whole thing becomes overwrought. Big is not necessarily great. Chest-pounding, wildly gesticulating heroes are annoying. Still, we must grant them the occasional moment of grandeur: when the singer's golden voice reaches calmly for the heights under the overbearing pressure of the music and each instrument has anxiously submitted to the tide, the man stands above the stormy waters of life, and you suddenly realize that he's very tall indeed, that his face and his voice give off enough light to rival the stars. If you hadn't seen him stand up, you wouldn't have realized that he's usually crawling on the ground.

As far as foreign popular music goes, I dislike those half-old, half-new sorts of songs the most. Collections like *One Hundred and One Classic Songs* carry with them the air of a nineteenth-century parlor, a feeling of dull contentment, gently refined and suffocating. Perhaps this stuffy feeling has to do with the vogue in those times for tight corsets, when everyone ate far too well. Their sadness seems less like sadness than gloomy discomfort. There's a love song called "At Dusk": "At dusk, When you remember me / Don't hold a grudge, my dear." From the sound of it, this is the voice of a proper lady who rejected a suitor many years before, for his own good, and for her own good as well. Without giving the affair much thought, she lives alone and grows old alone. Although her pride and her self-respect remain intact, she begins to feel apologetic as the end nears. That might be a gentle and lovely sentiment, if only we could ignore the years of slow death and decay in between. As it is, we can feel only annoyed by her belated emotional logic.

There's none of this sort of logic in Scottish folk songs. The ancient folk tune "Loch Lomond" was recently jazzed up by a popular American band and became a big hit for a time:

> You take the high road, and I'll take the low road
> And I'll be in Scotland afore you
> But me and my true love will never meet again
> On the bonnie, bonnie banks of Loch Lomond.

You can imagine the mountainous, foggy wastes of Scotland, its slopes covered in heather that grows as tall as wild grass, with soft lavender flowers that seem to float above the heather like a layer of muted purple mist. The air is fresh, vibrant, and cold. We only have that sort of cleanliness in *Shijing* (The classic of poetry).

Listening too much to most jazz music makes you feel groggy, like when you wake up much too late, the sunlight is bright and yellow, but you don't know what time it is, and you have no energy, no appetite, and nothing in your head. Those exaggerated, loping rhythms seem to pursue you, and yet they're quite comfortable at the same time. My favorite song is "Girl on the Police Gazette."[1] It wasn't very popular in China, perhaps because it was a little too innovative and avoided the usual "June," "moon," "blue," and "you" sorts of lyrics:

> Oh, my search will never cease for the girl on the police
>   gazette
> For the pretty young brunette
> On the pink police gazette

This is the very image of little people in the big city.

South American music is like a raging fire or the call of an overripe spring. Hawaiian music is very monotonous, always the metallic sound of plucked guitar. It's like late summer or early autumn when you have to put the wicker bed mats out on a bamboo pole to air in the sun. The flower-patterned Taiwanese mats and straw-colored wicker mats curl in the wind, their edges faded a golden sunny hue. You sit on the ground to nap with the brim of a straw hat pulled over your eyes. Not just you—your lover leans against your shoulder, the breath from his or her nostrils soughing like a blow-dryer in a hair salon. Wallowing in this extreme languor, you might grow quite annoyed if you didn't love each other very, very much, because the sense that all you're doing is killing time is all too clear. Tireless deep blue skies above, an ageless breeze, a sun that has shone and will go on shining for all eternity. But life itself is short, and so you are terribly agitated by everything that is eternal.

Of the various kinds of Chinese popular music, I dislike drum songs for their childish temper. The most famous singers sing unnaturally drawn-out phrases in one incredibly long breath, without their faces ever getting red or the veins in their necks popping out with the effort. And the audience has come expressly to see whether their faces will get red or their veins will pop out from the strain. A narrative song such as "The Great Western Chamber" expends enormous effort to portray the romantic longings of the main character Yingying but always seems like little more than the tiresome ramblings of a loquacious Beijing storyteller who loves to listen to himself talk.

I've only heard *tanci* story songs once.[2] A young man with a long, thin face was singing "Golden Phoenix." Every other phrase was punctuated by an extremely affirmative sort of grunt, and with every grunt, he would shake his head back and forth, as if he had got hold of a chunk of human flesh in his jaws and was unwilling to let it go. I suppose some of the audience derives a soft-core thrill from this sort of thing.

Relatively speaking, *shenqu* are fairly honest and down to earth.[3] These Shanghainese songs express a kind of "hurry up and get along" mentality that is matched by a special sort of music that sounds really rushed, like walking so fast your feet don't touch the ground and the wind whistles in your ears. The strangest thing is that when they sing about death, they use a similar sort of music, but the atmosphere seems completely different. When they sing, "Souls by threes and sevens wandering under heaven, souls by threes and sevens wandering under heaven, when the king of hell calls for them at the third watch, this job he won't botch, when the king of hell calls for them at the third watch, none of them will wake up in the morning," the notes fall like a hard, steady rain, repeating over and over again, in a noisy flurry of sound. It's as if some great event is about to happen, and the audience feels nervous, even a little panicky, but the musicians don't really have any feelings at all. For these common folks, even death has a distinctly human feel.

As for Chinese pop songs, it used to be that everyone was crazy for little-girlish singers, and so all the stars forced their voices unnaturally high and flat. A song like "Peach Blossom River" came out sounding like unintelligible nonsense syllables—"jia ah jia, ji jia jia ji jia ah jia"—through the little speaker of a wireless radio. Bemused foreigners would often ask how it could be that all Chinese girls' voices sounded like *that*? Things are much better now. But Chinese popular songs still lack a real musical foundation: it's as if someone decided that a new era needs new songs, and so they pound out new songs, come what may. That's why when I *do* happen to hear a pleasing tune like "Roses Blooming Everywhere," I can't help suspecting that it must have been copied from an American or Japanese song.[4] Late one night, the sound of music from a dance hall came floating through the air from afar. A sharp, thin female voice was singing: "Roses, roses, blooming everywhere!" In all of Shanghai, there were hardly any lights on, and the night seemed all the more empty and vast because of it. I still hadn't put out the lights. A row of windows with dark blue velvet drapes pulled shut, like the "heavy curtains of night" of literary cliché. The velvet curtains fluttered in the wind, their edges splattered pale and dusty gold by the light of the lamp. A strange sort of car tore hurriedly down the street, perhaps in pursuit of thieves, wailing as it went, like the steam whistle of a passenger ship. With its sad, attenuated whistle—wa! wa...wa!...wa—the ocean seemed to appear just outside my window. Departure aboard an ocean liner, a tale of fateful separation to chill one's very soul. The "wa...wa" sound gradually moved into the distance. On such a cruel night, a night so big and so broken, it was impossible to imagine that any roses would be blooming. And yet this woman, in a tiny and determinedly optimistic voice, was insisting that they were. Even if all that was really blooming were imitation silk flowers—ornamenting a mosquito net, a lamp shade, the brim of a hat, a sleeve, the toe of a pair of shoes, or a parasol—the fragile satisfaction they offered had a certain intimate, lovely, charm.

Epilogue
DAYS AND NIGHTS OF CHINA

IN THE days between autumn and winter last year, I went every day to buy vegetables. Twice, I was able to write a poem on the way to market, which left me both surprised and delighted. The first came when I saw the leaves falling from a French plane tree. One of the leaves fell very very slowly, holding its strangely graceful pose all the way down to the ground. I stood still to watch, but before it had touched down, I moved on so that I wouldn't seem to be staring blankly in the same place for so long. As I walked away, I turned back for one final glance. Afterward, I wrote this:

THE LOVE OF A FALLING LEAF

The big yellow leaf tumbles down
slowly, passing by the breeze
by the pale green sky
by the knifelike rays of the sun
and the dusty dreams of yellow-gray apartment buildings.
As it falls toward the middle of the road
you can see it means to kiss
its own shadow.
Its shadow on the ground
reaches out in welcome, reaches out
and seems to drift to the side.
The leaf moves as slowly as can be,
feigning middle-aged nonchalance,
but as soon as it hits the ground

a hand baked gold by the season
carefully palms its little black shadow
as if catching a cricket:
"Oh, here you are!"
In the autumn sun
on the cement ground
they sleep quietly together
the leaf and its love.

Another time, I went to the vegetable market when it was already wintertime. The sun was dazzlingly bright, but there was a damp, clean smell in the air like freshly washed laundry hanging in a neat array from a bamboo pole. The colors and patterns of the padded cotton gowns of two children wobbling somewhere around my feet had a certain similarity: one was the color of salted vegetables, the other of soy pickles, and both were covered with a deep, dark oily stain formed of innumerable smaller stains across the front, resembling the proverbial embroidered sack in which Guan Gong, the god of war, keeps his beard below his chin. There was another child, cradled in someone's arms, clad in a peach-red fake serge padded gown. That precious splash of color was cradled between the accumulated dirt and grime of a whole winter and seemed all the more poignant because of the filth, like a lotus blossom rising above the muck. As for the blue of blue cotton cloth: that is our national color. Most of the blue cotton shirts you see people wearing on the streets have been mended so many times that they are a patchwork of light and shade, as if they had all been rinsed by the rain, leaving an eye-opening bluish green. Our China has always been a nation of patches. Even our sky was patched together by the goddess Nüwa.

A tangerine seller puts down his carrying baskets to take a rest on the side of the road, his arms crossed in front of him as he leisurely watches the passing sights, the whites of his eyes clearly outlined by the contours of his flat, round face. But, in the split second after I pass by, he lifts his head abruptly, his lips split into a gigantic circle, and his chant seems to reach for the skies: "Two for a hundred silver dollars! Two for a hundred silver dollars! Come on, fellows! I'm practically giving them away!" I often hear his song from upstairs, and yet I'm still startled out of my wits, for how could it be coming from this man? The sound is so huge, and yet just seconds earlier he was standing and gazing quietly at the world around him. Now, he's holding his head up at an angle, his face beaming roundly like a full moon as he shouts merrily to the street, just like the Chinese in Sapajou's cartoons.[1] The Chinese in foreigners' cartoons are always carefree, crafty, and lovably capable of laughing off the bitterness of their lives, so much so that it almost seems a pleasure to be swindled out of a couple extra dollars by them. But when you think about it, the delightful atmosphere of such cartoons is quite heartbreaking.

There is a Taoist monk who walks the streets begging for alms, clad in a great adept's cloak made of faded black cloth. His hair is worn in a little gray coil on the crown of his head, not unlike the massed curls of a stylish modern woman. With his squinty eyes and hair pulled back across his temples, his sallow face has something of the look of an embittered woman who's fallen on hard times. It is difficult to tell how old he might be, but because of malnutrition, his body is tall and gaunt, seemingly stuck forever in the lanky frame of a seventeen- or eighteen-year-old. He holds a length of bamboo at an angle, beating out a slow rhythm with a mallet: "Tock...tock... tock." This, too, is a kind of clock, but one that measures a different sort of time: the time of sunlight slanting inch by inch across a lonely and ancient temple in the mountains. Time is like space: there are areas that are worth money as well as vast stretches of wasteland. Don't tell me that "time is worth more than gold." There are those who would sell their entire lives for a bowl of rice and find no takers. (They would even sell their next life, if they could, in the form of their children's and grandchildren's prospects for the future.) This Taoist monk has brought their worthless spare time into the high-speed bustle of the metropolis. Around him is a riotous profusion of advertisements, store fronts, the honking of automobile horns. He is the fabled dreamer of the dream of yellow millet, but he has awoken from his nap without actually having had the dream—and feels an altogether different kind of emptiness.[2] The Taoist walks over to the door of a hardware store and prostrates himself, but naturally they have nothing to give him, so he merely makes a kowtow to no one in particular. Having clambered back up to his feet, the "tock … tock … tock" resumes, and he crosses over to the cigarette stand next door and once again "makes obeisance to the earthly dust," kowtowing crookedly, his movements like the slow ooze of black water or the lazy bloom of a black chrysanthemum flower. To watch him is to feel that the dust of this world is piling ever higher, to know that not only will hopes turn to ash but anything and everything one touches will ultimately crumble to nothingness. I am rather carried away by this sentiment until I realize that if I continue to follow in his wake, he might ask me for alms as well. And with that, I hurry away.

The shopping basket of a servant woman coming back from market is full of coils of silver vermicelli noodles, like the unkempt hair of an old woman. There is another woman contentedly holding a crimson-lacquered tray piled with "longevity noodles" that are ingeniously folded into different layers, each suspended above the other. The bundle of noodles at the top is tied at the end with a peach-red strip of paper, like the red ribbon at the end of a little girl's ponytail. The pale rice-colored tresses dangle below, each strand as thick as a little snake.

Then there is the young girl who walks past holding a lidded wok. The handles on either side of the wok are threaded with blue cloth so that it is easier to carry. The indigo-colored strips of cloth look dirty but somehow make you feel that she shares an intimate bond with the wok, that "the heart connects to the hands, and the hands connect to the heart."

The hands of the apprentice in the butcher shop are swollen with cold. If your glance darts toward him as he noisily minces meat with a cleaver, it looks like he's chopping his own red, swollen fingers. A woman stands outside the counter, a prostitute who's no longer young, perhaps a madam in her own right or just doing business with a few other ladies of the same type. She still perms her hair, which sweeps behind her ears in a puffy cloud. Her face bears the traces of her former beauty, without scar or blemish, but still looks somehow pitted and uneven, and a little hesitant. She has a gold tooth, a black silk gown with rolled-up sleeves, and the loose threads of the worn sheepskin on the sleeves cling together in little petals of cloth, like white "maiden crab" chrysanthemums. She asks for a half pound of pork, but the apprentice busies himself with his mincing, and it is unclear whether he simply didn't hear what she said or is deliberately ignoring her. An uncertain smile moves across her face, and she stands outside the entrance, lifting her hands to straighten the tassels on her sleeves, revealing two golden rings and the bright red polish on her nails.

The proprietress of the butcher shop sits at a card table and lectures a relative just up from the countryside on the misdeeds of her sister-in-law. Her hands are folded into her pockets and her too-tight cotton-padded gown and blue cotton dust apron seem to tie her body up in knots, against which she struggles mightily, stretching her neck forward, her jaundiced eyes widening with the strain. And yet this is the kind of young woman that the local newspapers would refer to as a "young woman of not inconsiderable charm": "Well, you might think that what belongs to her brother belongs to her as well and that his house is hers, too. And that might have been true before, but not anymore." Her tone is neither one of accusation nor of reproach, and her eyes hardly seem to register the presence of her relative. She speaks with a contempt as deep as the sea, and her eyes stare blankly into the distance, as if she were gazing across the ocean. Again and again, she raises her voice and lets out a shout, like spitting into the ocean and knowing full well the pointlessness of the gesture. The relative, a long-stemmed water pipe dangling from his mouth, clad in a Chinese-style short jacket and trousers, and resting one foot on a wooden bench, consoles her: "All of that should go without saying. It's not worth talking about." But she continues bitterly, "She even went and sold those two pork hides her brother had saved." She raises her face to point to the wall behind them. High up on the partition, a few hooks have been driven into the wooden planks, but now there is only a blue cloth apron hanging from the wall.

At the store next door, Shanghainese *shenqu* songs pour volubly from the wireless, also deliberating endlessly on the long and short of various family affairs. First, a woman speaks her piece, and then a man chimes in with a loud, eloquent aria of his own: "A man of my years isn't getting any younger... If some untoward event should send me to the netherworld, who will be there to see me on my way?" I love to listen, my ears like fish in water, swimming in the music of his words. Turning the corner, the street suddenly becomes bleak. There is a red wall directly ahead, bricks painted in large clumsy white characters edged in blue with the name of an elementary school. Inside the campus grows a profusion of tall and desolate white trees. The gleaming white sky behind them casts the slightly slanted trunks in a shade of pale green. The radio is still playing *shenqu*, but the lyrics are no longer audible. I remember the lyrics from the beginning of a song cycle that I once read in a songbook: "With the first drum beat from the watchtower, the world falls quiet.... The tower is dark when the second watch sounds.... At the third watch, the tower is even more desolate...." The tone of the first line is imposingly grand, and I am very fond of the majestic images it calls to mind: of the China that has come down to us from the empires of the Han and Tang, of cities lit by a multitude of lamps slowly falling quiet with the sound of a drum.

I am holding a mesh shopping bag full of cans and bottles. There are two covered ceramic bowls full of tofu and soybean paste that need to be held upright, and a big bundle of cabbage hearts that needs to be kept at an angle so that it doesn't crush the eggs underneath. In short, I can proceed only with the greatest of difficulty. Although the rays of the winter sun are weak, it is noon, and I have walked quite a distance in the sun, so that its beams are like bees buzzing unrelentingly overhead, which makes me break into an itchy sort of sweat. I am truly happy to be walking underneath a Chinese sun. And I like feeling that my hands and legs are young and strong. And all this seems to be connected together, but I don't know why. In these happy moments—the sound of the wireless, the colors of the streets—a portion of all this seems to belong to me, even if what sinks sadly to the ground is also Chinese silt. At bottom, this is China after all.

When I get home, even before I have had a chance to pile the groceries in the kitchen, I sit down at my desk. Never before have I written anything so quickly; even I'm a bit shocked. After some revision, what I have is this:

DAYS AND NIGHTS OF CHINA

My road passes
across the land of my country.
Everywhere the chaos of my own people;
patched and patched once more, joined and joined again,
a people of patched and colored clouds.
My people,
my youth.
I am truly happy to bask in the sun back from market,
weighed down by my three meals for the day.
The first drumbeats from the watchtower settle all under heaven,
quieting the hearts of the people;
the uneasy clamor of voices begins to sink,
sink to the bottom ...
China, after all.

AFTERWORD

WE HAVE learned a great deal more about Eileen Chang and her work since the first edition of this translation was published seventeen years ago. Roland Soong, the executor of Chang's literary estate, has gone through her posthumous papers and published a wide range of previously unknown works, most notably three novels—*Little Reunions*, *The Fall of the Pagoda*, and *The Book of Change*—and two hefty volumes of correspondence between Chang and Soong's parents, Stephen and Mae Soong, covering all four decades of Chang's life in America. Thanks to these publications, we can now see that Chang devoted her later years to retelling and refashioning her early writings and to the work of self-translation, as if forever haunted by her early experiences of war, displacement, and permanent loss. With a clear view of Chang's work in exile, it is possible to discuss a "late style" that is distinct from that of the Shanghai years when she wrote the essays in *Written on Water*, while we can now appreciate this early masterpiece in light of her entire literary career.

Chang first emerged on the Shanghai literary scene in 1942, writing film reviews and cultural commentary for the English-language journal *The XX Century*. With wit, poise, and delight, the "young miss Chang," as she was soon known, captured Chinese ways of thinking and patterns of life for a non-Chinese audience. But the ambitious young author sought a larger readership and a deeper impact than was possible by writing in English alone. She refashioned her English essays in sumptuously stylized Chinese prose, and before long they were coming out in the leading popular journals of the time. Chang became an overnight literary sensation.

Several of these self-translations figured in the thirty essays collected in *Written on Water* when it was published in December 1944. There is nothing secondhand about them, however. They are all marked by an acute sense of urgency. In August of the same year Chang had brought out a collection of ten short stories, *Romances* (*Chuanqi*), and these two early volumes signal the advent of a great stylist writing in immediate response to the volatile times in which she lived. When the first printing of *Romances* sold out almost immediately, the new edition included a preface by Chang in which she famously declared: "Make yourself famous as early as you can! If success comes too late, the pleasure of it isn't as intense . . . Hurry! Hurry! Otherwise it will be too late! Too late!"

This same urgency is evident in the Chinese title of the essays, *Liuyan*, literally "flowing words," and in her reminiscences, she explains that she wanted to indicate that her writing was not meant to endure so much as to linger and then fade away. *Liuyan* also carries the meaning of "rumors" or "gossip," and this sense too is in play: her work is to flow freely and swiftly to reach the widest possible audience.

Readers versed in classical Chinese literature might speculate that the word *liuyan* alludes to the Song dynasty poet, essayist, and critic Su Shi's frequently quoted definition of prose writing: "[Prose] mostly resembles traveling clouds and flowing water (*xingyun liushui*)." And readers familiar with Western literature will make an immediate connection between Chang's title and the famous inscription on the poet John Keats's grave marker in Rome: "Here lies one whose name was writ in water." The title originally came to her in English, Chang says in her reminiscences. In her correspondence with the Soongs, the reference to the epitaph is further confirmed.

For Chang the urgency and brevity of the modern essay functions as a metaphor for the fragility and futility of modern life. The connection is further strengthened if we consider the historical background against which Chang wrote her essays. As *Written on Water* went to press in December 1944, China was still in the midst of a long and devastating war with Japan. Shanghai remained under Japanese occupation and there seemed no end in sight. Given this, Chang's title could be taken to express a certain ambivalence, as if she were caught between despair at destruction and a desire to make a mark before all is washed away.

Titles mattered to Chang. One of the essays in *Written on Water* is called "'What Is Essential Is That Names Be Right.'" Another, no less representative piece, bears the title "Whispers"—in Chinese, *siyu*, which means "private discussions" and is part of a phrase suggestive of the hushed tones and interruptions that accompany intimate exchanges. And the voice of the essay whispers, murmurs, and gossips. Chang reinvents prose, turning it into a stream of thoughts, a random scattering of scenes, from which nothing substantial emerges, only bits and pieces of life tinted with the haziness of childhood memories. Her technique closely resembles montage: flashbacks and moments of free association remind the reader of the blurred boundaries between memory and reality, past and present, fact and fiction.

Something of Chang's own life story emerges if we read "Whispers" in light of another essay, "From the Ashes." "Whispers" is written in the first person, and as it reaches its end Chang is entering adulthood, about to embark on a journey: "I passed my entrance examination, but because of the war I was unable to go to England and ended up being diverted to Hong Kong instead. Three years later, once more on account of the war, I returned to Shanghai without having finished my degree." This ending connects seamlessly with the start of "From the Ashes":

> There's already a considerable distance between myself and Hong Kong: one thousand miles, two years, new events, and new people. I would not have known how or from where to begin speaking of what I saw and heard in Hong Kong during the war, because the experience cut too close to the bone, affecting me in an altogether drastic fashion.

One thousand miles sets the two worlds apart, and her two years away already feel like a lifetime. If "Whispers" is a resounding beginning to Chang's incessant retelling of her childhood experiences,

"From the Ashes" works as a key index of people, places, and events in wartime Hong Kong, experiences that haunt her later works. These early essays are a key to understanding the more extensive narratives of *Little Reunions*, *The Fall of the Pagoda*, and *The Book of Change*.

Hong Kong is an important presence in the essays, but Shanghai looms even larger. "Notes on Apartment Life," "Seeing with the Streets," "Shanghainese, After All," and "Epilogue: Days and Nights of China" all constitute an homage to the city that saw Chang's swift rise to fame. "Notes on Apartment Life" is full of texture and nuance, a colorful symphony that amounts to a parable of war. Here private space is constantly intruded upon by external forces, and Chang's animated world of images, sounds, and objects brings to mind themes of unemployment, social unrest, and economic instability. Her tone is lighter in "Epilogue: Days and Nights of China," originally published as the epilogue to the expanded 1946 edition of *Romances*. She describes her morning ride on the elevator from her sixth-floor apartment to the awakening streets, where she mingles with the masses while making her way to the magnificently vivid world of the vegetable market. Chang's vision of urban modernity is situated somewhere between the glitz of the grand avenues and the lively but more subdued atmosphere of the back alleys.

Chang's vision of modernity is also situated at a bustling cultural crossroad. Her literary persona was a complex mix of multiple influences. There was Chinese literary tradition, itself intricate enough, along with the vibrant and unsettling modern vernacular literature that had taken shape in the twentieth century. References to both traditional and modern Chinese literature abound in *Written on Water*. At the same time, Chang possessed an in-depth knowledge of Anglophone literature, both the canonical texts taught in her English classes at the University of Hong Kong and the contemporary writers that were all the rage in colonial Hong Kong. Her father and aunt were both Bernard Shaw fans, and Shaw was a favorite of hers too. So were Somerset Maugham, Stella Benson, D. H. Lawrence, H. G. Wells, and Aldous Huxley, thanks to an extensive extracurricular reading list she was introduced to by her English teachers at the university. These authors and their works appear in her early fiction and essays, side by side with multiple references to the films and visual culture of the day. From Peking Opera to women's fashion, from the culture of the streets to highbrow aesthetic properties, from histories of dance to shows of European modernist paintings, from nostalgic rambles through classical Chinese literature to a fond tour of Shanghai cinema, Chang's breadth of knowledge is impressively on display throughout *Written on Water*.

What might these essays have meant to Chang herself in retrospect? Chang's unfinished travelogue, *Yixiang ji* (Chronicle of a strange land), written in a notebook as she traveled south from Shanghai to the rural region of Zhejiang Province in early 1946, provides some clues. Roland Soong, who unearthed this text from Chang's posthumous papers, has described it as "not only record[ing] in detail critical dates in Chang's life but serv[ing] as a constant blueprint for her later writings." And indeed this fragmented narrative signals the impending end of her Shanghai period, while also serving as a critical reflection on her early works.

The first-person narrator in *Chronicle of a Strange Land* is called Mrs. Shen. Describing a family compound in Hangzhou, where she stops for a time en route to Wenzhou, she paints an unusual scene from memory:

> Life is like my childhood servant. If you asked her to get something for you, she'd take all the time in the world before opening a large drawer from which she would at last remove a tiny bundle wrapped in a checkered handkerchief. Removing the pins, she would open the bundle to examine its contents, before wrapping it up again and returning it to its original spot. Then out would come another bundle, this one wrapped with a white bamboo cloth and tied with faded old shoelaces. She would open that one up, peer inside, and wrap it up in turn. She would

check bundle after bundle, frown, and wonder "huhn?" If it hadn't been for me fretting away at her side, she would have been at it forever, so intimate was she with all these objects that had been in her keeping for so long. If she couldn't find something there, no one could.

There is a reason that Chang's travel narrative dwells on this moment. The image of the servant undoing her bundles is a metaphor for the writer exploring memory. Chang's later career of incessant retelling and refashioning older narratives is much like opening one wrapped bundle after another.

Chang must have carried many of these imaginary bundles or packets around with her during her long years of exile. They became the foundation of her work. Some contained childhood fears and worries, moments of vexed pleasure, sounds, smells, colors, and other sensations. Some contained the three years of her college life that ended in a bloody battle that shook her to the core. In others yet there are scenes of daily life in Shanghai or impressions from her reading. As Chang wrote and rewrote the narratives of her own life, she went back to these bundles, each with its own little universe. And all these bundles are already present in the pages of *Written on Water*, the first glimmer of a unique literary world that in time would fill with figures and shadows of the past.

—Nicole Huang

NOTES

FROM THE MOUTHS OF BABES

1   The *Shanghai Evening Post and Mercury* was an American-owned English-language daily that was published from 1929 until the Japanese occupation of the city in 1941.

2   Su Qing (1917–1982) rocketed to literary fame in Shanghai during the Japanese occupation on the strength of her first novel, *Jiehun shinian* (Ten years of marriage).

3   Zhang Henshui (1895–1967) is considered the emblematic writer of the Mandarin Ducks and Butterflies school of popular fiction, His work, however, may more accurately be described as an amalgam of the romance fiction for which the school is named, new-style fiction (with its realist concern for social and political issues), and popular genres such as martial arts fiction. Zhang's best-selling 1929 novel *Tixiao yinyuan* (Fate in tears and laughter) is a representative example.

4   A classic of Ming dynasty vernacular fiction, *The Golden Lotus (Jinping mei)* portrays in meticulous detail the domestic intrigues, business dealings, and sexual excesses of Ximen Qing, a wealthy merchant, and his many wives and concubines.

5   Hongkew (Hongkou) was a district of Shanghai dominated by Japanese shopkeepers, soldiers, and colonial officials; it also played host to a large community of Jewish refugees during the war years.

6   "Lament for the Southland" ("Ai jiangnan") is the tune title *(cipai)* of a Song dynasty song lyric current in the tenth and eleventh centuries.

7   For a translation of this text, see Anton Chekhov, *Later Short Stories, 1888–1903*, trans. Constance Garnett (New York: Modern Library, 1999), 397–410.

8   *Dream of the Red Chamber (Honglou meng)*, written by Cao Xueqin in the 1750s and also known as *The Story of the Stone (Shitou ji)*, is the greatest masterpiece of Chinese vernacular fiction and one of Chang's primary

literary sources of inspiration. See Cao Xueqin, *The Story of the Stone*, trans. David Hawkes (Harmondsworth: Penguin, 1979).

9 Chang is reading examples of what would have then been thought of as new-style fiction. Mu Shiying (1912–1940) was one of the primary exponents of modernist fiction in the 1930s and a central figure in the New Sensation school of writing associated with the journal *Les Contemporains (Xiandai)*. Ba Jin (1904–2005) was a self-styled anarchist whose fusion of the rebellious concerns of May Fourth-era new-style fiction and the melodramatic imagination of the Mandarin Ducks and Butterfly school made his fiction enduringly popular with modern Chinese readers. His most widely read novel is *Jia*, published in English as *Family* (Garden City, N.Y.: Anchor, 1979).

WRITING OF ONE'S OWN

1 Chang initially wrote this essay in response to the prominent literary critic Fu Lei's criticisms of her serialized novella *Lianhuan tao* (Chained links). Fu Lei, a well-respected scholar and prolific translator of French literature, professed himself to be amazed by Chang's youthful talent. Writing under a pseudonym (Xun Yu) in an essay called "Lun Zhang Ailing de xiaoshuo" (On Eileen Chang's fiction), Fu first praises Chang's impeccable narrative techniques in stories such as "The Golden Cangue" and "Love in a Fallen City" and then moves on to criticize *Lianhuan tao* as trivial and "lacking in substance." Implicit in Fu's critique was a sense that Chang, in focusing on the "petty" and "passive" domestic lives and loves of largely female urbanites, was betraying the nationalistic and politically engaged ideals of earlier realist literature of the May Fourth Movement. Fu Lei's critique appeared in the same journal, *Wanxiang* (Phenomena), in which *Lianhuan tao* began its serialization in 1944. After producing this response to defend her work, Chang abruptly ended the serialization. The novella itself, about lower-class woman named Nixi who travels from one man to another and maintains her vitality and optimism against all odds, went unfinished.

2 The line is from a poem titled "Beating the Drum" ("Jigu"), from *Shijing* (The classic of poetry), the earliest and most influential poetic anthology in the Chinese literary tradition. The same line is cited by the male protagonist Fan Liuyuan in Chang's novella "Love in a Fallen City" ("Qingcheng zhi lian").

3   A Chinese narrative tradition based in part on the thirteenth-century vernacular drama *Xixiang ji* (The story of the western wing).

4   Chang is misquoting from the Tang poet Du Fu's 719 poem "Respectfully Presented to Venerable Mr. Wei: Twenty Couplets" ("Fengzeng Wei zuo chengzhang ershi yun").

NOTES ON APARTMENT LIFE

1   The line derives from Su Shi's (1037–1101) famous Song dynasty lyric set to the melody "Shuidiao gefou" (Song for the river tune).

2   Chang is referring here to a right-wing Chinese political party that was established in 1937 after the outbreak of the war with Japan, not its German namesake.

"WHAT IS ESSENTIAL IS THAT NAMES BE RIGHT"

1   In her title, Chang alludes to the words of Confucius in *Analects* 13.3. Asked by a disciple what the first priority in governance ought to be, Confucius replies. "What is essential is that the names be right." Without such a rectification of names, he continues, "words will not follow. If words do not follow, deeds will go unaccomplished; when deeds go unaccomplished, rites and music will not flourish; when rites and music do not flourish, punishment will not fit the crime; when punishments do not fit the crime, the common people will not know where to put hand or foot." See Confucius, *The Analects*, trans. D. C. Lau (London: Penguin, 1979), 118.

2   Wang Yunwu (1888–1979) was for many years the editor-in-chief of the largest and most influential Shanghai publishing house of the modern era, The Commercial Press, as well as the inventor of the "four corner" indexing system used in many Chinese character dictionaries.

3   Both are titles of popular novels of the late 1930s by Zhang Henshui (1895–1967). See "From the Mouths of Babes," note 3.

4   Chang refers here to Wen Kang's much-beloved early nineteenth-century martial arts novel.

5   Chang is playing here on a sequence of ludicrously diverse classical references and poetic allusions. Gongyang Huan evokes the name of the author of the Confucian classic *Gongyang zhuan*. Zangsun Didong uses an exceedingly rare and antiquated compound surname, paired with an equally abstruse term for "rainbow." Ming Di means something like "Esoteric Meditations," Bai Po implies "Pale Marsh," while Mu Lian alludes

to the half-immortal nephew of the heavenly emperor who demonstrated his filial piety by cutting down a mountain with an axe. Ying Yuan means "Cherry Ravine" and alludes to feminine beauty, as does the more bathetic Duan Dai, or "Broken Emerald" (*dai* indicates the greenish-black mineral that was often used to paint women's eyebrows and thus stands as a synecdoche for a lovely young maiden). Dongfang Maozhi was a famous court jester of the Han dynasty, Lin Yanchan implies "Maiden in Ethereal Mist," and Nü Gui carries the somewhat archaic connotation of a "maiden fair."

FROM THE ASHES

1   Our Lady's Hall was located on the hill behind the University of Hong Kong campus at 9 Po Shan Road. It was founded in 1939 by the sisters of the French Convent School as the university's first women's dormitory. Chang was among its earliest residents.

2   Fatima Mohideen (1920–1997), nicknamed Yanying by Chang, was Chang's best friend in college. Her father was a Sri Lankan of Arab descent and her Chinese mother was from Tianjin. Mohideen was born in Hong Kong and raised in Malay and Shanghai. A medical student, she began her studies at Hong Kong University, like Chang, in August 1939, and the two roomed together at Our Lady's Hall. After the war interrupted their schooling, the pair returned to Shanghai together in May 1942. Chang makes frequent references to "Yanying" in her writing, and she is the subject of the essay "The Sayings of Yanying," included in *Written on Water*, to which Mohideen contributed the original cover design.

3   Born in Hong Kong in 1904, Norman H. France spent the early part of his childhood in the colony and studied and worked mostly at Cambridge University before he was appointed Reader in History at HKU in 1931. He was killed near a military garrison at Stanley in Hong Kong on December 20, 1941, and was buried at Stanley Military Cemetery. He would return in Chang's later novels, as Mr. Andrews in *Little Reunions* and as Mr. Gerald H. Blaisdell in *The Book of Change*.

4   A late Qing dynasty novel by Li Boyuan (1867–1906) that exposed the foibles and corruption of the official class, first published in 1903.

5   The line is from a poem by the eighth-century poet Wei Yingwu titled "Chu fa Yangzi ji Yuan da jiaoshu" (On first setting out on the Yangzi River; sent to Collator Yuan the Senior).

6   The line derives from the famously cryptic and lyrical ninth-century poet Li Shangyin's celebrated poem *Jinse* (Brocade zither).

SHANGHAINESE, AFTER ALL

1   A school of prose writing pioneered by Zhang Huiyan and popular among literati during the Qianlong and Jiaqing periods (corresponding to the eighteenth century). Yanghu prose was slightly less severe and more inclusive than the stripped-down and resolutely classicist Tongcheng school with which it was sometimes associated.

2   These are all short stories and novellas Chang published in her 1944 collection *Chuanqi* (Romances).

SEEING WITH THE STREETS

"Seeing with the Streets" is a literal translation of an idiom (*daolu yimu*) that derives from the pre-Qin text *Guoyu* (Discourses of the states). The traditional understanding is that the idiom refers to the harsh rule of a Zhou king, during which passersby on the street, too scared to speak, could only signal their mutual understanding with their eyes. Eileen Chang gestures playfully toward this historical scenario toward the end of the essay by describing the Japanese military occupation of the city, and the arrest of a partisan.

1   From "Mooring on the Yao River," an eleventh-century poem by Wang An-shi.

2   Li Kui, also known as the Black Whirlwind, is one of the one hundred and eight heroes of the Ming dynasty martial arts adventure, *Outlaws of the Marsh (Shuihu zhuan)*. Renowned for his seemingly inexhaustible appetite for combat and killing, Li Kui is also portrayed as a devoted son. Ironically, however, his mother becomes a victim of a voracious tiger on account of his negligence as he transports her over a mountain ridge.

3   *Xiepu chao* (Tides of the Huangpu) was a popular crime novel and social exposé written in the early 1920s by Zhu Shouju (also known by his pen name Haishang shuomeng ren, or "Shanghai Sleeptalker").

4   A two-stringed bowed instrument.

A CHRONICLE OF CHANGING CLOTHES

1   This article appeared for the first time in the January 1943 issue of *The XXth Century*, a pro-Axis English-language journal published in Japanese-occupied Shanghai, under the title "Chinese Life and Fashions." Less than a year later, Chang translated, revised, and expanded the piece for publication in a Chinese-language journal *Gujin* (Past and present), retitling it

"Gengyi ji" (A chronicle of changing clothes). It was this version of the piece that was ultimately included in Chang's collection *Liuyan* (Written on water). The text presented here, along with original illustrations by Chang herself, is a triangulated translation into English of Chang's translation into Chinese.

2 Wang Zhaojun was a legendary second century A.D. handmaiden who was dispatched by the emperor to the Huns as a gesture of pacification.

3 Prospect Garden (Daguan yuan) is the large, idyllic, and elaborately wrought fictional space that serves as the principal setting of *Dream of the Red Chamber* (see "From the Mouths of Babes," note 8).

4 1907 or 1908.

5 An early form of modern drama that incorporated aspects of Chinese opera with Western dramaturgy and flourished in the decade after 1900.

6 Liu Bei (161–223), a warlord and military strategist of the third century, is most famously depicted in the beloved Ming dynasty novel *Romance of the Three Kingdoms (Sanguo yanyi)*.

SPEAKING OF WOMEN

1 Chang is lampooning the protofeminist arguments issued by prominent reformist intellectuals such as Kang Youwei and Liang Qichao as part of their abortive effort to modernize Chinese politics and society in the waning years of the Qing dynasty.

2 Eileen Chang here refers to Cybel, the female protagonist of O'Neill's play, not by her name but as "Mother Earth," *Dimu* (地母) in the original text. This is perhaps an attempt to assimilate Cybel to the Chinese Daoist pantheon, in which "Mother Earth" is an important deity. But more likely, Chang has noticed that O'Neill himself describes her thus: "Cybel has grown stouter and more voluptuous, but her face is still unmarked and fresh, her calm more profound. She is like an unmoved idol of Mother Earth." In all other instances, we have deferred to the standard English text, rather than directly translating Chang's Chinese renditions of the play script.

3 The Goddess of the Luo River, originally named Fu Fei and memorialized in a famous poetic rhapsody *(fu)* by Cao Zhi (192–232), was said to have drowned herself on account of an illicit love affair. Guanyin is a female bodhisattva revered as a goddess of mercy and compassion in Chinese Buddhist tradition.

BY THE LIGHT OF THE SILVER LANTERN

1 A version of this essay originally appeared as a film review entitled "Wife, Vamp, Child" in *The XXth Century*. See *The XXth Century* 4, no. 5 (May 1943): 392–393.

2 Nancy Chan (or Chen Yunshang) was one of the most celebrated stars of the wartime Chinese cinema. Originally from Hong Kong, she was catapulted to fame in Shanghai for her genderbending performance as Mulan in the 1939 blockbuster *Mulan Joins the Army*.

3 Bai Guang came to prominence as an actress, singer, and celebrity during the occupation period of 1941 to 1945 and was pigeonholed as a vamp in both her public roles and private life.

LET'S GO! LET'S GO UPSTAIRS

1 Henrik Ibsen's drama was first published in Chinese translation in a 1918 issue of *Xin qingnian* (New youth), the flagship journal of the New Culture Movement. The play had an enormous impact on contemporary debates concerning the status of women, traditional social arrangements, and the legacy of Confucian culture. Nora, who leaves behind her husband and her dull bourgeois existence in the original text, became an emblematic and controversial figure in China whose very name came to represent the emancipation of women from traditional social restraints.

2 Ke Ling (1900–2000) was a prominent playwright, essayist, and literary critic, as well as the editor of one of the period's most well-respected literary magazines, *Wanxiang* (Phenomena). He was also an early advocate of Eileen Chang's writing.

3 Cao Yu is perhaps the foremost modern Chinese playwright, whose work came to prominence in the late 1930s and 1940s.

SCHOOLING AT THE SILVER PALACE

1 This essay was originally published as a film review in the English-language journal *The XXth Century* and subsequently rewritten and expanded in Chinese. See Eileen Chang, "China: Educating the Family," *The XXth Century* 4, no. 4 (April 1943). The Chinese title of the essay, "Yingong jiuxue ji," seems to be a parody of the title of one of the most popular pedagogical novels of the first half of the twentieth century, Bao Tianxiao's *Xin'er jiuxue ji* (The schooling of Xin'er), which was an adaptation of a didactic and nationalistic Italian story for children, Edmondo de Amicis's *Heart (Cuore)*.

2 Yuan Mei (1716–1798) was a prolific and eccentric Qing poet and literary critic. His residence and garden, dubbed the Suiyuan, was populated in part by young women whom Yuan, in rather unconventional fashion, had taken on as his disciples. Zheng Kangcheng (also known as Zheng Xuan) was a scholar of the Eastern Han period.

PEKING OPERA THROUGH FOREIGN EYES

1 Chang published a version of this essay in English in the June 1943 number of *The XXth Century* (432–438) as "Still Alive."

2 A dramatic adaptation of the romance novel of the same title by Qin Shou'ou, the play opened at the Carlton Theater in January 1943, to great popular acclaim, and was made into a film in 1944 by the director Maxu Weibang.

3 Written in the Ming dynasty, *Shuihu zhuan* (The water margin) is one of the most beloved masterpieces of Chinese vernacular fiction, as well as an important progenitor of the martial arts novel.

4 The Hegemon of Chu is also a character in the opera *Farewell My Concubine (Bawang bieji).*

5 Zhuge Liang, a legendary military strategist of the Three Kingdoms period (third century A.D.) is immortalized in a number of vernacular dramas and works of fiction, including the Ming dynasty *Romance of the Three Kingdoms.*

6 Kun-style opera *(kunqu)* originated in Kunshan, Zhejiang province, and reached the zenith of its popularity in the late Ming and Qing periods. It is known for its elegant emphasis on poetic diction and mellifluous, woodwind-based music. The style has usually been associated with literati patronage, especially in the prosperous and cultivated southeastern coastal cities such as Yangzhou and Suzhou, in marked contradistinction to the more popular, northern roots of Peking opera.

THE SAYINGS OF YANYING

See "From the Ashes," note 2, for a discussion of Fatima Mohideen, called "Yanying" by Chang.

UNPUBLISHED MANUSCRIPTS

1 Chang's nephew was referring to an older work of vernacular fiction on the same historical theme.

2 The Chancellery style *(taige ti)* flourished among court officials and literati in the Yongle and Chenghua eras of the Ming dynasty and is known
for its meticulous attention to details of literary form and craftsmanship
(sometimes to the detriment of expression).

3 Zhang Ziping (1893–1959) was one of the founders, with Mao Dun and
Yu Dafu, of the Creation Society. His later fictional work was renowned
for its exploration of romance and sexuality. He was eventually tried and
imprisoned for his collaboration with the Japanese occupation.

4 See "From the Mouths of Babes," note 3 for a discussion of Zhang Henshui.

5 Li Shifang is known as one of the four great female impersonators of
modern Peking opera and was a disciple of Mei Lanfang.

WHAT ARE WE TO WRITE?

1 "Swallow's nest" is slang for a brothel. Chang is unable to go to the interior of China because Shanghai had at that point been separated from the
hinterlands by the war with Japan.

2 Shi Hui (1915–1957) was a noted stage and film actor and a talented
essayist.

BEATING PEOPLE

1 Li Hanqiu (1873–1923) was known primarily for popular fiction in the
Mandarin Ducks and Butterflies mode. The author of over thirty novels,
his most widely read work is *Guangling chao* (The tides of Guangling).

POETRY AND NONSENSE

1 Zhou Zuoren (1885–1967), brother of the so-called father of modern Chinese literature, Lu Xun, was one of the most distinguished essayists and
cultural figures of the Republican period.

2 Lu Yishi (pen name of Lu Yu, 1913–2013) was an active member of the
modernist poetry movements in Shanghai and Taiwan, working closely
with Dai Wangshu and others. After emigrating to Taiwan in 1948, he
published under the name Ji Xian.

3 Gu Mingdao (1897–1944) was the author of more than thirty romance,
historical, and martial arts novels.

4 For more on the popular success of Qin Shou'ou's *Qiu haitang* (Autumn
quince), see Chang's essay "Peking Opera Through Foreign Eyes" in this
volume.

5   All these writers were central figures in the development of modern Chinese verse forms.

WITH THE WOMEN ON THE TRAM

1   Chang's title borrows from a poem in the *Shijing* (The Classic of poetry) called "You nü tong che" (With the lady on the carriage), transposing its images of the courtship of a courtly beauty to a distinctly modern context.

WHISPERS

1   A beloved Ming dynasty vernacular novel detailing the military and political history of the Three Kingdoms period by way of the dramatic exploits of heroes such as Cao, Liu Bei, and Zhuge Liang.

2   Meng Lijun is said to have masqueraded as a boy in order to pass the civil service examinations and serve as prime minister of the Yuan dynasty. Her story has furnished the material for a number of vernacular stories and dramas.

3   *Journey to the West*, best known in Arthur Waley's abridged English translation, *Monkey*, is a Ming dynasty vernacular novel attributed to Wu Cheng'en and detailing the adventures of an intrepid monk and his companions (including the Sun Wukong, the magical monkey) during their quest to find and transport the sacred Tripitaka Buddhist scriptures from India to China.

4   A distinctively Shanghainese form of densely packed modern row housing, located off the main avenues along gated lanes.

5   Chinese intellectual and essayist whose series of best-selling English-language books on China and Chinese culture garnered him great renown in the 1930s and 1940s as a cultural emissary to the West.

6   A Republican-era crime novel written by Zhang Chunfan.

UNFORGETTABLE PAINTINGS

1   Chang seems to be mistaken here. The woman in the painting is Tahitian.

2   An important figure in modern Chinese painting, Lin Fengmian (1900–1991) studied Western painting as a young man in France and went on to serve as the head of the National Academy of Art in Hangzhou.

3   See n. 2 of the preceding essay.

4   *Bijin ga* are traditional Japanese paintings and prints of beautiful women (*bijin*), often geishas. *The Twelve Hours in the Pleasure Quarters of the Yo-*

shiwara was a series of prints created by Kitagawa Utamaru (1753–1806), a key *Ukiyo-e* woodblock artist.

5 The work described here does not exist. Chang seems to have conflated several different Utamaru paintings.

6 Tanizaki Junichiro (1886–1965), also the author of *Naomi (Chijin no ai)*, was a prominent modern Japanese novelist.

UNDER AN UMBRELLA

1 A celebrated columnist in the Shanghai tabloids of the 1930s and 1940s.

ON DANCE

1 Chang appears to be thinking of a Song dynasty song lyric by Yan Jidao (mid-eleventh–early twelfth century) to the tune "Zhegu tian" (Partridge weather).

2 From Anton Chekhov's 1895 story "Anna on the Neck" ("Anna na shee"). In the interest of accuracy, I have translated Chang's translation rather than citing a preexisting version. For a full translation of the text, see Anton Chekhov, *Later Short Stories: 1888–1903*, trans. Constance Garnett (New York: Modern Library, 1999), 304–317.

3 Chang seems to be mistaken here. The tango has its origins in Buenos Aires, Argentina.

4 Chang is playing on a phrase designating the third solar term in the traditional Chinese agricultural calendar, "the waking of the insects" *(jingzhe)* from hibernation in the springtime.

ON PAINTING

1 The line is from *Shijing* (The classic of poetry), a sixth-century B.C. collection traditionally said to be edited by Confucius.

ON THE SECOND EDITION OF *ROMANCES*

This essay was a preface to the second edition of Chang's first fiction collection, *Romances (Chuanqi)*, initially published in the same year as *Written on Water*.

1 A form of *pingju* (northern opera), deriving from rural Hebei province.

2 Zhu Baoxia was born in the northern Chinese city of Tangshan in 1914 and is credited as a pioneer in the popularization of *pingju* in Shanghai, where she first performed, to great acclaim, in 1928.

3 Chang is quoting here from the first two lines of a traditional educational primer, *Qianzi wen* (The thousand-character primer).

ON MUSIC

1 "Girl on the Police Gazette" was a 1937 composition by Irving Berlin performed by Dick Powell for the film *On the Avenue*.
2 *Tanci* is a musical genre, usually associated with the city of Suzhu, in which storytelling is set to musical accompaniment.
3 *Shenqu* is a popular genre of operatic songs in the Shanghainese dialect.
4 "Peach Blossom River" ("Taohua jiang") was a 1928 composition by the pioneering Chinese popular music composer, Li Jinhui. "Roses Blooming Everywhere" ("Qiangwei chuchu kai") was a popular song by Chen Gexin recorded in 1942 by Gong Qiuxia as the theme for an eponymous film.

EPILOGUE: DAYS AND NIGHTS OF CHINA

This essay was not included in the original edition of *Written on Water*. It first appeared as an epilogue to the expanded edition of *Romances* that was published in 1946.

1 Sapajou (the pen name of Georgii Avksent'ievich Sapojnikoff) was a White Russian refugee who served as a cartoonist for the *North China Daily News* in Shanghai from the late 1920s until the 1940s.
2 A Taoist parable in which a man lives an entire lifetime—brimming with intrigue, romance, worldly success, and failure—only to find upon awaking that it was all merely a dream, whose decades corresponded in the mortal world to the time it takes to cook a pot of yellow millet porridge.

OTHER NEW YORK REVIEW CLASSICS
For a complete list of titles, visit www.nyrb.com.